OLD TEXTS, NEW PRACTICES

OLD TEXTS NEW PRACTICES

Islamic Reform in Modern Morocco

ETTY TEREM

STANFORD UNIVERSITY PRESS
STANFORD, CALIFORNIA

Stanford University Press
Stanford, California

Printed in the United States of America on acid-free, archival-quality paper

Library of Congress Cataloging-in-Publication Data

Terem, Etty, 1967- author.
Old texts, new practices : Islamic reform in modern Morocco / Etty Terem.
pages cm
Includes bibliographical references and index.
ISBN 978-0-8047-8707-9 (cloth : alk. paper)
1. 'Imrani, Muhammad al-Mahdi ibn Muhammad, 1850-1923. Mi'yar al-jadid. 2. Fatwas--Morocco--History. 3. Malikites--Morocco--History. 4. Islamic renewal--Morocco--History. 5. Islamic law--Social aspects--Morocco--History. I. Title.
KBP494.53.T47 2014
340.5'922--dc23 2013048577

ISBN 978-0-8047-9084-0 (electronic)

Typeset by Bruce Lundquist in 10/14 Minion

To Shlomi, for being what matters most

Law doesn't just mop up, it defines. It doesn't just correct, it makes possible. What it defines, the meaning frames it sets forth, is an important force in shaping human behavior and giving it sense, lending it significance, point and direction. It is this sort of thing—law not so much as a device or mechanism to put things back on track when they have run into trouble, but as itself a constructive element "within culture," a style of thought, which in conjunction with a lot of other things equally "within culture"—Islam, Buddhism, etc.—lays down the track in the first place.

Clifford Geertz, "Off Echoes:
Some Comments on Anthropology and Law"

The law works by the translation of authoritative texts into the present moment, a kind of pushing forward of what was written in one context into another, where it has a necessarily somewhat different meaning. This is not a mechanical or technical process and its burdens and responsibilities cannot be cut short by any of the devices used to avoid them, such as resort to the "original intention" of the framers or the "plain words" of the text. It always requires an act of creation, a making of something new; yet the original text cannot be forgotten, for fidelity is always due to it. Indeed it is upon prior text that our right to speak at all depends.

James Boyd White, *Justice as Translation:
An Essay in Cultural and Legal Criticism*

CONTENTS

ACKNOWLEDGMENTS

This book began as a very different research project that investigated the *New Miʿyār* of al-Mahdī al-Wazzānī as a muftī's interpretation of his society, focusing exclusively upon Fāsī family life and kinship practices. As I was finishing that original research, I realized that the *New Miʿyār* tells a more significant and complicated story than the narrowly framed one I recounted. I recognized that al-Wazzānī's ambitious plan for his work and his new consciousness might offer fresh insights into the material he collected and the order into which he arranged it, many of which I had not yet fully explored. Focusing on the *New Miʿyār*'s overall meaning pushed me to conceive a more sophisticated reading of the assembled fatwās, emphasizing the way they corresponded to the new material and epistemological conditions shaped by Moroccan modernity. Perhaps more important, I became aware that an adequate interrogation of the entire work and the individual fatwās in it engenders a complex understanding of modern Islamic reformist thought that conceptually problematizes some scholarly works. As I undertook the task of reconceptualizing and rewriting, I had to confront my source again. Fortunately, the subsequent research effort was worthwhile. The opportunity to revisit the *New Miʿyār* was invaluable in refining my thinking and resulted in new and unexpected horizons of historical interpretation.

In the course of writing this book, I have received invaluable help and encouragement from many individuals, and it is a pleasure to acknowledge their support. My foremost thanks are due to Roger Owen, Susan Miller, and David Powers. I am grateful to Roger Owen, who helped me relate my work to larger concerns and questions in the field of Middle Eastern studies. His unflagging encouragement and good advice have always come to my aid when I needed them most. For his friendship and continuing interest in this project, I remain deeply indebted. I am also grateful to Susan Miller for her astute engagement with early drafts of this manuscript. Her critical comments and probing questions helped me find my own perspective and inspired the revisions that shaped this book. I am deeply grateful to David Powers, from whom I learned much of what I know about muftīs and fatwās. His influence on me and his contribution to this project have been profound and direct. He has been a teacher, meticulous critic, and friend. His advice and criticism have provided me with a constant source of inspiration and stimulation. I am also indebted to Wilfrid Rollman for generously sharing his deep knowledge of nineteenth-century Morocco with me. His critical suggestions on early drafts of the manuscript provided me with invaluable feedback. I would particularly like to thank him for his continuing support and intellectual companionship. I would also like to thank Dror Zeevi, who read early drafts of the manuscript and gave me unfailing support and incisive advice. I owe a special debt of gratitude to Aron Zysow for the conscientious corrections and generous advice he offered. His invaluable critique pushed me to maintain a sense of rigor in my interpretation and analysis of fatwās. I am also profoundly grateful to Jonathan Katz and Lawrence Rosen, who read the entire manuscript and offered me detailed suggestions and helpful feedback. Their interest in my work and generous criticism provided me with much-appreciated encouragement and support. My honest thanks go to them all, though the responsibility for any errors in this book is mine alone.

This project benefited a great deal from the friends and colleagues who read sections of the manuscript or chapters in draft form and offered valuable comments, engaged me in stimulating conversations, or recommended readings that sustained my thinking. In particular, I wish to thank Peri Bearman, Hannah-Louise Clark, Kenneth Cuno, Yoav Di-Capua, Jan Goldberg, Emily Gottreich, Jocelyn Hendrickson, Nimrod Hurvitz, Mohamed El-Mansour, Jessica Marglin, James McDougall, Najwa al-Qattan, Suzanne Smith, Susan Spectorsky, Itzchak Weismann, and Michael Winter. I would also like to thank Mostafa Atamnia, Hala Bahouth, and Ahmed al-Rahim for their assistance with difficult Arabic texts. I owe thanks to Daniel Williford, who kindly read the entire manuscript before it had been sent to publishers and saved me from various copyediting errors. Four people were directly involved in the production of the book: I was fortunate to work with Kate Wahl, the editor-in-chief of Stanford University Press, whose high professional standards made the publication process an encouraging and constructive experience. I am also thankful to Frances Malcolm and Mariana Raykov at Stanford University Press for their immense competence, attention, and patience and to Cynthia Lindlof, who skillfully copyedited this book.

Special thanks to my colleagues at Rhodes College for their camaraderie and friendship. I would particularly like to thank Brian Shaffer, who was very generous with his time on many occasions and has always offered me excellent advice. His wisdom, integrity, and modesty have guided me through the pressures of academic life. I am also grateful to Michael Drompp, Dean of Faculty, for his continued trust and support of my work. Without his patience and help, it would not have been possible for me to finish this undertaking. I want to thank most affectionately my friends and colleagues in the Department of History, who took an interest in my work, made useful comments on early drafts, and offered much encouragement.

Several modest but instrumental grants from Harvard University's Center for Middle Eastern Studies and Morocco Studies Program supported my early research. Harvard University's Humanities Center and the Andrew W. Mellon Foundation provided funding that enabled me to complete the dissertation. Rhodes College's Creative Advanced Planning (CAP)—Mellon Study Leave gave me the time to finish writing the book. In addition, I am grateful to the staff of the Middle East Division of Widener Library at Harvard University. Michael Hopper generously ordered Moroccan works at my request, and Karim Rouqui's ready availability as a source of advice was of tremendous help. Very special thanks go to Kenan Padgett, the interlibrary loan librarian at Barret Library at Rhodes College, for facilitating the completion of my research.

To my husband, Shlomi Sarfati, goes my deepest appreciation. He has lived with this project, always generously, through its many stages. With plenty of humor and joy, he endorsed al-Wazzānī's invasion into his life. I am lucky to have his love and support.

OLD TEXTS, NEW PRACTICES

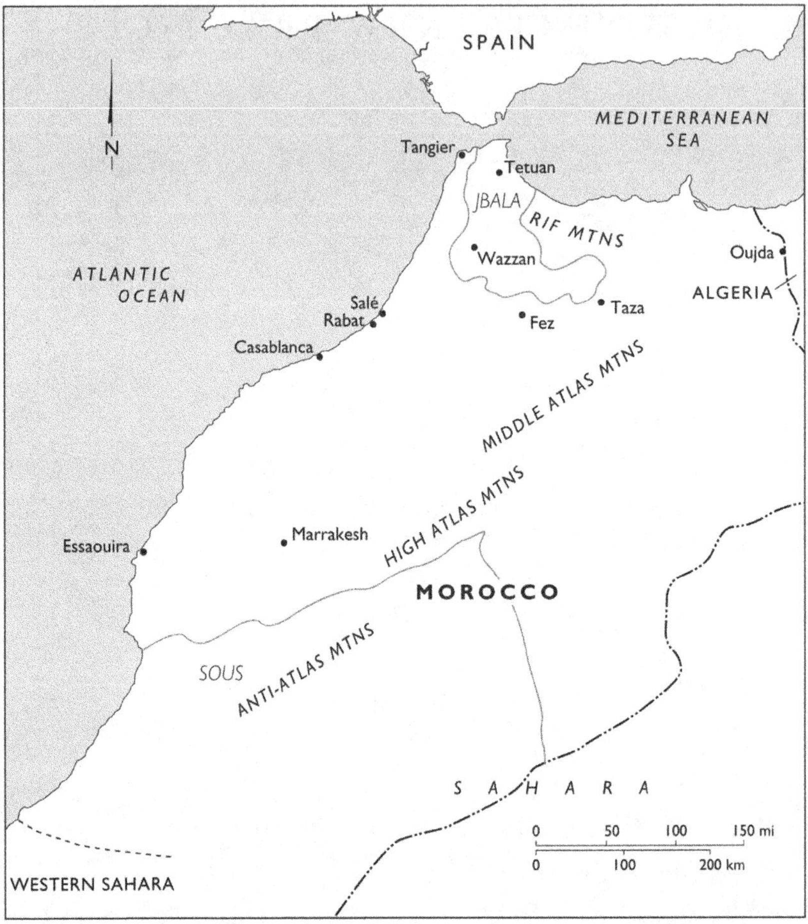
SPAIN
MEDITERRANEAN SEA
N
Tangier
Tetuan
JBALA
RIF MTNS
Oujda
Wazzan
ATLANTIC OCEAN
ALGERIA
Salé
Rabat
Taza
Fez
Casablanca
MIDDLE ATLAS MTNS
HIGH ATLAS MTNS
Essaouira
Marrakesh
MOROCCO
SOUS
ANTI-ATLAS MTNS
S A H A R A
0 50 100 150 mi
0 100 200 km
WESTERN SAHARA

Morocco

1 MODERN ISLAM AND THE RELIGIOUS REFORM TRADITION

IN 1910, at the height of a period of major crisis and change in Morocco, as fears about a full-scale French military occupation threatened the country with social disorder and anarchy, al-Mahdī al-Wazzānī (1849–1923), a prominent Moroccan Islamic scholar, published a massive eleven-volume compilation of Mālikī fatwās and named it *al-Mi'yār al-jadīd* (the *New Standard Measure*; henceforth, the *New Mi'yār*).[1] In all likelihood, al-Wazzānī began his project around 1902.[2] Enormous effort was involved in the compilation of the book. During a period of approximately eight years, al-Wazzānī toiled on countless manuscripts of Mālikī law and jurisprudence. He came across thousands of fatwās that had been issued in Morocco over the course of centuries of Mālikī legal activity, selecting individual fatwās to be included in his monumental work.

As a work of compilation, the *New Mi'yār* constitutes an assemblage of legal opinions issued by al-Wazzānī himself and by other prominent Mālikī muftīs, both contemporaries and predecessors. The scope of the work attests to a deliberate policy on the part of al-Wazzānī to produce a digest or encyclopedia of Mālikī law. It is immediately apparent that he carefully selected fatwās that tackle an ample spectrum of topics, and he gathered, copied, and arranged the material according to thematic criteria. Many of these legal opinions treat questions concerned with concrete social exigencies and everyday life of ordinary people that emerged within the context of the world in which al-Wazzānī lived: What are the ethical and legal duties of Muslims residing under European rule? Is emigration from non-Muslim territory an absolute duty? Is it lawful for Muslim merchants to travel to Europe? Is it appropriate to impose a market tax not stipulated by the Qur'ān? Is it legal to consume European-manufactured sugar?

Al-Wazzānī's compilation of fatwās was deeply rooted in a traditional, eclectic genre of classical Islamic texts.[3] Throughout Muslim societies, fatwās issued by distinguished jurists were regularly collected, either by the jurists themselves or by their students or associates, to be taught, transmitted, and interpreted.[4] In text-centered societies, assembling the greatest teachings of the previous generations not only reflects a deeply ingrained respect for precedent and established authority but assigns such authority and prestige to the compiler and the work.[5] Such fatwā collections can become paradigmatic examples of legal schools and juristic thought.

Al-Wazzānī's naming the finished work the *New Mi'yār* automatically implied continuity with a leading work of the Mālikī school, the *Mi'yār* of Aḥmad al-Wansharīsī (d. 1508), the most famous collection of Mālikī fatwās.[6] In the centuries after its compilation, this encyclopedic oeuvre was one of the most widely used legal texts by Moroccan 'ulamā'. Its juristic authority was considered impeccable, and it was regarded as an authoritative model within the Mālikī school. Al-Wazzānī's compilation resembles al-Wansharīsī's in its massiveness, chronological span, format, and apparatus. It is only natural to assume that al-Wazzānī's selection of the *New Mi'yār* as the title of his work was intended to echo the reputation of al-Wansharīsī's *Mi'yār*. Indeed, the modern editor of the *New Mi'yār*, 'Umar Bin'abbād, has referred to the collection as "one more brick, in terms of its content and size, and its scholarly significance and value that is added to the edifice [*ṣarḥ*] of great Moroccan authors in this field, such as *Kitāb al-Mi'yār* of Aḥmad al-Wansharīsī."[7]

The *New Mi'yār* is one of the central and most extensive texts of the Mālikī legal tradition written and published in pre-Protectorate Morocco (1860–1912) and is recognized as an important repository of the Moroccan juristic lore.[8] Despite its scope and vast spectrum of topics, no comprehensive study of the collection has been undertaken to date.[9] Who was al-Mahdī al-Wazzānī? What causes and motives led him to compile the *New Mi'yār*? Why was a *New Mi'yār* needed? What were his objectives for the work? And how did they shape the nature of the material he collected in it? This book is about a single text, the *New Mi'yār* of al-Mahdī al-Wazzānī, its nature and meaning. It aims at providing detailed analysis of a specific project of Islamic reform initiated by a modernist religious scholar.

ISLAMIC MODERNISM RECONSIDERED

A long-standing view, if not consensus, has dominated the scholarship on modern Islamic reformist thought in the late nineteenth and early twentieth centuries. This view, in broad outline, maintains that reformist thinkers promulgated a sharp critique of the classical Islamic scholarship and rejected the principle of legal schools.[10] More specifically, the concepts of renewal (*tajdīd*), revival (*iḥyā'*), and reform (*iṣlāḥ*) are understood to involve the recovering of a correct form of Islam exemplified by the Prophet and the "pious ancestors" (*al-salaf al-ṣāliḥ*). This focus of reformist Islam on the early community of Muslims posited a return to the basic authoritative sources, the Qur'ān and the *sunna* (the normative example of the Prophet). Central to Islamic reformism, as suggested by this narrative, are the notions of revival of the Prophetic *sunna* recorded in authenticated ḥadīth (traditions traced to Muḥammad), promotion of *ijtihād* (reasoning independent of precedent), and rejection of *taqlīd* (blind imitation of earlier authorities).

In its preoccupation with the Qur'ān and the corpus of the ḥadīth as the guide to the true essence of Islam, and the vehement opposition to *taqlīd*, modern reformism, as emphasized fairly consistently by scholars, denoted radical critique of the legacy and teachings of classical scholarship, the classical schools of law (*madhāhib*, sing. *madhhab*), and the religious establishment.[11] In one of the seminal texts on Islamic reform, Ali Merad articulates an outlook shared by many commentators on this orientation that characterized Islamic modernism:

> By preaching tirelessly for a return to first principles, the reformists were led to voice severe criticism of the orthodox Schools and their teachers. In their eyes, the Schools generally identified themselves with trends hostile to reason and science; they hindered the research carried out by *idjtihad* and consequently helped to stop the cultural progress of the community; they in fact gave priority to the study of *fikh* over knowledge based on the Kuran and on the Prophet's *Sunna*; they placed the authority of the "doctors" higher than the authority of the only legitimate and worthwhile *madhhab*: that of the Salaf.[12]

Accordingly, reformist 'ulamā' have been often construed as the opposite of conservative 'ulamā'. In their attitude toward Islamic tradition, conservative 'ulamā' were depicted as defenders of the classical interpretations of the orthodox schools who rejected any form of change and were content with blind adherence to juristic opinions developed hundreds of years ago. Moreover, Muslim reformers, it has been often argued, were concerned with the sociopolitical consequences of modernization and the overwhelming Western challenge, so they espoused a dynamic and flexible understanding of Islam and provided the underpinnings for the renewal and revival of Islamic tradition. Conversely, conservative ʿulamāʾ have been tagged as protectors of the status quo who were detached from the changed conditions of the time and hostile to modern ideas and practices.[13]

Recent scholarly efforts to investigate and characterize the multifaceted movement of modern Islamic reform in the late nineteenth century and the beginning of the twentieth century have aptly criticized some of the implicit assumptions underpinning the historiography of modern Islamic reform. Critics have observed that for decades, Western scholars often told the story of Islamic modernist reformism as reflecting the subjective viewpoint of a few modernist intellectuals of the early twentieth century associated with the modernist network in Cairo, with whom they had most contact and on whose writings they principally relied.[14] Ultimately, the conceptual preoccupations invoked in the works of major reformists such as Jamāl al-Dīn al-Afghānī (d. 1897), Muḥammad ʿAbduh (d. 1905), and Rashīd Riḍā (d. 1935) became a fundamental typology on which the study of modern Islamic reformism is based.[15] I agree with this dissatisfaction.[16] The type of reformism that emerged in Egypt undoubtedly deserves close attention.[17] My general concern here, however, is with conceiving the broad movement of modernist reform, which developed within the intellectual/epistemological, geographical, and political diversity of Islam, in terms of the ideas and principles that are intimately linked to a single network of Muslim reformers.[18]

More specifically, my principal concern is with automatically associating Islamic modernism with a sharp critique of the medieval scholarship and rejection of the principle of legal schools. The problem with this conception of modern reformism is the implication that thinkers who abided by consensual precedent, invoked the authority of the conventional legal schools, and were important members of the religious leadership in their communities did not (indeed, could not) offer any change as a basis for Islamic revival and reform. This study offers a new way of conceptualizing Islamic reformers and their projects. Redefining such an established view uncovers yet another chapter in the narrative of the origins of modern Islam.

Over the past few decades, a growing body of literature on tradition and religious authority in Islam has aimed at offering new approaches to thinking about Islamic tradition and historical change.[19] The emergent view posits Islamic tradition as a sphere of fundamentally variable and shifting truths and principles rather than a set of stagnant beliefs and understandings. Scholars have argued that definitions of what constitutes Islamic tradition emerge within competing discourses and arguments, further eroding the simpler association of Islamic tradition with a fixed, essentialized body of knowledge. Interrogations of the concept have been particularly fruitful in redirecting the attention of scholars from prominent formulations of tradition as "traditional" that simply mimics the past to complex conceptions of pursuing continuity and coherence with the past. This approach is connected to the idea that appeal to tradition does not always entail opposition to change but can effectively enable it, that innovation may be articulate entirely within the terms of an age-old tradition. It is this body of knowledge on which I draw. My own view is profoundly inspired by the works of Talal Asad, an anthropologist of religion, and Daniel Brown, a scholar of Islam.

Asad understands Islam as "a discursive tradition" consisting of ongoing discourses in a variety of historical circumstances that seek to orient practitioners regarding the authorized practices. For him,

> These discourses relate conceptually to *a past* (when the practice was instituted, and from which the knowledge of its point and proper performance has been transmitted) and *a future* (how the point of that practice can best be secured in the short or long term, or why it should be modified or abandoned), through *a present* (how it is linked to other practices, institutions, and social conditions).[20]

Moreover, Asad argues that Islamic tradition is constituted and reconstituted not only by ongoing interactions between the present and the past. For him, interpretative debates, confrontations, and conflicts are intrinsic to the constitution and development of Islamic tradition, as of others. In Asad's view, central to the concept of tradition is orthodoxy, which conveys the correct authoritative doctrine. As he suggests, orthodoxy "is not a mere body of opinion but a distinctive relationship—a relationship of power. Wherever Muslims have the power to regulate, uphold, require, or adjust *correct* practices, and to condemn, exclude, undermine, or replace *incorrect* ones, there is the domain of orthodoxy."[21]

Particularly instructive to my thinking is the conception of power and change. The construction and reconstruction of Islamic orthodoxy, or the definition of what constitutes a Muslim, emerges in conditions of conflict and contestation of interpretations; "incorrect" concepts, beliefs, and practices are dismantled and replaced with "correct" ones. Furthermore, Asad suggests in a related article that because orthodoxy "aspires to be authoritative," what is involved in the process of determining orthodoxy "is not a simple ad hoc acceptance of new arrangements but the attempt to redescribe norms and concepts with the aid of tradition-guided reasoning." In fact, for Asad, those who speak for Islamic orthodoxy "cannot speak in total freedom: there are conceptual and institutional conditions that must be attended to if discourses are to be persuasive."[22] From this point of view, then, a reconfigured orthodoxy necessarily engages Islamic forms of reasoning and is firmly rooted in the Islamic discursive tradition.

Closely related to this position is Daniel Brown's approach to the relationships between Islamic tradition and modernity. He points out,

> A tradition emerges from the prism of modernity as a multi-colored spectrum of responses. Some responses will show the effects of modernity much more dramatically than others, but none will be entirely untouched. At the same time, each color of the spectrum, each different response, is clearly rooted in the tradition. All responses to modernity from a religious tradition, and even those that seem to have left the tradition altogether behind, maintain a certain continuity with the tradition, just as each band of the spectrum is present in the light entering a prism.[23]

Brown invokes the transforming relationships of modernity and tradition. His point is that in the modern competition over the definition and content of tradition, there are no nonmodern formulations of tradition. He urges us to imagine tradition as "refracted by the prism of modernity." For him, modern Muslims are engaged in an ongoing process of *rethinking* the traditions in which they participate. All responses to modernity from a religious tradition are at the same time fundamentally shaped by the modern as well as anchored within tradition. This is to say that "the most radical opponents of tradition are not departing from the tradition" and "the most conservative defenders of tradition cannot help but reshape the very tradition that they seek to preserve unchanged."[24]

The point that Brown's insight illustrates for me is that the opposition between modern reform and Islamic intellectual tradition that underlies so many discussions of modern Islam assumes a simplistic understanding of the relations between tradition and modernity. Fidelity to the large body of Islamic classical knowledge, and adherence to earlier rulings and precedents authorized by the *madhhab*, does not simply signify "traditional" as opposed to "modern" Islamic thought. Put differently, while some reformist thinkers aimed at defending the Islamic legal tradition through the implementation of norms they considered as "truly" Islamic, these thinkers were also modern and reformulated Islam through the prism of historical time and in light of the new social circumstances and structural changes produced within modernity.

Asad and Brown invite me to imagine tradition as consisting of alternative, even rival, interpretations that by a culturally specific continuous argument and disagreement over the content of that tradition constitute and reconstitute orthodox doctrine. The latter is firmly grounded in Islamic texts, beliefs, and practices. Moreover, modernity has a constitutive effect on tradition; it informs/imposes a distinctive pattern of rethinking tradition. This pattern is a fundamentally *modern* one.

I argue that precisely such a competition between interpretations characterized the period in which al-Mahdī al-Wazzānī operated, and such a reconstitution of tradition was his *New Mi'yār*. Larger political and socioeconomic transformations that characterized the Moroccan nineteenth century stimulated a widespread reexamination of Islamic law and scrutiny of social and legal norms. Many among the religious scholars and jurists of the period were particularly dissatisfied with the state of the Mālikī legal tradition and called for a reevaluation of its definitive doctrinal authority. In composing his *New Mi'yār*, al-Wazzānī reacted against this negative assessment of Mālikī jurisprudence and sought to defend and reinforce its preeminent authority.

In approaching the *New Mi'yār* from this vantage point, my goal is to provide a way of conceptualizing the relations between Islamic tradition and modern religious reform that is different from that proposed by existing scholarship. I want to demonstrate that Islamic ideas of revival and reform were not the privileged intellectual monopoly of reformist thinkers who articulated a critical position toward the classical legal tradition. In fact, al-Wazzānī's reform project aimed at the revival and renewal of the authority of Mālikī scholarship by introducing a new Mālikī orthodoxy.

THE MAKING OF THE *NEW MI'YĀR*

Al-Mahdī al-Wazzānī was a distinguished Moroccan religious scholar (*faqīh*, pl. *fuqahā'*) of the late nineteenth century. He was born in 1849 in the city of Wazzān in northern Morocco to a sharīfan family of the celebrated 'Imrānī line, which claimed lineage to the Prophet Muḥammad through his descendant and founder of Fez, Mawlāy Idrīs. As a youth, al-Wazzānī left Wazzān for Fez, where he studied Islamic law at the Qarawiyyīn University. After completing his studies, al-Wazzānī wrote legal treatises, taught at the Qarawiyyīn, and issued fatwās, engaging in the various roles of the trained legal scholar.

By the time al-Wazzānī completed the writing of the *New Miʿyār* in 1910, the Moroccan state and society had undergone a period of approximately sixty years of far-reaching changes that constituted an accelerated passage to modernity.[25] Beginning in the second half of the nineteenth century, the Moroccan state and society experienced new circumstances arising from two interrelated historical developments: the growing disparity in power between Morocco and Europe, which prompted ever-increasing foreign interference in Moroccan affairs, and the modernizing projects initiated and led by the Moroccan state (henceforth, the Makhzan).[26]

The French occupation of Ottoman Algiers in July 1830 had fateful repercussions for Morocco. Shortly thereafter, Europe affirmed its economic and military superiority at Morocco's expense. Throughout the remainder of the nineteenth century England, France, and to a lesser extent Spain and Germany aggressively competed for influence in the internal affairs of the Moroccan state. Between the mid-nineteenth century and the beginning of colonial rule in 1912, Moroccan sovereignty was repeatedly challenged by European powers. The sultan's armies suffered crushing military defeats at the hands of modern European armies in 1844 (the battle of Isly against France) and again in 1859 (the Tetuan war against Spain), forcing the Makhzan to sign a truce and humiliating peace treaties. The financial cost of the wars and the large war indemnity forced the Makhzan to accept foreign loans, which bankrupted the Moroccan state. The unfavorable commercial treaties concluded with European states (beginning with England in 1856) opened Morocco to an increasingly aggressive European economic expansion that the Makhzan was unprepared to meet.[27] As foreign governments increasingly undermined the sovereign rights of the Moroccan sultan, the system of granting consular protection to native Moroccans became widespread and much abused. By the last decades of the nineteenth century, the protection offered by the foreign powers symbolized the transformation of the foundations underlying the relations between the Islamic ruler and his subjects.[28] Moroccan writings of the time manifest the anger and frustration of particular sectors of the population with the inability of the state to stop European encroachment.[29]

Confronted by Europe's political, military, and economic superiority and a deepening economic crisis, the Makhzan initiated reforms in the government, the financial system, and the army. The second half of the nineteenth century marked a period of extensive Makhzan-led reform that was meant to place more political, fiscal, and religious authority in the hands of the state.While foreign advisers played a prominent role in shaping various reforms, there were also members of the Moroccan bureaucracy and merchant elite, familiar with administrative, socioeconomic, and technological developments in Europe, who were active in these reforms and their implementation.[30] In the course of the reform process, local praxis and social ideals were considerably modified and replaced with new and innovative institutions and practices. This intensive process of centralization and reform of the Moroccan state prompted considerable local resistance and generated internal unrest in Moroccan society.[31] The reform effort of the second half of the nineteenth century, however, proved mostly ineffective in preventing greater European intervention in Moroccan affairs. The convening of the international Madrid conference in 1880, at which the European powers addressed their competing ambitions regarding Morocco, further exposed the unequal relationship of power between Europe and Morocco that culminated in military occupation and the establishment of the French and Spanish Protectorates in 1912.

By the latter part of the nineteenth century, concerns regarding European hegemony, the corresponding weakness of Islam, and dissatisfaction with the state of politics and religion emerged as central issues for many religious thinkers. The new historical conditions encouraged a special preoccupation with Islamic law. Doctrinal questions and theological considerations took on particular significance and became the focus of intense debates and heated conversations.[32] This preoccupation with Islamic law in turn triggered a larger reexamination of the Mālikī legal tradition and a call for religious reform. In the face of crisis and change, Moroccan 'ulamā' searched the tradition in which they were grounded for the explanations for the apparent weakness of Islam. Leading Moroccan jurists offered a radical critique of Mālikī jurisprudence (*fiqh*) and vigorously insisted that the renewal of religion (*tajdīd*) was necessary for the revival of the Moroccan Muslim community.[33]

In the course of these years, al-Mahdī al-Wazzānī, in addition to being a writer of treatises, a muftī, and a professor of law, compiled two collections of Mālikī fatwās. The writing of the *New Mi'yār* was preceded by the *Exalted Gift*, a short and less-known compilation.[34] Al-Wazzānī devoted considerable energy to these two projects, and as I am going to suggest, for him, making fatwā compilations was not only the mere assembling of a collection. Rather, collecting the material was a creative act of making new constructions that effectively represent and communicate the unique modern Moroccan existence.

Like most classical collections of fatwās, al-Wazzānī's *New Miʿyār* is structured according to the standard categories of Islamic law, or sharīʿa jurisprudence. The collection encompasses a wide array of subject matter that covers almost every conceivable area of life. The fatwās range from treatments of marriage contracts, dowries, divorce, alimony, and child custody to considerations of questions concerning inheritance and pious endowments; ritual duties, such as prayer, fasting, and alms giving; crimes against religion; rules of evidence and court procedure; and many other issues. It is worth noting that the legal deliberations touch upon the entire spectrum of private and communal life and reveal the enormous variety of matters that al-Wazzānī considered central to his oeuvre. In addition, it must be stressed that the *New Miʿyār* represents an Islamic conception of law. It is arranged according to the conventional branches of *fiqh* and in line with the traditional comprehensiveness of sharīʿa jurisprudence. As a work of *fiqh*, it embraces acts of worship (*ʿibādāt*) and interpersonal relations (*muʿāmalāt*). In other words, the *New Miʿyār* does not represent a new understanding of the nature and role of the law; rather, it is a legal text within the conventional *fiqh* tradition.

As mentioned, in creating the *New Miʿyār*, al-Wazzānī collected fatwās from a wide range of sources—from his own work, from those of his contemporaries, and from canonical texts central to the Mālikī tradition. As a literary work, the *New Miʿyār* reflects al-Wazzānī's self-conception as both a compiler of Mālikī knowledge and wisdom and a muftī. In the first role, al-Wazzānī studied manuscripts comprising the school's doctrine—law manuals, commentaries, treatises, and fatwā compilations. He then selected and copied individual fatwās that he considered as authoritative statements within the Mālikī school. Finally, he assembled and arranged the material in separate, thematically unified chapters (*bāb*, pl. *abwāb*). In editing the material and preparing chapters, al-Wazzānī took a dynamic and creative role of juxtaposing different authorities, consciously creating original links and eliciting new arguments.[35] In the second role, that of a muftī, he treated legal disputes between individuals, requests for fatwās from judges, and questions arising from actual judicial practice.[36] In addition to gathering his own material, al-Wazzānī chose to present dozens, if not hundreds, of fatwās issued by his predecessors, which he disputed in order to introduce new legal opinions firmly grounded in Mālikī mainstream scholarship, thereby emphasizing the act of recovering and restoring the correct practice from within Mālikī intellectual tradition using familiar forms of reasoning. In this way, al-Wazzānī created "new yet old" constructions that featured a creative dialogue between his own cultural world and the Mālikī heritage.[37]

In both roles, however, al-Wazzānī relied primarily on the traditional commentaries and classical and medieval literature of the Mālikī *madhhab*. His sources include some of the most authoritative works of legal doctrine and celebrated compilations of fatwās of the Mālikī school, such as the *Muwaṭṭa'* of Mālik b. Anas (d. 795), *Mudawwana* of Saḥnūn (d. 854), *Risāla* of al-Qayrawānī (d. 996), *Fatāwā* of Ibn Rushd (d. 1126), *Mukhtaṣar* of Khalīl (d. 1374), *Ajwiba* of Ibn Lubb (d. 1380), *Nawāzil* of Ibn Hilāl (d. 1504), *Kitāb al-Mi'yār* of al-Wansharīsī (d. 1508), and *Mawāhib al-Jalīl* of al-Ḥaṭṭāb (d. 1547). At the same time, he compiled much material from early modern and modern works of distinguished Mālikī legists such as *al-'Amāl al-Fāsī* of 'Abd al-Raḥmān al-Fāsī (d. 1685), *Nawāzil* of al-Majjasī (d. 1688), *Sharḥ al-Zurqānī* of al-Zurqānī (d. 1710), *Kitāb al-Nawāzil* of al-'Alamī (d. 1715), and *al-'Amal al-Muṭlaq* of Sijilmāsī (d. 1800). In addition, he incorporated manuscripts and commentaries of prolific jurists of the first half of the nineteenth century and his contemporaries such as 'Ali al-Tasūlī (d. 1842), Muḥammad bin al-Madanī Gannūn (d. 1885), and Muḥammad bin Ja'far al-Kattānī (d. 1927). Whether the library he used while conducting his research was the Qarawiyyīn's, his own private library, or those of his colleagues, the canonical works of *les grands docteurs* of the Mālikī *madhhab* that are central to the tradition predominate.[38]

These sources span many centuries and capture and communicate the accumulated juristic patrimony of the Mālikī school. This is a significant determinant of the ideological orientation and cultural function of the *New Mi'yār*, giving a particular color to the work. The *New Mi'yār* is intimately linked to a specific intellectual community and textual culture, thereby bound to be shaped by the methods of reasoning, modes of argumentation, and foundational principles that conform to this legal tradition. This strong connection to the Mālikī discursive tradition pushes to the fore the obvious uniqueness of the *New Mi'yār*. On the one hand, fundamental domains of the text, including attitudes, beliefs, judgments, sensitivities, vocabulary, and so on, operate within the Mālikī tradition; and on the other, it is inevitably rooted within the cultural world of its author, his motivations, and temperament. My point is that al-Wazzānī's *New Miʿyār* is a document of a certain milieu at a certain moment, a product of its time, bearing traces of a particular intellectual tradition.

READING FATWĀS

It should be clear by now that this book investigates the *New Miʿyār* as a cohesive and original work, consciously and deliberately created by a single author. From this perspective, *Old Texts, New Practices* differs from other studies that are based on fatwā compilations. Most such works have tended to neglect the compilation's own literary form and function and treated almost exclusively selected fatwās as a subject of critical discussion and source material for historical construction. Fatwā compilations have been principally studied as a mine of texts waiting to be investigated.[39] In this book I move away from this preoccupation.

As the following chapters demonstrate, I am interested in the *New Miʿyār* as a single text. It seems to me that this conceptual framework is a more instructive and fruitful one since it encourages me to consider fatwā texts within the compositional context of the entire work. Consequently, what is important to me is not only to read fatwās but also to explore the author of the compilation and his consciousness, the historical context from which the compilation emerged, the creative act of producing it, its content, and its meaning in the mind of its author. To put the same point in another way, central to this book's concerns is the view of the *New Miʿyār* as a radically ideological text original to the period. Al-Wazzānī was not a passive clerk copying the sayings of his predecessors in a schematic method, and the *New Miʿyār* is not a scrapbook or a random compilation of fatwās. Rather, it possesses a particular character and espouses a particular point of view.

In an effort to penetrate the nature and meaning of the *New Miʿyār*, I have sought ways to conceptualize the relationship between al-Wazzānī and the individual fatwās that make up his compilation. In this study, I have approached the law from a particular historical perspective, itself the result of my encounters with the works of cultural anthropologists.[40] As is undoubtedly clear by now, law, as understood here, interacts with a particular historical reality. It fits a particular place, time, and society. It takes place within a certain culture and projects its internal logic. The role and importance of the law are inseparable from its connections to a wide range of cultural practices and its dialectic interaction with a specific society.

Specifically, I have drawn on Brinkley Messick's investigation of the muftīship as an indigenous institution of worldly interpretation.[41] For Messick, muftīs are worldly interpreters who apply Islamic law to practical life problems; their fatwās constitute an application of a "distinctive notion of text" to the factual world, representing a mode of thought that serves to "bring Islamic-legal knowledge into the world and the world into knowledge." As he suggests, "Muftis are intermediate figures" who "have functioned at the interpretative interface of theory and practice in Islamic law for many centuries."[42] In other words, Messick views the muftīship as an institution representing an interpretative activity that crafts meaning for a society in its own terms by relating an indigenous notion of text to a particular set of circumstances.

Muftīship, Messick emphasizes,

> was not only an institution through which rarified scholarly disputes and the received wisdom of the jurists were brought down to earth in communicable form as "guidance" for the common people. It was also the channel through which mundane, earth-hugging realities, including new factual developments, were formally noticed by and reflected upon by qualified scholarly minds, leading to analogical extensions of the body of legal knowledge. In a dialectical manner, locally generated questions were related to locally interpreted jurisprudence.[43]

As muftīs offered their opinions on what the Islamic view entailed, they were also engaged in a continual process of developing legal doctrine on new topics in response to concerns and events in their communities, creating new texts and regulating new cases. For Messick, the muftī's fatwā provides an example of an interpretative genre that is clearly identified as "native" interpretation by the people themselves. In his view, fatwās are "neither oriented towards, nor dependent upon, communicating with outsiders." As such, they represent indigenous thought, comprising an interpretation of reality, for indigenous consumption.[44]

Inspired by Messick's conceptualization of the muftīship, I argue that al-Wazzānī's discourse invokes a pattern of sophisticated interaction between Mālikī legal doctrine, sources of legal authority, and the rhetoric of legal argumentation, on the one hand, and sociocultural assumptions, customary practices, and sensibilities particular to his society, on the other. In other words, Messick invites me to argue that al-Wazzānī formulated in his *New Mi'yār* an interpretation of the world anchored in Mālikī tradition for a particular Muslim society. The point I wish to emphasize is that even though the *New Miʿyār* transmits Mālikī memory and tradition and features a multiplicity of voices, it bears the personal, subjective creativity of an individual author's voice, rooted in his own cultural world, and thereby builds upon his interpretation of his society.

This book presents a twofold argument. First, in composing the *New Miʿyār*, al-Wazzānī reacted to—or against—Islamic ideas of revival and reform that encouraged a radical critique of Mālikī legal tradition and a call for a reevaluation of its definitive doctrinal authority and special status in the Moroccan intellectual scene. Al-Wazzānī's *New Miʿyār* intended to restore and reinforce the preeminent authority of the Mālikī legal tradition by composing a new Mālikī orthodoxy. Second, in the *New Miʿyār*, al-Wazzānī, in fact, formulated his interpretation of the world anchored in the Mālikī discursive tradition for a particular Muslim society. In elaborating his interpretation, al-Wazzānī both challenged and accommodated the changes in his age. His goal was to infuse Mālikī thought with meaning relevant to his changed world. Thus, a critical concern in his *New Miʿyār* was to establish a discourse that consciously preserved long-standing Mālikī doctrine and knowledge as the substance of a contemporary ethical Muslim life. In the process, al-Wazzānī actively transformed the contents and forms of Mālikī scholarship. For al-Wazzānī, redefining Mālikī tradition and thought as an effective regulator of contemporary social relations and Islamic morality was necessary to ensure its preservation and continuity in the context of the changes that marked Moroccan modernity. In other words, the story of al-Wazzānī and his *New Miʿyār* alters the focus of our attention away from (the usual and misleading) narrative that defines Islamic modernism as a rupture with tradition and toward the distinctive shape of discourses, consciousnesses, and intellectual projects that emerged in a modern Muslim world.

THE STRUCTURE OF THE STUDY

My trajectory in the succeeding chapters is as follows: Chapter 2 looks at al-Mahdī al-Wazzānī's biography. In particular, this chapter focuses on the question of what experiences, institutions, and professional roles shaped al-Wazzānī's identity and his vision of the world. I argue first that al-Wazzānī was an adherent of the Mālikī school of sharīʿa jurisprudence and a highly trained Mālikī *faqīh*. I also suggest that he was deeply involved in the exigencies of everyday life. My portrait is of a man who was a distinguished scholar and at the same time rooted, in a variety of ways, in the world he inhabited. He was a respected member of the community of Moroccan scholars, deeply involved in the legal and social affairs of the local population, and a loyal counselor in the service of the Moroccan sultan. In addition to his professional, authoritative knowledge of Islamic law, his position within society granted him intimate acquaintance with social and cultural life, political changes and conflicts, and doctrinal conversations and debates. Al-Wazzānī was a broadly respected and venerated *faqīh* among his fellow *fuqahā'* and in the popular sectors of society, and this affected his self-definition and expanded his sense of his intellectual abilities.

In Chapter 3, I examine the concrete historical circumstances within which the *New Mi'yār* was created. I argue that the new historical conditions of the late nineteenth and early twentieth centuries encouraged a special preoccupation with Islamic law and informed conversations and debates about Mālikī jurisprudence, its content, and nature. Concerns about the declining state of Islam emerged as a critical issue for religious thinkers. They firmly believed that religious reform and the renewal of religion would benefit social and political life. Al-Wazzānī viewed the dissatisfaction with the state of the Mālikī legal legacy as a direct challenge to the special position and authority of Mālikī *fiqh* and ultimately to his position as keeper of knowledge and interpreter of law. Thus, I maintain that in his *New Mi'yār*, al-Wazzānī searched for a solid basis for defending and restoring Mālikī legal tradition by composing a new Mālikī orthodoxy.

While these two chapters are concerned with al-Wazzānī and the concrete historical content of the changes that marked Moroccan modernity within which the *New Mi'yār* emerged and acquired its form and meaning, the next three chapters examine the very nature and meaning of the compilation. The chapters are organized thematically and focus on an analysis of five fatwā texts, which deal with sociolegal issues that experienced dramatic structural and conceptual transformations in al-Wazzānī's time. Together, the three chapters offer a way to penetrate al-Wazzānī's juristic interpretation and argumentation as well as his compositional mechanics and methods.

Chapter 4 focuses on the expansion of contact with foreigners as the growing disparity in power between Morocco and Europe became particularly acute during the second half of the nineteenth century. Specifically, I analyze two texts composed by al-Wazzānī. The first is a fatwā originally issued by al-Wazzānī himself on Muslims becoming protégés of foreign powers represented in Morocco. Al-Wazzānī's juristic argumentation is an unequivocal condemnation of Muslim protégés and a rejection of the discourse that authorized the practice. The second text is an extensive editorial comment, combining materials from separate sources, gathered and arranged by al-Wazzānī. In it, he disputes a famous fatwā issued by Aḥmad al-Wansharīsī on the legal duty of Muslims who voluntarily reside under non-Muslim rule to migrate from the realm of unbelief. Here, al-Wazzānī contested older ways of interpreting the world and accommodated the changes created by the new historical conditions. In both texts, I demonstrate how al-Wazzānī explicitly delegitimized and marginalized certain interpretations and authorized others in order to both challenge and accommodate the historical change dictated by Moroccan modernity.

Chapter 5 investigates the sociolegal domain of kinship and domestic life as new historical conditions emerged and altered circumstances and consciousnesses in the Moroccan countryside and cities. I examine two fatwās issued by al-Wazzānī. The first one tells the story of a dispute over family property (*ḥubs*). The second fatwā focuses on a family conflict between a woman and her brother-in-law, who refuses to pay her maintenance (*nafaqa*). In both cases, al-Wazzānī contests interpretations that sought to enhance gender asymmetry and male dominance. Instead, he suggests a restructuring of the patriarchal social order to reflect changes in family arrangements and household composition. I argue that al-Wazzānī denounced and rejected older answers that became irrelevant and legitimized others that accommodated the new historical conditions.

Chapter 6 looks at the increased Moroccan trade with Europe and the diffusion of new tastes for European-manufactured items. I explore one text assembled by al-Wazzānī that deliberately combines material from several sources written in the course of the nineteenth century. Al-Wazzānī compiled this text in response to rumors circulated in the last quarter of the nineteenth century that imported sugar from Europe was processed with pig's blood. The text unequivocally authorizes the consumption of imported sugar and reinforces the drinking of three other popular stimulant beverages. I show how al-Wazzānī's composition authorized an interpretation that accommodated new customs and changing tastes.

Finally, in Chapter 7 I reflect on the complexities of change in Islamic law. I focus on the Islamic commitment to argument and debate in a shared style of discourse and its role in shaping the direction and nature of that change. I argue that al-Wazzānī's commitment to compile in his *New Miʿyār* the most authoritative opinions within the Mālikī school of law as a medium for the transmission and preservation of tradition did not preclude innovation and creativity. In fact, precisely by pretending merely to present original, earlier texts, the *New Miʿyār* regularly offered new interpretations of the law and allowed for considerable flexibility in the adaptation of the law to new historical conditions and changing social needs. This complex dialogue between new consciousnesses and age-old voices of tradition is instructive for thinking about modern Islam.

2 RELIGIOUS KNOWLEDGE AND AUTHORITY IN PRECOLONIAL MOROCCO

TRACING al-Mahdī al-Wazzānī's life and career is problematic because of sparse information scattered through varied sources that contain biographical and autobiographical fragments and the nature of the evidence these records provide. Particularly, two kinds of historical sources recount the life of al-Wazzānī: the biography (*tarjama*, pl. *tarājim*), and a sort of premodern curriculum vitae (*fihris* or *fahrasa*).[1] An examination of these biographical and autobiographical literary genres offers the historian access to the intellectual life, human networks, and academic institutions of a religious scholar. Although they provide evidence that links the individual with the religious and scholarly centers of his society, these records leave us in the dark about many aspects of life that interest us. Information that falls outside the scope of the piety and scholarly authority of the individual under study is not part of the record. For example, there is no mention of marriages, and, with certain exceptions, women do not appear in the record. Thus, the family and household context in which learning occurs is difficult to ascertain. Moreover, economic position and political interests are not part of these sources.

In addition, these genres construct the individual for a specific, known audience, the community of religious scholars, employing the language and rhetorical structures of the *fuqahā'*. In other words, these records represent the *faqīh* in a highly stylized manner; the text itself and the message embedded in it constitute a discursive construction expressed in the language and rhetoric that originated within the community of the *fuqahā'*. Thus, typically, the data these documents contain consist of cultural glosses and metaphors that demonstrate a set of normative religious virtues and pious behavior that pose challenges to our understanding of the social world of the individual under examination. In the absence of other direct sources that record the life of al-Wazzānī, my strategy is to start with the solid evidence available in the extant material and amplify the substance of his life story from additional sources.

FRAGMENTS OF BIOGRAPHY

Al-Mahdī al-Wazzānī was born in the northern Moroccan city of Wazzān in 1849 (1266 AH). His father, who moved to Wazzān before al-Mahdī's birth, came from the Ghumāra Berber tribe that inhabited the Jbāla foothills of

Northern Morocco

northern Morocco. The latter constitutes a group within one of the principal Berber groups in Morocco, the Maṣmūda Berbers.[2] In addition, al-Wazzānī asserted a sharīfan status by claiming an ʿImrānī origin. The ʿImrānīs from the Ghumāra claim a long genealogy that links them to the house of the Prophet Muḥammad and his descendant and founder of Fez, Idrīs bin Idrīs.[3] We can imagine that years later, al-Wazzānī's status as a sharīf of the celebrated ʿImrānī line would grant him a special religious status and authority as a prominent *faqīh* in Fez. Presumably, it would further have imbued him with a sense of distinction and prominence as well as great respect from his fellow *fuqahā'* and his society.[4]

The ʿImrānī *shurafā'* of northern Morocco, like other *shurafā'*, enjoyed religious prestige and reverence and may well have benefited from a wide range of privileges in the form of donations, tax exemptions, decrees of distinctions, and land grants. The biographical dictionaries give little help on al-Wazzānī's fortune or his family's wealth. In all likelihood, as a prestigious family by virtue of descent and knowledge, al-Wazzānī's family was among those who did well. Edmund Burke indicates that al-Wazzānī was a businessman who owned land north of Fez.[5] If so, perhaps his family's private property contributed to his economic ascendancy.

Perhaps al-Wazzānī's father took him as a boy on trips north to his birthplace in the Jbāla region, not far from Wazzān. There, the young al-Wazzānī must have learned about the celebrated Idrīsī *shurafā'* and the special importance of the Idrīsī line in Fez.[6] Surely, al-Wazzānī must have traveled, accompanied by his family, to one of the most venerated holy shrines of the Idrīsī line in Morocco, the sanctuary (*ḥurm*) of the great sharīfan saint, Mawlāy ʿAbd al-Salām Ibn Mashīsh (d. 1228) in the Jbāla region.[7] If so, he may have witnessed acts of worship associated with the cult of saints, such as making vows, offering sacrifices, praying at the tomb, boisterous *dhikr* (a repetitive form of prayer) ceremonies, and ecstatic singing and dancing. Al-Wazzānī would surely have taken away with him some images and memories of the annual pilgrimage and the Sufi customs and fests that went along with it.

Wazzān was a renowned sacred center. Located between Fez and Tangier, Wazzān dominated the Jbāla tribal region and was a transit place for an influx of people and goods from the north. The sharīfs of Wazzān, as Idrīsī *shurafā'* and a celebrated saintly lineage, enjoyed a great degree of respect and regional power, especially among the tribes of the Jbāla and the Rif in northern Morocco. Like other *shurafā'*, the Wazzānī sharīfs were granted many privileges, such as entitlement to oversee large estates in the environs of Wazzān that extended over the lands of several tribal territories, including that of the Maṣmūda.

The city was also the focus of intense worship and spiritual activity centered on the Sufi order (*ṭarīqa*) of the Wazzāniyya. The lodge of the Wazzāniyya (*zāwiya)* was the scene of pilgrimages, zealous chanting, dancing, and other ecstatic activities associated with mystical practices.[8] There the young al-Wazzānī was inducted into the Wazzāniyya *ṭarīqa* by Sīdī al-Ḥājj ʿAbd al-Salām al-Wazzānī, head of the *zāwiya*, and Sīdī ʿAbd al-Jabbār al-Wazzānī, the Makhzan-appointed governor of the city.[9] Al-Wazzānī later recounts two stories about debates he had as a young student at the ages of fourteen and eighteen with two of his teachers about the existence and virtues of saints (*awliyāʾ*), prophets

Sīdī al-Ḥājj ʿAbd al-Salām. Source: *France-Maroc: Revue mensuelle illustrée, organe du Comité des foires du Maroc* 3 (March 1919): 65. Harvard College Library Afr 1306.1F.

(*anbiyāʾ*), and other pious people.[10] According to al-Wazzānī's narrative, in the two instances, he expressed his unquestioned belief in God's intercessors (*awliyāʾ Allāh*) and the idea of powerful protégés of God acting as intermediaries for the Muslim community.[11] However, his teachers, distinguished jurists themselves who were partisans of Islamic jurisprudence and committed disseminators of exoteric sciences (*ʿilm ẓāhirī*), condemned these beliefs as innovations that need to be purged from the Islamic community and explicitly criticized al-Wazzānī for his reprehensible beliefs. «Despite the direct accusations his teachers leveled against him, al-Wazzānī, as suggested by his narrative, was persistent in defending his position and evidently convinced his teachers to reconsider their beliefs. These stories illustrate that al-Wazzānī was seriously engaged in attaining religious knowledge derived through mysticism (*ʿilm bāṭinī*) from a young age. The image he conveys of himself is of a disciple and a partisan of the cult of saints.

With this in mind, it appears that the world in which al-Mahdī al-Wazzānī grew up, the Jbāla and Wazzān, was a locus of intense devotion centered on a celebrated *zāwiya* and included important sites of Sufi activity. We can imagine that these early encounters with Sufism might have influenced his worldview, cultural style, and tone and were likely to have had an important and enduring influence on his thinking. Perhaps this intimate acquaintance with Sufi mystics and principal practices made him more aware and accepting of Sufi teachings and ideas later in his life.

During the latter part of the nineteenth century the Wazzānī sharīfs became important figures in the politico-religious Moroccan landscape. In the course of the second part of the nineteenth century the *zāwiya*'s relationship with the Moroccan sultan, Mawlāy Ḥasan (r. 1873–94), deteriorated steadily, partly because of the sultan's transgression of the *zāwiya*'s traditional rights. This tendency became particularly obvious in 1875 when the sultan violated the *ḥurm*-related customs and disregarded the Wazzānī sharīfs' religious privileges.[12] The sharīf of Wazzān, Sīdī al-Ḥājj ʿAbd al-Salām al-Wazzānī, was deeply offended and saw in the sultan's behavior an insult to his religious prestige. The incident turned into a major political crisis when, in 1884, fearing for his own life, the sharīf of Wazzān finally placed himself under the protection of France, thereby openly defying the authority of the sultan as the head of the Islamic community.[13] The sharīf's behavior provoked considerable opposition and significantly undermined the prestige of the *zāwiya*. The point to be highlighted is that al-Wazzānī, who maintained close contacts with the city of Wazzān and its prominent sharīfs over the years, especially with ʿAbd al-Salām himself and his son the sharīf al-ʿArabī, who became the spiritual head of the *zāwiya* upon his father's death in 1892, might have been valued by the sultan for his political connections and ties. Such connections could conceivably have been viewed as a means of sustaining the relationships between the Wazzānī sharīfs and the sultan.[14]

His years as a youth in Wazzān brought other experiences to al-Mahdī al-Wazzānī. There the young al-Wazzānī received formative Islamic education in the local Moroccan intellectual tradition.[15] The first step in acquiring an Islamic education in Morocco, as elsewhere in the Muslim world, is memorization of the Qur'ān in its proper recitation. Biographies of Moroccan men of learning in the late nineteenth and early twentieth centuries underscore the important role played by close relatives in shaping their attitudes toward learning. Such a pattern of Qur'ānic instruction was integral to a child's upbringing and development. Biographical dictionaries indicate that men of learning most often came from households in which the father or another close relative was literate and actively encouraged Qur'ānic recitation and study. This pattern of domestic authority is central in al-Wazzānī's upbringing as well. Al-Wazzānī came from a learned family. His father was literate, and one of his brothers was a muftī.[16] Al-Wazzānī's father was closely involved in the early education of his sons. With his father and other scholars al-Wazzānī memorized the Qur'ān according to the most popular method of recitation in Morocco, *riwāyat warsh*, at the mosque school in Wazzān.[17]

When al-Wazzānī was ten years old, his father died, but al-Wazzānī continued his studies of the religious sciences.[18] He acquired fundamental skills in reading and writing in Arabic, grammar, and Islamic law. The pedagogical style was one of rote instruction with a heavy emphasis on memorization. Although the names of the earlier books he studied are not mentioned in the records, the standard literature that most of the learned men of his generation studied can be reconstructed from other biographies. He most likely memorized one or two grammar books in addition to two manuals of Mālikī law.[19] These treatises were recognized as standard beginner's texts, commonly the first books after the Qur'ān that students memorized. The result of such training was a basic exposure to the foundation of the religious sciences, which later allowed al-Wazzānī to pursue studies at a center of higher learning such as the famous university of the Qarawiyyīn.

It seems that the world around young al-Mahdī al-Wazzānī was informed, beyond Sufi brotherhood activities, also by the typical Moroccan form of primary Islamic education. By all accounts, al-Wazzānī was engaged in a considerable and lengthy learning process, according to the specialized tradition of instruction of his time. He recited the Qur'ān, memorized short, abridged classical Mālikī manuals, read works devoted to mysticism, and acquired a solid base for later study. Already at this level of training, al-Wazzānī was inscribed into an intellectual world marked by specialized knowledge elaborated in authoritative texts orally transmitted through methods of recitation and memorization. These elements of intellectual activity and scholarship would be further developed throughout the course of his advanced study in Fez and would become more pronounced in his writings.

PURSUING KNOWLEDGE IN FEZ

To complete his studies, al-Wazzānī left Wazzān for Fez, where he studied Islamic law with distinguished scholars. As the most prestigious center of Islamic scholarship in Morocco, Fez drew many students who came to pursue advanced studies in the juridical sciences at the Qarawiyyīn University.

Founded in the ninth century, the Qarawiyyīn together with the many student dormitories throughout the city, made Fez an important center of Moroccan cultural life. Within the Qarawiyyīn milieu, students of rural origin (*āfāqīs*) were readily distinguishable from the students from Fez itself. Whereas the latter continued to live with their families at home, the students from other cities and from rural Morocco were accommodated at one of the seven dormitories scattered throughout the city. As a student, al-Wazzānī most likely stayed at the Saffarīn madrasa where students from Wazzān and the Jbāla region usually resided.[20]

Al-Wazzānī's teachers at the Qarawiyyīn included highly regarded scholars such as the distinguished *faqīh* and prolific writer Abū 'Abdallāh Muḥammad b. al-Madanī Gannūn (d. 1885),[21] the well-known teacher Aḥmad Bannānī (d.1888),[22] the Sufi shaykh Abū Muḥammad al-Ḥājj Ṣāliḥ b. al-Tādilī (d.1889),[23] the *qāḍī* of Meknes Abū al-'Abbās Aḥmad b. al-Ṭālib b. Sūda (d. 1903),[24] the *faqīh* Ja'far b. Idrīs al-Kattānī (d. 1905),[25] the Mauritanian mystic and shaykh Muḥammad Muṣṭafā Mā al-'Aynayn al-Shanjīṭī (d. 1910),[26] and the *faqīh* Abū 'Abdallāh Muḥammad al-Qādirī (d. 1913).[27] Under their guidance, al-Wazzānī studied the following areas of Islamic scholarship: the Qur'ān; Mālikī law, including the *Muwaṭṭā'* of Mālik b. Anas and the *Mukhtaṣar* of Khalīl b. Isḥāq; jurisprudence, including the *Jam' al-Jawāmi'* of Ibn al-Subkī; and the major collections of traditions (*aḥādīth*, sing. *ḥadīth*) of the Prophet, including the *Ṣaḥīḥ*s of Bukhārī and Muslim, *Shamā'il* of Tirmidhī, and *Kitāb al-Shifā* of Qāḍī 'Iyāḍ.[28] These authoritative texts, some composed by great Mālikī jurists, were central to al-Wazzānī's training as well as to the intellectual formation of his generation.[29]

Al-Wazzānī's teachers were all distinguished intellectual figures of turn-of-the-century Morocco. Al-Madanī Gannūn was a prominent religious scholar and *shaykh al-jamā'a*, or supreme juristic authority of Morocco.[30] He was a

The Qarawiyyīn mosque-university in Fez. Source: *France-Maroc: Revue mensuelle illustrée, organe du Comité des foires du Maroc* 4 (June 1920): 137. Harvard College Library Afr 1306.1F.

prolific writer and one of the leading advocates of Islamic reformist ideas at the Qarawiyyīn University. A highly independent thinker, Gannūn was particularly preoccupied with the growing signs of decline of muftīship and *iftā'* (the process by which muftīs issued legal opinions) and sought to encourage the revival of independent legal reasoning (*ijtihād*). In addition, he was critical of the prevailing Sufi practices associated with mystical orders that he perceived to be dangerous innovation (*bid'a*) and to represent false Sufism (*al-taṣawwuf al-muzayyaf*).[31] His ethic of piety and religious asceticism placed

The Bū 'Ināniyya madrasa in Fez founded by the Marīnid sultan Abū 'Inān (r. 1348–58). The madrasa operated simultaneously as a mosque, school, and dormitory. The student rooms surround the large courtyard used for prayer and lesson circles. Photograph by author.

him in opposition with the ruling elite and led to his imprisonment by Sultan Muḥammad IV (r. 1859–73).[32]

Ja'far bin Idrīs al-Kattānī was an accomplished religious scholar, and during the latter part of his life he was the *shaykh al-jamā'a*, like Gannūn before him. He was a disciple of Shaykh 'Abd al-Kabīr al-Kattānī, a prominent Sufi and the leader of the Kattāniyya brotherhood, who in the late nineteenth century became a highly revered mystic and spiritual leader. Ja'far al-Kattānī's strong commitment to Sufi doctrines and the teachings of mysticism, especially his expressed support of unorthodox practices, such as special chanting and the use of musical instruments, led him to fundamental doctrinal disputes with Gannūn, who condemned less-orthodox mystics for exceeding established sharī'a norms.[33]

Mā al-'Aynayn was a celebrated *'alim*, prolific writer, and head of the 'Ayaniyya brotherhood. He authored more than three hundred books and pamphlets on mystical devotion, religious sciences, and jurisprudence.[34] He had strong links with the Moroccan Makhzan during the reigns of Mawlāy Ḥasan (r. 1873–94) and Mawlāy 'Abd al-'Azīz (r. 1894–1908), and during the same period the 'Ayaniyya *zāwiyas* enjoyed the patronage of the Makhzan. Mā al-'Aynayn was known for his political and military opposition to European encroachment on Morocco and for his orthodox Sufism and mystical forms of worship. Critical of what he viewed as the moral and religious corruption caused by the profusion of brotherhoods, he stressed the need to make the brotherhoods into one and called for a reform of religion in light of the two most authoritative sources, the Qur'ān and the *sunna*.

This highly diversified educational background is an emblem of precolonial Moroccan intellectual, cultural, and religious life. A succinct consideration of the biographies of al-Wazzānī's peers, members of the Moroccan learned religious elite, illustrates that it was not a rare instance for a Moroccan *faqīh* in the last decades of the nineteenth century to receive his education at the hands of three prominent and influential scholars who contemplated texts, arguments, and practices founded on different Islamic concepts and semantics. As will become clear, dramatic structural and discursive transformations that marked the world in which al-Wazzānī lived and operated compelled the elite 'ulamā' to engage moral criticism and define authorized practices, concepts, and institutions for sustaining a moral Muslim community. Or, to put it in Talal Asad's language, to make claims about what is and what is not Islamic.[35] My own view is that al-Wazzānī's training was partly constituted by the modern conditions that altered the language, the concepts, and the values of the people in his world.

From his teachers, al-Wazzānī would have been introduced to the major concerns of religious scholars in Morocco of his day, concerns that would be at the center of his scholarly project years later. What attitude should one take toward Mālikī doctrines and legal opinions? Could a muftī base his fatwā on an opinion established in a legal school other than his own? How could a jurist employ *ijtihād* and in what connection? How was one to think of the practice of *taqlīd*? What were the accepted views on the use of *qiyās* (analogical reasoning) as a source for the derivation of legal opinions? Is it permissible for Muslims to be divided into Sufi orders? What was the religious obligation toward *bidʿa* that could not be justified by the Qurʾān and the *sunna* of the Prophet? Were practices associated with the cult of saints considered to constitute *bidʿa*? Were they contradicted by the doctrine of *tawḥīd* (the belief in the oneness of God)? Was incorporating practices involving ascetic excess and ecstatic utterance acceptable? Was it legitimate for a Muslim to travel to Europe? What was the responsibility of Muslims toward *jihād* (defense of Muslim territory) and *hijra* (migration from the realm of unbelief)? Can one arrest the processes of social and moral decay of the day? What attitude should one take toward laxities such as coffee drinking and tobacco smoking? We can imagine al-Wazzānī asking these scholars questions, listening to their answers, and participating in heated conversations with them.

The training al-Wazzānī received at the Qarawiyyīn was representative of turn-of-the-century Mālikī scholarship and characteristic of Muslim pedagogy. There was neither a fixed length to the course of study nor a sharply defined curriculum. Intellectual life and culture were strongly associated with Islamic knowledge.[36] Studies at the Qarawiyyīn focused on religious sciences (*al-ʿulūm al-sharʿiyya*) and supporting disciplines (*al-ʿulūm al-musāʿida*). The jurisprudence of the sharīʿa was the primary subject of training, and oral transmission through recitation (*riwāya*) was the foremost mode of learning.[37]

In his work on Islamic education, anthropologist Dale Eickelman is concerned with a Moroccan qāḍī who studied at the illustrious Yūsufiya University in Marrakesh in the 1920s and 1930s. Drawing on literary sources such as teaching licenses, biographies, and autobiographies, Eickelman describes a pedagogical style that entails recitation and memorization. The educational process, he explains, was "intermediate between oral and written systems of transmission of knowledge. Its key treatises existed in written form but were conveyed orally, to be written down and memorized by students."[38]

Al-Wazzānī's autobiographical sketch (*fahrasa*) verifies Eickelman's assessment. In it, he provides a list of the texts he studied, how they were studied, and with whom. These are the "recited texts" studied in the pattern of *arwīhi ʿan*, indicating the standard recitational-commentary lessons guided by a teacher. In this cultural world the passing on of knowledge was highly personalized, and there could be no advanced knowledge that had not been received directly from the teacher. Authoritative knowledge had to be transmitted by way of teacher to student.[39] Through this format of instruction al-Wazzānī was introduced to Mālikī law, jurisprudence, and *ḥadīth*. This religious knowledge was not easily attained. The learning path was long, rigorous, and arduous, and its ultimate goal was to produce the Moroccan *faqīh*—a fully trained jurist.

BEYOND HIGHER ISLAMIC LEARNING

Wael Hallaq has demonstrated the extent to which a Muslim jurist may function in different juristic roles that are not always clearly distinguished from each other, such as qāḍī, muftī, author-jurist, and professor. As Hallaq argues, biographical and autobiographical literature establishes that the legal career of an accomplished jurist was typically one that successfully fulfilled all these roles.[40] As we shall see, al-Mahdī al-Wazzānī was a representative of this feature of Islamic legal culture. After completing his studies, he wrote juridical treatises, taught at the Qarawiyyīn, and issued fatwās, engaging in the various roles of the trained legal scholar. As a professional jurist and thinker, he was deeply embedded in the Mālikī legal tradition, which through the centuries became closely associated with the Maghrib.[41] In light of Hallaq's typology of the legal profession, it can safely be stated that al-Wazzānī's legal career represents the highest Mālikī scholarship and professionalism by the standards of his time.

By virtue of the nature of his work, al-Wazzānī was not only an accomplished legal scholar but was also deeply engaged with the intellectual and social world that he inhabited, including the scholarly community of Moroccan jurists and the wider Moroccan society. As already mentioned, Brinkley Messick has expressed the point that the muftī is an intermediate figure, "retaining the purity of the madrasa while approaching the rough and tumble of the mahkama."[42] Messick underscores the role of the muftī as a mediator who was associated with the theoretical transmission of knowledge and at the same time was involved with the mundane social world around him. This point is best conceptualized with respect to al-Mahdī al-Wazzānī, who was a professional Mālikī *faqīh* and at the same time closely involved in the social and intellectual arenas of Moroccan life.

Engaging in Writing (*taʾlīf*)

A story is narrated about a devoted al-Wazzānī, who, while writing in the small hours of the night under the light of an oil lamp, as was his habit, would carelessly let his turban catch fire. On such occasions, al-Wazzānī, supposing that the smoke filling the room was coming from the kitchen, would then summon his wife from bed to put down the fire.[43] There is, of course, an element of legend in this story; however, this image of al-Wazzānī is of an assiduous scholar who was seriously engaged in writing. Al-Wazzānī was a prolific author who wrote numerous treatises, commentaries on grammar texts and Mālikī law, and multivolume fatwā compilations, many of which have not been edited and published. Writing, as Hallaq argues, "was an essential part of any distinguished legal career," and the mere absence of a list of the treatises written by the jurist from any biographical notice speaks volumes.[44]

One focus of al-Wazzānī's jurisprudential writings was elucidating commentaries on the expansive *ʿamal* literature, which consists of a series of works written in the fifteenth through seventeenth centuries, containing actual judicial decisions that became the authoritative doctrine of the school.[45] Confronted with issues not squarely covered by the Text of God, distinguished qāḍīs across the Muslim lands and throughout history modified and adapted the sharīʿa in their court decisions to meet the needs of the Muslim community that were arising from new social realities. These qāḍīs, drawing upon their understanding of the truth of Revelation, further elaborated and modified Islamic law; their judicial decisions served as a vehicle for legitimizing existing practices and local customs that were at variance with the divine sharīʿa.

Although the *ʿamal* is not peculiar to Moroccan or Mālikī legal practice, it is in the Moroccan legal context that *ʿamal* played a dominant role as an official source of the law. Beginning at the end of the fifteenth century, Moroccan judicial practice and decisions were used as a dominant guide to juridical reasoning and were incorporated into fatwās.[46] The explanation for the special authority of the *ʿamal* in Morocco lies in the assumption of later Moroccan jurists that the authoritative opinions of Mālik, the founding master of the Mālikī legal school, and of the great legal experts (*mujtahids*) of the school make up the foundation of the dominant judicial practice of the *madhhab*. Thus, this corpus of knowledge came to represent the most original and authentic judicial practice associated with the opinions of the generations that were closest to the Prophet Muḥammad and his Companions.[47]

But there is another salient explanation for the paramount importance of the *ʿamal* in the Moroccan context that bears preliminary consideration here. In his detailed study of the Moroccan legal system Jacques Berque suggests that the *ʿamal* literature acquired an authoritative status in the Moroccan legal tradition because it introduces the issue of "customary practices" as a significant source of the law. Berque further argues that the incorporation of custom into law effectively permitted religious scholars the consideration and regulation of local practices that were not stipulated by the revealed texts. Ultimately, this process generated new legal norms and legal rules that clearly emanated from local customs.[48] In other words, for Berque, the centrality of the *ʿamal* literature in Mālikī jurisprudence was a consequence of its operation as a tool of acclimatization of Islamic law into Moroccan society. It may be argued that by incorporating custom into Mālikī jurisprudence, Mālikism appealed to the illiterate tribal and rural societies of Morocco whose laws were unwritten and based on local traditions.[49]

Al-Wazzānī authored four extensive commentaries on three celebrated *ʿamal* collections of the Mālikī school. He wrote two commentaries on *al-ʿAmāl al-Fāsī* of ʿAbd al-Raḥmān al-Fāsī (d. 1685), a classic text containing more than two hundred judicial decisions that formed part of the judicial practice of Fez.[50] In addition, he authored a commentary on a commentary on *Tuḥfat al-Ḥukkām* of Ibn ʿĀṣim (d. 1427), an authoritative manual of Andalusian *ʿamal*, as well as a commentary on a commentary on the *Lāmīya* of ʿAlī al-Zaqqāq (d. 1507), a procedural guide for judges.[51] Both commentaries were still taught as part of the curriculum at the Qarawiyyīn in the 1920s, indicating the appreciation of al-Wazzānī's work by Moroccan jurists.[52]

Undoubtedly, al-Wazzānī held the *ʿamal* works in high esteem, since he extensively referred to them as principal authoritative sources in his *New Miʿyār*. I argue that it is quite instructive that al-Wazzānī complemented the *ʿamal* literature with his commentaries and used the *ʿamal* opinions as a dominant corpus on which to base his fatwās. This reliance on classical Mālikī legal compilations presumably could offer the historian an access point to al-Wazzānī's intellectual orientation and interpretative attitude. Al-Wazzānī's writings represent a certain kind of scholarship, one that stresses the authority of previous decisions and solutions of distinguished Mālikī jurists. It implies a specific style of interpretation and reasoning that identifies the school's foundational principles and legal doctrines and derives legal opinions from it. Al-Wazzānī was named by one of his biographers as a skillful writer and a knowledgeable jurist who "never turned away from Mālik's doctrine."[53] In the course of my study of al-Wazzānī, I have come to agree with this view of al-Wazzānī as a committed Mālikī jurist in a fundamental sense. As we shall see in the following chapters, al-Wazzānī was not only a leading advocate and practitioner of Mālikī jurisprudence of his day but would also strive actively to shape and reconfigure the content of Mālikī legal tradition.

As mentioned previously, al-Wazzānī also authored two extensive fatwā collections. Like his commentaries on *ʿamal* literature, this intellectual endeavor illuminates al-Wazzānī's scholarly style and his orientation as a legal interpreter. Al-Wazzānī's fatwās represent a deep and thorough understanding of Mālikī doctrine and teachings. As a principle, they consist of opinions of established sources of authority, combined and revised to create essentially new compositions. Like his commentaries, his fatwā scholarship demonstrates his dynamic engagement with a mature legal discourse and exemplifies the scope of his interpretative thought within the *madhhab*.

In addition, al-Wazzānī wrote his *fahrasa*—perhaps the most explicit intellectual statement that connects al-Wazzānī to the Mālikī school. In his *fahrasa*, al-Wazzānī gives a meticulous account of the principal books he studied and with whom. Through his relations with particular teachers and specific texts, al-Wazzānī establishes his intellectual posture and scholarly commitment to the Mālikī school.

Furthermore, a closer look at the complete list of al-Wazzānī's writings reveals his perspective on Moroccan Sufism and mystical tradition. A prominent aspect of Moroccan Islam is that Sufism and Mālikism have intertwined since the eleventh century. According to Vincent Cornell, who studies Sufism in premodern Morocco, many of the most important Sufis and saints of early Moroccan Sufism were legal specialists. This alliance between Sufism and Mālikism, he explains, was in part due to the ethical perspective of the Mālikī *madhhab*, which emphasized the complementarity between inner belief and outer practice. As a result, a particular brand of Sufism emerged in Morocco that was heavily influenced by the law or, as Cornell puts it, a type of "juridical Sufism."[54] This form of Sufism "is epistemologically subservient to the authority of the religious law" and fosters a "praxis-oriented approach, which is based on the jurisprudence of inter-personal behavior."[55]

In al-Wazzānī's age, many established scholars identified and diagnosed the problems confronting the Muslim community as caused by the spread of Sufi beliefs and practices conceived as heretical and a threat to the fun-

5

ابن شقرون والأربعة عن الشيخ التاودي المتقدم

فصل وأما صحيح الإمام مسلم
ابن الحجاج القشيري رضي الله عنه

Al-Mahdī al-Wazzānī. Source: *Hādhihī fahrasa*, lithograph (Fez: al-Maṭbaʿa al-Ḥajariyya, 1896): 5. Harvard College Library, HX5YNU.

damentals of Islamic monotheism (*tawḥīd*). In particular, prevalent beliefs and popular practices informed by the cult of saints were criticized as un-Islamic. As already noted, al-Wazzānī was himself a Sufi practitioner of the Wazzāniyya Sufi order and, in his juristic roles as a muftī and author-jurist, he addressed different beliefs and practices associated with Sufism in fatwās and independent treatises.

Al-Wazzānī argues fervently in support of zealous mystical practices in matters of worship. He supports particular rituals that involve dancing, singing, and ululations in prayers and ritual processions. He advocates the celebration of annual religious fairs (*mawāsim*), promotes the belief in the powers of Sufi saints (*awliyā'*), and defends ritual visits to shrines and saints' tombs (*ziyāra*). In his essays, al-Wazzānī further stresses the centrality of the relationship between shaykh and disciple on the individual's path to attain proximity to God. He defends opinions that authorized recourse to the intercession of saints (*tawaṣṣul*) and declares its effectiveness.[56] It is obvious from his many treatises that al-Wazzānī viewed the more intense Moroccan Sufi practices and fervent Sufi worship as within the boundaries of normative Islam.

For example, in his treatise *Al-Nuṣḥ al-khāliṣ li-kāffat al-muslimīn bi'l-tawaṣṣul ilayhi ta'ālā bi-aṣfiyā'ihi al-muqarrabīn* (Sincere advice to all Muslims to approach God the sublime through his close friends), al-Wazzānī engages the discourse of critique and reform of his contemporaries, two Egyptian *fuqahā'*, one of them the influential nineteenth-century reformer and grand muftī of Egypt, Muḥammad 'Abduh.[57] The text is probably the principal statement by al-Wazzānī on the beliefs and practices associated with the cult of saints and is often mentioned by his biographers because it includes a commentary on 'Abduh's ideas on the subject. It was written in response to a question addressed to al-Wazzānī by a fellow Moroccan jurist who was surprised by a fatwā issued by the two Egyptian scholars. Al-Wazzānī's treatise takes the form of an extended fatwā. In it, al-Wazzānī engages point by point the two legal opinions issued by the Egyptian jurists and gives his definitive position on the issue.

The legal opinions issued by 'Abduh and his colleague promote long-standing arguments within Islamic tradition pertaining to the un-Islamic nature of Sufi doctrines and practices associated with the cult of saints. The two scholars fiercely contest the practice of using saints and other pious people (*ṣāliḥin*) as a means of approaching God (*tawaṣṣul*) and appealing to them for aid or intercession. They assert that the belief in a holy person's ability to invoke divine consideration is disgraceful to the Islamic faith.[58] Their message repeatedly illustrates that God alone has the power to benefit and to harm and that the meaning of *tawaṣṣul* through saints is merely emulating and mimicking humans. These practices, they maintain, were later accretions to the Qur'ān and the *sunna* of the Prophet Muḥammad, contradict the behavioral example of the Companions (*ṣaḥāba*) and their Successors (*tābi'ūn*), and were denied by the ranks of the early legal specialists (*mujtahids*) who upheld the normative values of Islam. Hence, they condemn all such acts and beliefs as *shirk* (associating persons or things with God), the antithesis of *tawḥīd*, and treat them as *bid'a*.[59]

The underlying message of al-Wazzānī's treatise is that the two jurists' condemnation of these beliefs and practices stems from their misinterpretation of the doctrine of *tawḥīd*. The veneration of saints as a means of approaching God and the belief that they have the power to aid the needy are licit and do not contradict *tawḥīd* since they do not detract from God's uniqueness and omnipotence. Al-Wazzānī regards intercession as permissible and Islamic so long as people remember that saints could not grant requests themselves but could only ask God to do so. For him, it is obvious that God is the source of all power and authority, and his deputies act as intermediaries for others before the ultimate source of authority.[60] He underscores that "the belief that any effective action, either [inflicting] harm or [extending] favor come from them [i.e., the virtuous and pious], or that they share with God in this [i.e., deciding on sanction or blessing], is harmful. The very adherence to them, however, without believing in innovation, is not dangerous."[61] Thus, al-Wazzānī asserts, *tawaṣṣul* through a saint is inseparable from the belief in God's unity.

In support of his claim, al-Wazzānī finds confirmation that *tawaṣṣul* through created beings (*makhlūq*) is licit in a central source of religious authority and ethical behavior. He recounts a story about the second caliph, 'Umar b. al-Khaṭṭāb, who sought the provision of rain (*istisqā'*) through the aid and intercession of al-'Abbās b. 'Abd al-Muṭṭalib.[62] Disputing the Egyptian jurist's argument, al-Wazzānī asks rhetorically:

> Tell me, oh Arab brother, do you accuse 'Umar b. al-Khaṭṭāb, Commander of the Faithful [*amīr al-mu'minīn*] of infidelity for this action? Do you accuse those who were present with him from among the Companions [*ṣaḥāba*] and the Successors [*tābi'īn*] of infidelity for they put between themselves and Allāh a mediator [*wāsiṭa*] from the people, and plead Allāh through al-'Abbās? Did they associate someone with God, in this action, and no one among them stood up resolutely for the right religion?[63]

Clearly, for al-Wazzānī, sainthood and intercession were jurisprudentially validated forms of Islam. It is important to emphasize that most of the Moroccan *fuqahā'* of al-Wazzānī's generation were Sufi practitioners who recognized both dimensions of religious knowledge, the exoteric (*'ilm ẓāhirī*) acquired through study of the authoritative sources and the esoteric (*'ilm bāṭinī*) attained through mystical practices. Generally speaking, in the late nineteenth and early twentieth centuries, the overwhelming majority of Moroccan *fuqahā'* belonged to relatively moderate Sufi orders and opposed Sufi beliefs and practices of worship that fell outside the boundaries of sharī'a.

Al-Wazzānī's discursive strategy in his treatises is particularly important. Together with his own arguments, counterarguments, interpretations, and explications, al-Wazzānī invokes selective citations and statements of earlier Mālikī authorities, and through this textual strategy his arguments acquire the backing of a highly authoritative tradition. In other words, by invoking the interpretations of earlier Mālikī authorities and great Andalusian and Moroccan jurists, such as Ibn Rushd (d. 1126), Qāḍī 'Iyāḍ (d. 1149), Muḥyī al-Dīn Ibn al-'Arabī (d. 1240), Ibn 'Arafa (d. 1400), Ibn Hilāl (d. 1504), Aḥmad al-Wansharīsī (d. 1508), 'Abd al-Qādir al-Fāsī (d. 1680), 'Abd al-Raḥmān al-Fāsī (d. 1685), and al-Ḥasan al-Yūsī (d. 1691), along with Qur'ānic exegesis and ḥadīth reports of Bukhārī and Muslim, al-Wazzānī seeks to legitimize indigenous Sufi beliefs and practices as a juridically acceptable form of Islam.

The bigger issue, as I see it, is that in his writings, al-Wazzānī emerges as a legal interpreter who operated entirely within the framework of the Mālikī school, employing authoritative texts and dominant opinions of the leading jurists of his school as his sources. In other words, al-Wazzānī was, as classified in Islamic legal studies, a *muqallid* (practitioner of *taqlīd*), or an "affiliated muftī" who was highly proficient in the fundamental Mālikī texts and the methodology of legal reasoning and who was capable of deriving legal rulings on the basis of his school's principles and general precepts.[64]

In all of al-Wazzānī's works, the most sustained juristic strategy is the absolute commitment to the Mālikī school of law and the preservation of the interpretative authority of great Mālikī jurists. He argues forcefully against stepping outside the particular doctrines and methods of his law school and tries to prove that crossing *madhhab* boundaries constituted a serious error, which amounted to mocking Islam and deviating from the straight path.[65] In explaining the reason for his unequivocal position, al-Wazzānī establishes an analogy between a Mālikī *faqīh* who crosses *madhhab* boundaries to justify his opinion and a Muslim layman who, despite his lack of legal knowledge, attempts to exercise independent reasoning. The *faqīh* was, in the eyes of al-Wazzānī, a misguided scholar because in his effort to issue legal advice, he, in effect, solicited rules and opinions issued by jurists he did not know, who used juridical tools and modes of argumentation foreign to him. As in the case of the layman who is ignorant of the law, the Mālikī *faqīh* is ignorant of legal knowledge of other schools of law. Al-Wazzānī goes on to say that in issuing a fatwā, this *faqīh*, even if he possesses masterly knowledge of the texts and rules of the *madhhab* of Mālik, should exclusively limit himself to the teachings and methodology of the Mālikī school.[66]

As has been argued by Sherman Jackson, *taqlīd* "should not be understood as primarily a movement in search of the content of previous interpretations. It was, rather, an attempt to gain authority for one's interpretation by associating it with the name or doctrine of an already established authority-figure." Jackson's point is that *taqlīd* was a central feature of Islamic tradition, a fundamental medium for endowing interpretations with authority.[67] More recently, Wael Hallaq has shown that *taqlīd*, as indicating loyalty to a legal doctrine and adherence to a legal authority, was the product of expansion and development of the Islamic legal tradition, "a development that was ineluctable [and] . . . symptomatic of a more monumental event, namely, the rise and final coming to maturity of the *madhhab*." In other words, rather than treat *taqlīd* as representing "the declining glory of Islam," Hallaq suggests that it is an "expression of the internal dynamics that came to dominate and characterize the *madhhab* as both doctrinal entity and a hermeneutical engagement." Furthermore, he argues that the dynamics of *taqlīd* within a *madhhab* did not simply indicate "the mere reproduction of the predecessors' doctrine" but were at times an expression of "juristic activity associated with *ijtihād*." For him, "in the pages of the average juristic text or law manual, the author-jurist inevitably indulges in every variety of *taqlīd*, ranging from simple restatement of authority to quasi-*ijtihād* of a sort."[68] Building on Jackson and Hallaq, I argue that it is precisely this approach to the authoritative legal doctrines of the Mālikī *madhhab* that characterizes al-Wazzānī's arguments and reasoning and led one of his biographers to name him "a cornerstone [*rukn*, pl. *arkān*] of the Mālikī *madhhab*."[69]

Another of al-Wazzānī's biographers named him "the seal of scholars in Morocco."[70] This designation seems to conceive al-Wazzānī in terms of a jurist, whose qualifications in all areas of the law identify him with a rank of achievement long extinct, thereby distinguishing him from succeeding generations of legists. Al-Mahdī al-Wazzānī appears to have been a Mālikī scholar of high caliber, a knowledgeable *ʿālim*, and an expert of jurisprudence who in his writings exhibited deep legal scholarship and understanding of Mālikī doctrine and was able to reason on the basis of the school's principles and texts.

Teaching at the Qarawiyyīn

In his professional role as a professor at the Qarawiyyīn, al-Wazzānī taught law and grammar, which were at the heart of the curriculum, and consequently was referred to as *al-ʿālim al-kabīr*—a term reserved exclusively for the most outstanding scholars of the community of learning.[71] In his lessons, al-Wazzānī taught the *Ajrūmīya*, a famous work of grammar, and a certain work of *sharḥ* (commentary) by shaykh Mayyāra.[72] During his career as a teacher, al-Wazzānī had many students. Among his close disciples were Sultan ʿAbd al-Ḥafīẓ, the well-known historian ʿAbd al-Raḥmān b. Zaydān, and Shaykh ʿAbd al-Ḥayy al-Kattānī. Other of his distinguished students were ʿAbd al-Ḥafīẓ al-Fāsī, ʿAbd al-Salām Ibn ʿAbd al-Qādir Ibn Sūda, and Muḥammad b. Muḥammad Makhlūf, who became prominent writers themselves and al-Wazzānī's principal biographers.

In their biographies of al-Wazzānī, the three writers emphasize their studies with him through the instruction methods of *qirāʾa* or *riwāya* (oral recitation). The image of him they convey is of a teacher who was "devoted to spreading Islamic knowledge in his writings as well as in his teaching."[73] His biographers recall al-Wazzānī as an exceptional teacher who was not only well read in Mālikī legal scholarship but also transmitted his knowledge, insisting on the comprehension of meaning and the elaboration on interpretation of the text.

As an influential teacher at the celebrated Qarawiyyīn University and a prominent member of the vibrant scholarly community of Fez, al-Wazzānī was exposed to the most contemporary ideas and trends and circles of teachers and students from Morocco and from the wider Muslim world. Prominent teachers at the Qarawiyyīn, colleagues of al-Wazzānī, traveled to the Ḥijāz to perform the pilgrimage and to Egypt and other parts of the Arab East in their pursuit of religious knowledge. For instance, Muḥammad bin ʿAbd al-Kabīr al-Kattānī, Muḥammad b. Jaʿfar al-Kattānī, ʿAbdallāh b. Idrīs al-Sanūsī, and Abū Shuʿaīb al-Dukkālī, among others, stayed for long periods in the Arab East and developed close cultural ties with local learned elites. For Moroccan scholars, the Arab East always represented the seat of religious authority as exercised by the great jurists of Islam. Therefore, they were eager to link local scholarship with the prestigious traditions of Arab East learning.[74]

In addition, various newspapers and journals from important intellectual centers of Islam circulated in Morocco and were available to Moroccan ʿulamāʾ, for instance, *al-Manār*, *al-Ahrām*, *al-Liwāʾ*, and *al-Muʾayyd* from

Cairo; *al-Rā'id*, *al-Ṣawāb*, and *al-Ḥāḍira* from Tunis; and *Kawkab Ifrīqiyā* from Algiers.[75] These newspapers not only introduced a wealth of new and exciting information particular to modern developments in the Middle East and North Africa at the turn of the century; they also ran articles on Morocco that engaged contemporary tensions and concerns central to a society undergoing dramatic transformation. Though al-Wazzānī himself did not perform the pilgrimage to Mecca nor did he travel to the Ḥijāz or the Arab East in pursuit of knowledge, his exposure was not parochial by the standards of his time. Rather, through his personal contacts with scholars and reading the Arabic-language press, he was not only introduced to contemporary Islamic thought but was critically engaged with it.

Al-Wazzānī was well aware of the social and political views of Muḥammad 'Abduh and his famous student Rashīd Riḍā and corresponded with them on matters pertaining to Islamic social and legal norms in the context of new social realities and needs. In a letter (*risāla*) to 'Abduh that was published in the celebrated journal *al-Manār*, al-Wazzānī addresses the issue of a Muslim eating meat slaughtered by Christians and Jews (*ahl al-kitāb*, people of the book).[76] The letter takes the form of a short fatwā that was given to the Moroccan minister of war Muḥammad al-Gabbāṣ, who posed a question to al-Wazzānī on the issue. It was written in response to an intense public debate in Egypt triggered by 'Abduh's most famous and controversial legal opinion, known as the Transvaal fatwā.[77] In his opinion, issued in 1903, 'Abduh responded to three questions pertaining to the practice of Islam and faith of Muslims residing outside Islamic sovereignty. In it, overturning a well-established legal opinion, 'Abduh declared that it is permissible for a Muslim to eat meat slaughtered by Christians even when the latter's slaughtering habits are different from those practiced by Muslims. In his *risāla*, al-Wazzānī confirms 'Abduh's view and condemns his opponents as *ba'ḍ al-māriqīn min al-din* (some of those who deviate from religion).[78]

Firmly rooted in the political and social conditions of his age, al-Wazzānī participated in controversies and heated discussions about ethical behavior among Muslims in the context of the challenges and changes facing the Moroccan state and society of his time. One of his strongest arguments against the growing foreign interference in Moroccan affairs was written in response to an article published in the Algerian journal *Kawkab Ifrīqiyā* in 1907. The article posits that when asked by Sultan Mawlāy 'Abd al-'Azīz to issue a legal opinion that legitimized European assistance in the process of reform and reorganization of the Moroccan state and consolidation of the position of his Makhzan, the 'ulamā' of Fez authorized the sultan's position.[79]

The article set off intense public debate, led by the Fāsī elite who sought a clarification of the 'ulamā' of Fez. Al-Wazzānī, among other jurists, replied, ultimately denying the "pure lie" fabricated by the journal. He went on to identify the editor of the journal as a liar, stating that "it is necessary to stay away from his lies, and not to pay attention to his vain fables and fairy tales. The issue is widely known; it is mentioned in *al-Mukhtaṣar* [of Khalīl] and the commentaries, and recognized by the youngest of children. His saying [i.e., Khalīl's]: seeking the help of the polytheist [*mushrik*] is prohibited, means that, seeking the help of the unbeliever [*kuffār*] is not allowed to Muslims."[80]

Finally, according to Muḥammad al-Manūnī, an important historian of modern Morocco, al-Wazzānī was involved in the promulgation of a constitution modeled upon the Ottoman constitution.[81] For a brief period in 1909–10, a very small constitutionalist movement was able to gain the support of Makhzan officials and members of the 'ulamā'.[82] Morocco's scholarly community was exposed to Ottoman legal reform through travel to the Arab East and the various Arabic newspapers and journals that became available in the late nineteenth and early twentieth centuries. Two constitutions were drafted; their language demonstrates the extent to which Morocco was drawn to the language of reform in the Arab East.[83]

The importance of the Moroccan constitutionalist movement lies in that it represented an attempt to consolidate relations of power sharing between the Makhzan and 'ulamā'.[84] The two constitutions called for the establishment of consultative assemblies and elected councils that together with the sultan would oversee the entire state apparatus, but both had very little resonance at the time. Since I was unable to find more information about al-Wazzānī's actual activity in the records of the time, I do not read too much into his involvement. All of the evidence I have, however, suggests that as a renowned professor at the Qarawiyyīn and a prominent member in the Moroccan scholarly community, al-Wazzānī was intellectually engaged with the cultural, social, and political conditions of his day and with the challenges facing the Muslim communities of his time.

Issuing Fatwās

By virtue of the nature of his juristic role as a muftī, al-Wazzānī was significantly engaged not only with the intellectual community of his peers and colleagues but also with the social world of Moroccan society in general and Fez in particular.[85] Before I proceed any further, a general comment on the nature of the office of the muftī in Morocco in the late nineteenth century is in order. Generally speaking, during the period under study here, there was no state-sponsored and hierarchically organized legal system (such as in the Ottoman Empire). There was no chief muftī or shaykh al-Islām in Morocco who served as the head of an intricate religious institution. Furthermore, the office of the muftī was not institutionalized in the sense that it was not associated with a professional occupation. Individual *fuqahā'* acquired their status as muftīs by attaining individual scholarly accomplishments in the religious sciences and by assuming a particular code of conduct that was associated with men of learning.[86]

Jacques Berque has observed in his perceptive portrait of a nineteenth-century Fāsī *faqīh*: "The scholar has been attached always, by a thousand-year tradition, to the affairs of the city. Only rarely has he given himself over to extreme abstraction or vanity. . . . His personality was shaped within the horizons of the city."[87] Berque has argued that the *faqīh* typically was not a retiring purist who distanced himself from the affairs of the community of which he was a part. Rather, he inhabited social life and operated within it. Berque's insight illuminates al-Wazzānī's profile as well.

During his career, al-Wazzānī delivered thousands of fatwās, the vast majority of which he collected in his two multivolume fatwā compilations. As a muftī in Fez, al-Wazzānī applied his knowledge of law beyond the confines of the Qarawiyyīn to address the affairs and needs of a Muslim community. A Mālikī by training and intellectual posture, al-Wazzānī brought Mālikī law to bear on actual problems and conflicts faced by late nineteenth-century Moroccan society. Al-Wazzānī's fatwās express his interpretation of Mālikī jurisprudence that supports his opinions and thoughts. He addresses sociolegal problems as a professional legist, with recourse to his specialized and authoritative knowledge of the law.

In addition to his legal knowledge, al-Wazzānī's fatwās require his understanding of actual social practices and local customs. Furthermore, because many of the questions posed to al-Wazzānī concerned the most ordinary realities of the Moroccan people, he was in effect intimately linked to their specific social circumstances. In the process of issuing fatwās, al-Wazzānī's point of departure was the facts of an actual inquiry, emanating from a concrete and particular social reality, as presented to him by the questioner.[88] By means of his fatwās, al-Wazzānī related his legal-religious knowledge to the sociolegal questions under his review and, therefore, was entrenched in the particularities of his social-historical setting.

Al-Wazzānī's fatwās address an impressive range of matters covered in sharīʿa scholarship. In many of these fatwās, he touches on the social concerns emerging in a society undergoing a fundamental restructuring of its institutions and social arrangements and tackles an array of tensions relating to the peculiar character of Moroccan modern development. For instance, he considered questions about the production and consumption of illicit products such as tobacco, hashish, wine, and coffee. He authorized beliefs and practices associated with the cult of saints such as *tawaṣṣul* through saints ritual visits and pilgrims to shrines, and the vocalization of rhymed praises during prayer. He discussed beliefs in omens and amulets and expressions of awe and zeal during the visitation of tombs. He justified the imposing of non-Islamic market taxes (*maks*, pl. *mukūs*) and disputed the obligation of Muslims to perform migration (*hijra*) from the abode of unbelief (*dār al-kufr*). He reflected on trade with the non-Islamic world, scrutinized the intermingling of Muslims and foreigners, and explicitly condemned the practice of Moroccans requesting the protection (*ḥimāya*) of foreign powers.

In describing the impact his fatwās had on the community of belief, the principal biographical sources indicate that people strove to acquire and benefit from his works, that "they carried his work to the Sudan, Algeria, and Tunisia,"[89] and that "they issued fatwās only after consulting his work, and never turned away from it because it includes the saying of earlier masters and contemporary scholars."[90] Surely, al-Wazzānī was considered during his life an example of a distinguished muftī who was proficient in the legal rulings and texts of the Mālikī doctrine.

In short, al-Wazzānī's juristic career as a prominent muftī, an influential professor, and an accomplished author of legal works reveals two significant themes. First, al-Wazzānī was a devoted Mālikī jurist who grounded his work in classical Mālikī legal teachings and thought. Second, he was actively involved with the scholarly community and with the larger Moroccan society. An intermediate figure, al-Wazzānī was situated in a special position within his society and culture. He was a legal expert and thinker who knitted together his juridical-religious knowledge with the social world around him. By virtue of his position, he was impressively knowledgeable in Mālikī doctrine and the authoritative school opinions, he was well aware of the intellectual and cultural trends and debates of his time, and he was intimately acquainted with social behavior and cultural patterns that informed Moroccan life. Undoubtedly, al-Wazzānī was recognized by his peers as one of the most prominent Mālikī jurists and enjoyed great veneration and respect from the general population. More significantly, we can imagine that al-Wazzānī defined and perceived himself as a capable jurist and a distinguished *faqīh*.

JOINING THE MOROCCAN NOTABILITY (*KHĀṢṢA*)

As I have pursued al-Mahdī al-Wazzānī, I realized that he must have identified himself not only as an accomplished jurist and legal authority. As I demonstrate in the following chapters, al-Wazzānī's *New Mi'yār* is more than a mere collection of fatwās compiled by a prominent jurist. Rather, it is a decisive instrument for the transmission, preservation, and re-creation of Mālikī legal culture, and its author must have imagined himself as a figure who could serve in this creative role as a leader of the intellectual and legal Mālikī tradition. What endowed al-Wazzānī with this sense of leadership and authority?

At the Qarawiyyīn University, al-Wazzānī acquired more than the expertise in the sciences of law and jurisprudence and the title of *faqīh*. Susan Miller has suggested, in the context of her discussion of the Moroccan *faqīh* Muḥammad al-Ṣaffār, that the association with the scholarly establishment of Fez offered a scholar an entry into the *khāṣṣa*, the upper ranks of Moroccan society.[91] In the Moroccan context, the *khāṣṣa* is referred to as the "people of tying and untying" (*ahl al-ḥall wa'l-'aqd*), which include *shurafā'*, 'ulamā', heads of religious orders, leading *a'yān* families, Makhzan officials, and wealthy merchants who are treated with respect and reverence. Here, as I delineate al-Wazzānī's association with the Moroccan power elite, I share Miller's view. As a respected sharīf and a highly regarded *faqīh*, al-Wazzānī seems to have quickly occupied an esteemed position among the *khāṣṣa* of Moroccan society. Soon, in addition to his career in teaching at the Qarawiyyīn and as muftī, al-Wazzānī became a counselor to Sultan 'Abd al-'Azīz (r. 1894–1908).[92]

A *faqīh* was by definition a significant figure in his society: "the master of religious science is at the same time the master of the right tone."[93] Sharī'a, or the Divine law, was more than a legal discourse; it was also a living tradition, "the right path," an ethical code as well as a body of law. Islamic knowledge was tied closely to nonreligious spheres of knowledge and thus encompassed a code for proper conduct.[94] Valued for his thorough knowledge of Islamic law and religiously prescribed behavior, al-Wazzānī was often drawn into the sultan's service.

The years in which al-Wazzānī lived, the last decades of the nineteenth century and the opening decades of the twentieth, were filled with political and social changes and crises. During this period, Moroccan sovereignty was considerably challenged by the European powers. Humiliating military defeats, loss of territory, and a fiscal crisis of major proportions plainly underscored the weakness of the Moroccan government in the face of European aggression. At the same time, the Makhzan and political elite initiated a reform effort that was directed toward centralization of the state apparatus and represented a significant transformation of the Moroccan state and society. Many of the changes and reform were viewed as illegitimate by certain segments of Moroccan society and were met with local resistance and social unrest.[95]

The historian Mohammed Kenbib has suggested that, by the end of the nineteenth century, the Makhzan was a mere shadow of its former self. He summarizes the increasingly untenable predicaments of the Moroccan state:

> In truth, the center of power in the country lay no longer in Fez or Marrakesh but rather in Tangier where [the foreign] legations dictated their demands, pressured the courts of justice, imposed the dismissal of governors and *qāḍīs* who were hostile to foreigners and their protégés, and requested punitive expeditions against tribes who were declared guilty and held collectively responsible for the interception of caravans, etc. . . . The foreign ministers worked to establish the reality of "states within a state." The latter was no more than an instrument for those who worked toward its destruction. Hence, the gulf that was instilled between the "unfit" and weak Makhzan and the majority of the population.[96]

In numerous instances during the period under discussion, in an attempt to reconcile the various pressure groups and bolster its own legitimacy, the Moroccan Makhzan drew on the spiritual and social authority of the 'ulamā'. At the beginning of the nineteenth century, the Moroccan 'ulamā' did not constitute a formal ecclesiastical group associated with distinctly defined interests. Nevertheless, the symbolic importance of their authority as guardians of the Divine law, or the people of knowledge (*ahl al-'ilm*), should not be overlooked.[97]

In his important book *Religion and Power in Morocco*, Henry Munson examines the political role of Islam in medieval Morocco (with the emergence of the Almohad state in the first half of the twelfth century) and throughout the postcolonial period. According to Munson, the cultivation of a relationship between the Makhzan and the 'ulamā' was a salient feature of the Moroccan religio-political system in the pre-Protectorate period. Although the 'ulamā' lacked the power to implement their views, they still had considerable influence deriving from their religious knowledge and interpretative authority. The sultans who strove to acquire legitimacy through religious and juristic channels could not dispense with the religio-legal elite.[98] Specifically, the Makhzan of ʿAbd al-ʿAzīz often sought the acceptance of the ʿulamāʾ for its attempts at reform and its policies toward European aggression.

In at least three such instances, al-Mahdī al-Wazzānī was called upon to act as a loyal servant and supporter of the Moroccan sultan ʿAbd al-ʿAzīz. One occasion occurred during the Makhzan's efforts to suppress the Abū Ḥimāra revolt, which seriously threatened Makhzan's authority. In October–November 1902, Jilālī b. Idrīs al-Zarhūnī al-Yūsufī (Abū Ḥimāra, in Moroccan dialect, Bū Ḥmāra) called upon the people of Fez and the tribes of the Taza and Oujda regions (northeast of Fez) to support him in his efforts to end the reign of Sultan ʿAbd al-ʿAzīz and claim the throne.[99] The Abū Ḥimāra rebellion met with much sympathy from the Moroccan ruling elite and the general population. Its appeal was based on a growing sense of anger and frustration with the ruling sultan, who increasingly was viewed by certain segments of Moroccan society as an illegitimate ruler. The sultan's failure to meet the challenge of European interference in Moroccan affairs, and rumors that rapidly spread throughout the country that Mawlāy ʿAbd al-ʿAzīz was "selling Morocco to the Christians," served to undermine the ruler's legitimacy.[100] Alluding to the considerable discontent with Sultan ʿAbd al-ʿAzīz are the attributes "fool" (*mahbūl*) or "madman" (*majnūn*) ascribed to him.

Although it directed enormous financial and military resources against Abū Ḥimāra's forces, the Makhzan was unable to effectively suppress the prolonged rebellion. The resulting damage to the sultan's stature in the eyes of the people is easy to imagine. In March 1903, in an attempt to counter Abū Ḥimāra's threat and repair his damaged authority, Sultan ʿAbd al-ʿAzīz called upon some of the most prominent ʿulamāʾ of Fez, al-Wazzānī included, to sign a fatwā condemning Abū Ḥimāra's revolt and declaring allegiance to the sultan.[101] In the fatwā, the ʿulamāʾ denounced the rebellion, arguing that supporting the rebel and refusing to obey the sultan could lead only to anarchy and to violence against Muslims. They posed the following question: "How does it suit a wise Muslim to follow this ignorant anarchist [*al-fattān al-jāhil*] in refusing to submit to the Commander of the Faithful [*amīr al-muʾminīn*] while submitting to the devils [*al-shayāṭīn*], succumbing to corruption, and getting involved in terrible things?" The ʿulamāʾ repeatedly stressed the idea that obedience to the Moroccan sultan was obedience to God and that disobedience was a conspiracy with the devil against God's law: "Whoever obeys the sultan obeys the merciful God and His Prophet; and whoever refuses to obey the sultan obeys the devil and enters into a war on the side of the misguided and hopeless people [*ahl al-ḍalāl wa'l-khasrān*]."[102]

Since al-Wazzānī merely signed a fatwā that was written by a secretary of the Makhzan and echoed its official position, it is virtually impossible to know what al-Wazzānī's opinion on Abū Ḥimāra's revolt really was. Nevertheless, it is important to note that al-Wazzānī was clearly seen as a distinguished figure in his society whose opinion commanded obedience and enjoyed the confidence of the sultan and his Makhzan officials. In addition, al-Wazzānī's support was considered necessary for the success of this fatwā in reaffirming the legitimacy of the sultan's rule and the illegitimacy of Abū Ḥimāra's revolt.

Al-Wazzānī also acted on behalf of the sultan as a member of the council of notables (*majlis al-a'yān*).[103] The year 1904 further consolidated the challenge of European imperialism and seriously impaired the sultan's ability to rule. It was the year that Great Britain and France signed the Entente cordiale, granting France a superior position in Moroccan affairs. The new agreement allowed for an increasing involvement of France in the Moroccan state with less interference from the other European states. Several months after the signing of the Entente cordiale, the sultan was forced to accept a French mission to Fez. The mission was led by Georges Saint-Réné Taillander, the ambassador of the minister of France. Its purpose was to discuss with Sultan 'Abd al-'Azīz a French proposal for a military, fiscal, and administrative program of reform for Morocco. The inability of the Moroccan sultan to meet the challenge of European intervention set off what is known as the First Moroccan Crisis, during which Moroccan critics openly voiced their discontent against the Makhzan's collaboration with France on the question of reforming the state.[104]

The French delegation arrived in Fez in January 1905. Prior to the arrival of the Taillander mission, a group of 'ulamā' met with Sultan 'Abd al-'Azīz and delivered a legal opinion in which all aspects of Morocco's crisis were attributed to the actions of foreigners. They specifically took issue with the idea that France's project of reform was crucial to guaranteeing material and moral advancement:

> We are hurt when we hear that we are in a state of decline [*inḥiṭāṭ*], and witnessing our condition makes us sad. However, every fact has its reason. We wonder about the cause of our decadence [*maṣā'ib*]. . . . It is clear to us that the foreigners are the fundamental cause of our sufferings, and that they are the cause of

> our decline, discord, internal strife, and destruction. . . . How do these foreigners benefit us? What are the new sciences that they taught us? And what did we gain from them? We spent our wealth for them, and they [in turn] misled us and spread decay [*fasād*] among us.[105]

Concerned with the domestic radicalization of opinion regarding the French mission and reform, the sultan convoked a consultative council of Moroccan notables. The council members were chosen to act as representatives of Moroccan opinion and as advisers to the sultan in evaluating French reform proposals. In fact, a later generation of Moroccan nationalists has seen in the *majlis al-aʿyān* the beginnings of a representative government in Morocco.

Al-Wazzānī was one of forty notables from the major cities and tribes of Morocco selected to participate in the council. Five meetings took place between the French delegates, the sultan's ministers, and fifteen members of the council of notables who were considered politically moderate, al-Wazzānī included.[106] Following a series of negotiations, the council of notables rejected the French proposals for reform and called for the convening of an international conference to discuss the question of Moroccan reforms and modernization. The Moroccans hoped that an international forum would better serve their interests in limiting French demands. The Makhzan undertook preparations for a conference to be held in the Spanish town of Algeciras the following year.

An accomplished *faqīh* and a trusted consultant of the sultan, al-Wazzānī was sent to Tangier, Algeria, and Tunisia to gather opinions on the position that should be taken by the Moroccan representatives on the French reform proposal.[107] Here, al-Wazzānī emerges as an informant and ambassador of the sultan. He was a prominent dignitary of the sultan, who executed his orders beyond Morocco and represented his power to local officials and the Moroccan population at large. It seems in this instance that al-Wazzānī must have been valued for his personal contacts and political connections, ones cultivated over the years as a distinguished sharīf and a prominent *faqīh*. In Algeria, his route included Tlemcen, Algiers, and Constantine. In Tunis, he stayed twenty days and met with many members of the local learned religious elite. The biographical accounts report that many scholars, aware of al-Wazzānī's juristic reputation and legal knowledge, sought to study with him some of the books he could transmit and to receive certificates (*ijāzas*) from him.

Finally, in 1907 Sultan ʿAbd al-ʿAzīz again turned to al-Wazzānī, requesting his opinion regarding the proper course of action in a serious conflict with France. By 1907 the very survival of the Makhzan of ʿAbd al-ʿAzīz was at stake.

Despite some gestures in the direction of internationalizing the reform effort of the Moroccan state, the signing of the Algeciras Act in May 1906 had consolidated, in effect, French intervention in Moroccan political and economic affairs. The inability of the sultan to defend Morocco from the imposition of colonial rule met with the disapproval of many Moroccans.[108] Moroccan critics accused ʿAbd al-ʿAzīz of delivering Morocco into the hands of the Europeans and of driving the Makhzan to bankruptcy with extravagant spending on tasteless European entertainments. Discontent with the sultan intensified when rumors seemed to confirm that he had completely fallen under the spell of the Christians and converted to Christianity. In the eyes of many Moroccans, Sultan ʿAbd al-ʿAzīz was unfit to rule any longer.

The growing discontent erupted in violence; throughout the country European nationals, and especially the French, came under physical assault. In March 1907 Émile Mauchamp, a French doctor working in Marrakesh, was murdered by an angry crowd. The ensuing French retaliation led to the occupation of Oujda, a city located to the northeast of Fez not far from the Algerian border.[109] A few months later, in July 1907, in a deadly attack on a train of the company that was building Casablanca's port, nine European employees were killed. Riots broke out in Casablanca at once, and the European quarter and the customs house were pillaged. In retaliation, the French navy bombarded the city, followed by the landing of two thousand French troops in August.[110]

In the face of unprecedented French military aggression and Moroccan anxiety and opposition, the sultan again sought the advice of some of the most prominent ʿulamāʾ and *aʿyān* of Fez on the correct manner of dealing with the crisis. In August 1907 two prominent ministers in the Makhzan of Sultan ʿAbd al-ʿAzīz met with esteemed members of the Moroccan *khāṣṣa* in Fez, al-Wazzānī included. Briefing them on the official position, the ministers explained the French aggression in Casablanca, drawing on the French narrative and justification and referring to it as the result of, "on the one hand, the good will of the French government to settle the dispute that persisted for a very long time, and on the other hand, its concern to secure the safety of its nationals and other Europeans, which the Makhzan, overwhelmed by the rural disorder, was no longer able to guarantee."[111] In short, the ministers instructed the members of the Moroccan elite to defend the Makhzan for its failure to alter the political situation with France.

We may never know how al-Wazzānī really viewed ʿAbd al-ʿAzīz and the Makhzan's policy toward the French encroachment. Yet this information, however fragmented and brief, tells us that al-Wazzānī was closely associated with the innermost circle of the sultan, often advising him on matters of legality and proper conduct, and entrusted with representing an official viewpoint to the Moroccan public. It can be argued, especially in the absence of additional information, that al-Wazzānī was merely a rubber stamp of the Makhzan and was no more than a loyal servant of the sultan who did what he was told to do. Whatever the case, I believe that for al-Wazzānī, the sultan's recognition and endorsement was anything but an ordinary liaison, and it must have empowered him and elevated his status in the eyes of himself and the community of which he was part. It may have well confirmed and strengthened his special position among his peer 'ulamā'. It must have aroused in him a sense of importance and eminence and undoubtedly validated his intellectual qualifications and legal knowledge. For sure, these direct ties with the entourage of the Moroccan sultan and the power elite of the country situated al-Wazzānī in the most dominant political center of his society. Al-Wazzānī was surely aware of the many political and social changes and challenges that marked the period.

Al-Mahdī al-Wazzānī died in Fez on Wednesday, September 13, 1923 (Ṣafar 1342), at the age of seventy-six and was buried outside Bāb al-fuṭūḥ in Fez.

Al-Wazzānī's grave. Photograph by author.

3 THE RHETORIC OF MOROCCAN MODERNITY

AL-MAHDĪ AL-WAZZĀNĪ'S generation was shaped by a sense that an acute crisis was imminent. By the latter part of the nineteenth century, new historical conditions emerged throughout the Mediterranean. European hegemony constructed new relations of power that resulted in the consolidation of the military occupation and colonization of Algeria by France, the Ottoman military defeats and loss of territories in the Balkans after 1878, the occupation of Tunis by France in 1881, and the occupation of Egypt by Britain in 1882. During this same period, Morocco was undergoing significant changes, which entailed the restructuring of state and society. Beginning in the mid-nineteenth century, Morocco entered a crucial phase of reform. The army, the government, and the financial system underwent a profound series of transformations. Like the Ottoman and Egyptian reforms, the Moroccan effort was crucial to guaranteeing the ability of the state to deal effectively with the external and internal forces that challenged its sovereignty.

These new historical conditions of the late nineteenth century encouraged a special preoccupation with Islamic law and informed conversations about Islamic tradition, its content and nature. Confronting a radically changed world, Moroccan 'ulamā' took issue with the tradition in which they were grounded, contemplating reasons for the unfolding Islamic degeneration and seeking solutions relevant to the dilemmas of their time. Concerns about the dismantling of Islamic authority emerged as a critical issue for religious thinkers. Firmly rooted in the Islamic tradition and committed to guaranteeing the revival of the Moroccan Muslim community, they firmly believed that reform (*iṣlāḥ*) and renewal (*tajdīd*) of existing norms and beliefs would benefit social and political life.

The late nineteenth-century preoccupation of Moroccan religious thinkers with reform and renewal was deeply embedded in Islamic thought and jurisprudence. Sunnī Islam holds that every hundred years a scholar who is considered a renewer (*mujaddid*) emerges to revive and regenerate Islamic thought and practice.[1] As has been demonstrated by scholars of Islam, over time, the concepts of reform, revival, and renewal became salient features of the Islamic tradition and came to represent a form of criticism crucial to guaranteeing the continuity of a moral Islamic society.[2] Moreover, the contemporary Moroccan discourse that elaborated on Islamic revivalism was emblematic of a broader formulation of discontent and expectations across the Muslim world. As new historical conditions emerged in the late nineteenth century, the writings of many Muslim scholars and jurists invoked reform and revivalism as the explicit response to the challenges of the time.[3]

Many late nineteenth-century Moroccan religious scholars attributed the weakness of the community of believers (*umma*) and its government in the face of European aggression to a fundamental departure from the correct understanding and application of the Qur'ānic revelation. According to this view, Moroccans had strayed from the pure *sunna*, the practice of the Prophet, and had being poisoned by dangerous innovation (*bid'a*) and blind adherence (*taqlīd*) to the teachings of classical law books and commentaries. Departure from the truth of Revelation was viewed as the critical illness afflicting contemporary Islam, and the corpus of knowledge known as *fiqh* understood as embodying such a deviation. These thinkers were deeply convinced that the sanctity of the sharī'a was being violated and that the renewal of religion (*tajdīd*) was necessary for the revival of Moroccan society. The desire to arrest the moral and social decline was accompanied by the assurance that all could be set right by returning to the authentic Islam of the Prophet and the first generation of Muslims, the *salaf al-ṣāliḥ*. This could be done only by returning to the original sources, the Qur'ān and the *sunna*, where the true essence of Islam can be found.[4]

These thinkers emerged out of the same intellectual milieu as al-Wazzānī. Some, such as Aḥmad b. Khālid al-Nāṣirī (d. 1897), Muḥammad bin 'Abd al-Kabīr al-Kattānī (d. 1909), Muḥammad b. Ja'far al-Kattānī (d. 1927), 'Abdallāh b. Idrīs al-Sanūsī (d. 1931), Abū Shu'aīb al-Dukkālī (d. 1937), and Muḥammad

b. al-Ḥasan al-Ḥajwī (d. 1956),[5] were prominent teachers at the Qarawiyyīn University in Fez and al-Wazzānī's peers. Others were al-Wazzānī's teachers and students, such as Abū ʿAbdallāh Muḥammad b. al-Madanī Gannūn (d. 1885), Muḥammad Muṣṭafā Mā al-ʿAynayn (d. 1910), Sultan ʿAbd al-Ḥafīẓ (r. 1908–12), ʿAbd al-Ḥafīẓ al-Fāṣī (d. 1964), ʿAbd al-Ḥayy al-Kattānī,[6] and ʿAbd al-Raḥmān b. Zaydān.[7] Their teachings and writings emphasize primarily religious subjects and concerns, invoking reform and revival of the Islamic intellectual tradition as imperative for facing new challenges dictated by Moroccan modernity. Their aims were to improve the understanding of the precepts of Islam and their application in order to ensure that daily life was conducted in harmony with Islam.[8]

There is a lack of sufficient scholarly works on Islamic reformist thought in Morocco in the late nineteenth century and the beginning of the twentieth century. Moreover, most of the available studies assert continuity between turn-of-the-twentieth-century reformist thought and the nationalist *salafiyya* movement, which emerged in the late 1930s. These works thus subsume late nineteenth-century thinkers and twentieth-century nationalists under one ideological rubric, the Moroccan *salafiyya* movement.[9] Such generalizations can be misleading. My research does not aim at a detailed analysis of the various Islamic reformist approaches that emerged in Morocco at the turn of the twentieth century. However, my discussion illuminates several arguments that are most closely associated with the works of many of these religious thinkers. My study reveals that these writers did not produce a single, homogeneous line of thought, nor did they constitute a unified movement. It is important to reconstruct the specific reformist projects initiated by each of these scholars before we can create proper typologies and examine their thoughts in comparison with later nationalist thinkers and activists.[10] With this in mind, in analyzing the intellectual context from which the *New Miʿyār* emerged, I have tried to avoid undue generalizations regarding the content of reformist thought as fully as possible and to focus on specific thinkers and their texts. In addition, I refer to the studied thinkers as scholars, jurists, or reformers and not as members of the *salafiyya* movement.

Islamic reformist thought in Morocco at the turn of the twentieth century was connected to reformist tendencies in the Arab East, especially those in Egypt and the Ḥijāz.[11] Some Moroccan reformers were exposed to Muslim reformers while on the pilgrimage to Mecca; others came under the influence of ḥadīth scholars in Egypt and the Ḥijāz while on the pilgrimage or as students at al-Azhar in Cairo. For instance, Muḥammad bin ʿAbd al-Kabīr al-Kattānī, his cousin Muḥammad bin Jaʿfar al-Kattānī, and ʿAbdallāh b. Idrīs al-Sanūsī performed the pilgrimage to Mecca and spent time in Cairo and Medina, where they met reformers and educators from all over the Islamic world. Al-Sanūsī also lived many years in Damascus and Istanbul and traveled throughout Egypt and Syria. Abū Shuʿaīb al-Dukkālī spent years studying jurisprudence at the famous al-Azhar University in Cairo and later taught religious studies in Mecca.

In addition, several works on ḥadīth and Qur'ān exegesis of prominent Muslim reformist thinkers were published and widely disseminated in Morocco—including *Nayl al-awṭār*, a law manual based on ḥadīth of Muḥammad al-Shawkānī (d. 1834) of Yemen, and *Rūḥ al-maʿānī*, a commentary on the Qur'ān of Maḥmūd al-Alūsī (d. 1854) of Baghdad.[12] Both scholars promoted, in varying degrees, the reformist ideas of the fourteenth-century Ḥanbalī thinker Ibn Taymiyya, who was renowned for his support of *ijtihād* and critique of *taqlīd* and what he considered heretical practices and beliefs, and were instrumental in advocating investigation of the Qur'ān and the canonical ḥadīth corpus.[13]

The famous reformer Muḥammad ʿAbduh traveled twice to North Africa (in late 1884 and early 1885 to Tunisia, and in 1903 to Tunisia and Algeria) and met with Moroccans.[14] Reformers, such as Muḥammad ʿAbduh, Rashīd Riḍā, and Shakīb Arslān, corresponded with Moroccans, and their ideas were known in the country.[15] As I demonstrated in the previous chapter, al-Wazzānī himself was well informed of their writings and on occasion responded to ʿAbduh's fatwās, interpretative teachings, and reformist ideas. In addition, the influential journals *al-ʿUrwa al-Wuthqā*, which was strongly associated with the reform project of al-Afghānī and ʿAbduh, and *al-Manār*, which was most closely associated with the work of Riḍā, its chief editor, were circulated in Morocco.[16]

The journals introduced Moroccan readers to the extensive transformation of Egypt and these thinkers' campaigns for reform and occasionally published articles on Moroccan contemporary questions and concerns.[17] It can be assumed that some of al-Afghānī's, ʿAbduh's, and Riḍā's criticisms and reformist ideas were known in Moroccan intellectual circles. The recognition of an intellectual link between Moroccan reformist thought and reformist circles in the Arab East is vital in providing deeper insights into this orientation. However, it is imperative to avoid inadequate generalizations that assert the coherence of these diverse and complex intellectual projects until such time as a substantial study that examines and compares the different intellectual trends becomes available.

Several studies on Islamic reformist tendencies in Morocco at the turn of the century have established that these conversations and concerns were not a distinctive contribution of late nineteenth-century thinkers; a pattern of rethinking tradition had been established well before the mid-nineteenth century. Throughout the second half of the eighteenth and early nineteenth centuries, controversies and debates about authentic tradition and authoritative texts were kept alive in Morocco. Islamic legal scholarship and the excesses of Sufi practices were subject to scrutiny and reevaluation, and revival of the study of ḥadīth became a central focus of Islamic reformist ideas.[18]

Yet it is important to note that alongside this continuity the particular historical circumstances of the late nineteenth and early twentieth centuries gave these ideas new force.[19] The Moroccan reformist discourse of the late nineteenth and early twentieth centuries can hardly be understood outside the context of European aggression and the apparent weakness of Islam. In contrast with the past, late nineteenth-century Moroccan reformers inhabited a changed, modern world deeply engaged with overpowering colonial modernity. In fact, the reasoning internal to turn-of-the-century Islamic reformist discourse was that a regeneration of Islamic knowledge and restoration of Islamic practices were crucial to guaranteeing the revival of the Islamic community and its struggle against European power.

A good case to exemplify this point is Muḥammad bin Jaʿfar al-Kattānī's forceful discussion in his *Naṣīḥat ahl al-Islām* (Frank counsel to the people of Islam), which was first published in 1908.[20] A primary focus of the text is that a deviation from the text of God and adoption of innovative and corrupted ideas from Europe made the Muslim lands in general, and Morocco in particular, vulnerable to European aggression and subjugation. A return to the rules of God would uplift Muslims from their state of moral and social degeneracy and ensure liberation from colonial Europe.

These Islamic reformist ideas shaped an intellectual discourse that could be used to understand and address the challenges to Islam. It generated a meaningful discourse that was both critical and constructive. On the one hand, Mālikī jurisprudence and Sufism were severely criticized. On the other, Moroccan thinkers asserted that the authentic tradition entailed a return to the Qur'ān and *sunna* and the path of the *salaf*. I am going to suggest that in composing his *New Miʿyār* and selecting his material, al-Mahdī al-Wazzānī carefully reacted to or against this particular local discourse and the consciousness that shaped it. More specifically, the *New Mi'yār* was aimed at restoring and reinforcing the preeminent authority of Mālikī jurisprudence by advocating a new Mālikī orthodoxy.

DEBATES ABOUT SHARĪ'A JURISPRUDENCE

A central problem in Muslim thought concerns the gap between the divine sharī'a as represented by the paradigmatic sources, the Qur'ān and the *sunna*, and the human understanding and elaboration of the two fundamental sources known as *fiqh*. Throughout Islamic history, this gap between the divine sharī'a and its human versions has generated critique and discontent. The late nineteenth- and early twentieth-century preoccupation with religion and Islamic law, and the discussions of reviving Islam, focused the attention of many Moroccan scholars on the question of the nature, status, and authority of Mālikī *fiqh*. Prominent jurists, such as 'Abdallāh Muḥammad Gannūn, Aḥmad al-Nāṣirī, Muḥammad b. 'Abd al-Kabīr al-Kattānī, Muḥammad b. Ja'far al-Kattānī, 'Abdallāh b. Idrīs al-Sanūsī, Abū Shu'aīb al-Dukkālī, 'Abd al-Raḥmān b. Zaydān, and Muḥammad al-Ḥajwī, criticized the way the Qur'ān and *sunna* traditionally had been interpreted and rejected the elaboration that classical scholarship had appended to these basic texts. Mālikī *fiqh* came to be viewed by many of the learned religious elite as disorganized, difficult to access, and generally unsuited for the times.[21]

Some jurists insisted that it is extremely difficult to work with the Mālikī corpus of knowledge. In their view, the sheer quantity of texts caused confusion and prompted disorder that often made the essential task of "finding" the law cumbersome if not impossible. The rules were scattered throughout a large number of works and had to be extrapolated from various manuals. The multiplicity of the texts brought about inevitable difference of opinions and inconsistent quality of views.[22] Scholars of this period widely recognized *fiqh* manuals as rigid and dogmatic, representing extreme academic intellectualism and legal reasoning that had no relevance for the modern world. Referring to the way leading scholars perceived Mālikī *fiqh* in the period, Malika Zeghal argues that "the proponents of religious reform considered the treatises of Mālikī *fiqh*, those manuals on which many 'ulamā' based their definition of the legal norm (sharī'a), as a monolithic and rigid casuistry that was the result of a blind imitation of the ancient jurisprudential system without regard for reality."[23]

Within sharīʿa jurisprudential discourse, the advocates of religious reform identified two spheres that required special attention: the culture of study and the practice of *iftāʾ*, or the process involved in issuing fatwās by the muftī. They argued that an increasing deterioration of religious scholarship, particularly in the study of Islamic law, resulted in a dramatic decline of *iftāʾ*. In other words, Moroccan reformist ideas represented a critique of the study of *fiqh* as well as legal procedures. In effect, reformist ideas discredited the basis of current religious jurisprudence and redefined the conduct of religious scholarship.[24]

The Decadence of Religious Studies

The desire to reorganize society according to the sacred law made many jurists concerned about the stagnant state of religious studies. It was believed that Muslims would recognize and apply the proper Islamic codes of social behavior through the spread of education. Thus, many among the Moroccan reformers sought to reform the content of Islamic education. They criticized the texts that were studied, the methods of instruction, and the culture associated with knowledge in general. They sought to revise much of the curriculum that most scholars followed.[25]

A prominent feature of the intellectual and institutional landscape of Morocco that was severely criticized by reform-minded scholars was the ideal of study. In the view of these scholars, knowledge (*ʿilm*) was focused squarely on the religious discipline that was embodied in Islamic law and the related sciences. This tendency to regard the sharīʿa as the exclusive, all-consuming object of reflection was seen as significantly restricting the nature of knowledge, instruction, and intellectual tradition.[26] Al-Nāṣirī, for example, insisted that other sciences, such as medicine, history, and geography, must also be studied and called for incorporating these disciplines into the curriculum.[27]

A concurrent concern was with the content and texts studied at the Qarawiyyīn. A major consequence of the rise of *fiqh* and its predominant role in instruction was the subordinate status of the study of *tafsīr* (the exegesis of the Qurʾān) and ḥadīth in the curriculum. *Fiqh* manuals were widely studied, while ḥadīth collections were relegated to a marginal position in the curriculum, and *tafsīr* disappeared altogether as a subject of study. Al-Wazzānī documented the locally studied texts of his time in his curriculum vitae (*fahrasa*). There, he reinforced the view that the science of ḥadīth at the Qarawiyyīn was limited. According to al-Wazzānī, the *Saḥīḥ* of al-Bukhārī and *al-Shamāʾil* of al-Tirmidhī were the most frequently read collections of Prophetic ḥadīth.

Next on al-Wazzānī's list were Qāḍī ʿIyād's *Kitāb al-Shifā* and Mālik's *Muwaṭṭa'*, while the *Saḥīḥ* of al-Muslim was the least read text.[28] Al-Wazzānī's statement seems to indicate that the jurists of his generation were less ḥadīth oriented and often read only one or two canonical ḥadīth collections.

A succinct report by Muḥammad bin ʿAbd al-Kabīr al-Kattānī underscores al-Wazzānī's statement: "As for the knowledge of ḥadīth, we do not find an advocate of it. If you ask someone to draw a conclusion from the ḥadīth about any trivial matter, he gets mad as if you committed a religious sin. And he responds with words of jurists or scholars of the school [imāms]."[29] In enumerating the disciplines and lists of books that a scholar of the time must study, Muḥammad bin Jaʿfar al-Kattānī stressed the change of orientation of the curriculum and the ultimate disinterest in the study of ḥadīth sciences at the time:

> In the past, the ʿulamā' devoted most of their work to [the study of ḥadīth], to the extent that there would be many thousands of students [eager to learn ḥadīth] in each of the many ḥadīth sessions [*majālis*]. However, these days this [practice] diminished, interest [in the study of ḥadīth] decreased, and there is no more than a frail impression of past effect of these [ḥadīth sessions]. Furthermore, nowadays the effect of [the study of ḥadīth] is gone, and its reputation and benefit vanished.[30]

In addition to questioning the centrality of *fiqh* as a body of knowledge in the local scholarly tradition, many leading thinkers viewed with disapproval the overreliance on abridgments of *fiqh* works (*mukhtaṣarāt*), condensed summaries of doctrinal classics. In contrast to the originality of foundational *fiqh* texts such as that of Mālik, these abridged works offered a derivative, compressed, and complicated synopsis of the doctrinal views.[31] For example, al-Wazzānī's contemporary, the historian Aḥmad al-Nāṣirī, who wrote extensively on the ossification (*jumūd*) afflicting religious studies, decried the devastating effects of the abridgment genre on Islamic knowledge: "The reason for the decline of knowledge [*ʿilm*] in Islam and the decrease of talent within it is people's preoccupation with abridgments [*mukhtaṣarāt*] that are incomprehensible and their avoidance of the books of earlier masters that are simple to understand and clear in their reasoning."[32]

Specifically, the well-known *al-Mukhtaṣar* of Khalīl (d. 1374) stood at the center of fierce debates and controversies. This manual of Mālikī jurisprudence had become the standard textbook for teaching jurisprudence at the Qarawiyyīn, replacing more substantive, original books composed by the founder of the school and his early followers. Arguing against the primacy of *al-Mukhtaṣar* of Khalīl, Muḥammad al-Ḥajwī makes the point that it is not sufficient for any person who seeks to engage in the elaboration of legal opinions and arguments to pursue merely knowledge of the Arabic language and the *Mukhtaṣar* of Khalīl and its commentaries, which was regarded by many scholars of the time as the primary legislative source and a substitute for the Book and the *sunna*. He insists that the grave consequence of this exclusive use of the *Mukhtaṣar* is that, in practice, many scholars do not understand their legal decisions, which in turn leads to mistakes in issuing fatwās and pronouncing legal rulings.[33]

Standing alone, *al-Mukhtaṣar* of Khalīl is often barely comprehensible and thus requires interpretative commentaries that further complicate its study. Al-Ḥajwī reports that it took scholars forty years to complete the study of *al-Mukhtaṣar* and its different commentaries.[34] Distinguished scholars criticized its modest literary qualities and its key role as the most widely disseminated of all sharīʿa texts and sought to limit its study and influence on Mālikī legal thought. In the mordant words of one of al-Wazzānī's contemporaries, "We are adherents of Khalīl; if he errs we err as well; if he is right, we are right too."[35]

Furthermore, the paramount importance of the vast body of *ʿamal* literature, the authoritative judicial practice, in the process of instruction was seen as symptomatic of the corruption and deterioration of local scholarship tradition. As noted previously, the *ʿamal* literature consists of a series of works drawn up beginning in the fifteenth century, and it comprises the prevailing opinions of the *madhhab* resorted to in court practice. As a body of knowledge and a source of law, *ʿamal* writings represent a qāḍī-made law. In seeking to solve a case of law, qāḍīs were obligated to adopt the widespread opinion (*mashhūr*) of the *madhhab*. However, basing their rulings on existing local customs and dominant practices, judges might follow what was called a "preferred opinion" (*rājiḥ*) or even a "weak opinion" (*ḍaʿīf*) in place of the widespread opinion of the *madhhab*. The opinions that gained authoritative status were included in *ʿamal* works.[36] Generally speaking, this selective appropriation of "preferred opinions" demonstrates the significant and fundamental process of change in Islamic law.

However, after the seventeenth century these works became classics in their own right, remaining a source of secured and standard knowledge for centuries. By the late nineteenth century, manuals that included the prevailing practices applicable only to one region or locale gained wide circulation and were deemed to represent the doctrine of the *madhhab*. Many of the Moroccan jurists of the period were concerned with the authoritative status of the *ʿamal* literature. For al-Ḥajwī, it best illustrated an excessive veneration of early scholars by the jurists of his time, resulting in the stagnation of law and precluding independent thought.[37]

Finally, fundamental to reformist discourse on the state of sharīʿa scholarship was the basic pedagogical activity associated with the local intellectual and institutional tradition. Distinguished jurists at the Qarawiyyīn such as Muḥammad Gannūn and al-Ḥajwī identified the principal instructional methods of recitation and memorization as the cause of a wider crisis in understanding and interpreting the sacred texts.[38] Some ʿulamāʾ warned that the reliance on the method of oral repetition of a particular text (*riwāya*) is a dangerous practice that discourages intellectual activity. They held that memorization (*dhākira*, *ḥifẓ*) restricts and simplifies the learning process by preventing sophisticated reflection on the real meaning of the written text and discovery of the law. The method of recitation and memorization of a text was followed and complemented by memorization of its commentary (*sharḥ*). The interpretative extension of the textual corpus was such that even supercommentaries became authoritative. The effect was that texts were rarely studied in the original; consequently, the text remained obscure (*ghumūd*) and incomprehensible (*ighlāq*).[39]

ʿAbd al-Ḥayy al-Kattānī objected to *riwāya*, arguing that many ʿulamāʾ actually fabricate the character and circumstances of their training through recitation and memorization. He says in this regard:

> When you approach the greatest [scholar] and ask him about the particular circumstances of his recitation of *Ṣaḥīḥ*, for example, with his teacher, he would tell you, I read it with him. If you, then, ask him did you read it in its entirety, he would say [that he read] only part of it. This is also the case with his teacher and the teacher of his teacher. . . . [Reporting] the recitation of an entire book for nothing more than a part of it is an obscene lie and a despicable fraud. Moreover, we see those [jurists] who undertook recitation with a shaykh who had recited with his shaykh only a part of *Mukhtaṣar* [of Khalīl] but nonetheless reported that he memorized with him the six books [of ḥadīth] and *Muwaṭṭāʾ* [of Mālik]. . . . We, therefore, consider instruction through recitation, which many Moroccans pursue, and the chains of transmission [*asānīd*], which they report, nothing to cheer about.[40]

A concurrent concern for the learning process underlies Ibrāhīm Ḥarakāt's comment on the issuance of fabricated licenses (*ijāza*s), certificates that attest to the study of a particular text through recitation and permit its transmission, in pre-Protectorate Morocco. He argues that *ijāzas*, a hallmark of membership in the scholarly community, were distributed irrespective of the qualifications and training of the students.[41]

The Decline of the Fatwā

The decay of the study of Islamic law led in turn to a further crisis in *iftā'* (the issuance of fatwās). The jurisprudential crisis embodied in the technical reception and transmission of Islamic knowledge and the prominence of *fiqh* manuals as instructional standards culminated in jurists' crafting a mass of weak and incorrect fatwās. According to advocates of Islamic reforms, especially Gannūn and al-Ḥajwī, poorly trained and unqualified jurists, incapable of practicing *ijtihād*, issued fatwās that led to many faulty and misguided legal opinions.[42]

The practice of *iftā'*, the jurist's most important task, underwent decline and stagnation. Gannūn's disdain for the fatwās given by his contemporaries is evident in this statement: "It is known that [the activity of] *iftā'* involves the elucidation of God's rule [*ḥukm*] in a particular legal case [*nāzila*]. It should not consist of unnecessary excessiveness or neglect, nor should it be supported by empty language, fallacious arguments, and tricks, which is precisely the prevalent practice of muftīs today."[43] For al-Ḥajwī, muftīs based their fatwās on *taqlīd*, referring their legal opinions to precedents in the school compendia without knowledge of the argumentation in the Qur'ān and the *sunna* or in the foundational *fiqh* works of the *madhhab*. Recovering the original and authentic intention of the Text of God was replaced by reciting passages from condensed abridgments and elaborated commentaries from memory.[44] According to al-Ḥajwī,

> Most of the works from which fatwās are derived enumerate legal cases [*furū'*] without offering any proof, except of [reference to] the *Muwaṭṭā'* [of Mālik] and its commentaries and the *Mudawwana* [of Saḥnūn]. I was surprised to read fatwās of some of the later scholars. They issue legal opinions that are guided by naïve thinking without referring to any text of the earlier scholars. In this way, one finds legal cases [argued by] al-Zurqānī that are commentaries on [legal opinions] of Khalīl and others, and people accept that with the utmost ease. Furthermore, even if one issued a fatwā referring to the Qur'ān, the *sunna*, or *qiyās*, he then set off an uproar and was insulted.[45]

Commenting on the stagnation or ossification (*jumūd*) of *fiqh* at the turn of the century, historian Muḥammad al-Fallāḥ al-'Alawī portrays the art of *iftā'*, arguing that the *fuqahā'* confined their juristic activity to a limited form of *tarjīḥ*, making certain opinions preponderant over others, and a narrowly defined *ikhtiyār*, preferring one already-established opinion over another, within the Mālikī *madhhab* alone. It follows, therefore, that the province of all jurists, a true and creative *ijtihād*, ceased, and instead the activity of issuing fatwās came to consist mainly of citing the sayings of earlier jurists and copying their teachings.[46]

More important, the blind imitation of past rulings and opinions had resulted in the issuance of fatwās detached from reality. In a frank "counsel" (*naṣīḥa*), Muḥammad Gannūn criticizes the conduct of the muftīs of his time, accusing them primarily of drawing conclusions without engaging in active and independent reflection on the principles of the case and without reference to social practice and reality. He further asserts that by the late nineteenth century, muftīs were no different from any other artisans or craftsmen who knew only their profession.[47] In professional terms, Gannūn argued that the muftīs abused their profession by recycling doctrinal solutions to problems that no longer held any social resonance.

Finally, for many Moroccan reformers the landmark of the jurisprudential crisis was the proliferation of opinions offering contradicting norms. In their view, the divergent legal opinions issued by jurists led to the improper practice of Islam and to social injustice. Illustrating the utter confusion that arose from the jumble of opinions and variety of collections during the late nineteenth century, the historian Muḥammad Ḥajjī explains that "for each question there were various rulings and opinions: this one ruled according to the saying of Zayd, that one gives a decision based on the teaching of ʿAmr, yet another issues a fatwā relying on someone else altogether. The result was conflicting answers that obscured the ways of truth and justice for the people."[48] For many legal specialists, the muftīs of the period gave religion and religious knowledge a bad reputation. This is best illustrated in the following remark of Muḥammad al-Ḥajwī: "In our time ignorance triumphed and the fatwā has become easily accessible to anyone who dares to reach out his hand to grab it, even if the hand is paralyzed and the palm of the hand is clumsy."[49]

During his reign, between 1908 and 1912, Sultan ʿAbd al-Ḥafīẓ put into practice some of his reformist thought. Critical of Islamic scholarship and legal literature in its present state, he embarked on a project of revitalizing Islamic knowledge and reordering the legal corpus. One aspect of this effort can be seen in his endeavor to regulate and systematize the process of issuance and dissemination of fatwās. Notably, 'Abd al-Ḥafīẓ limited the community of muftīs, that is, those scholars who engaged in the task of articulating the law and issuing fatwās, and was actively involved in collecting and publishing legal works and fatwā collections.[50] One such work was al-Wazzānī's *New Mi'yār*.[51]

CRITIQUE OF SUFISM

Advocates of reformist ideas insisted that the ills of Moroccan society were exacerbated by un-Islamic doctrines and practices that sharply contradicted Islamic norms. Prominent jurists at the Qarawiyyīn such as al-Madanī Gannūn, al-Nāṣirī, Mā al-'Aynayn, and al-Dukkālī viewed Sufi excesses as a major factor contributing to Morocco's inability to address the challenges of the time. To be sure, many of the scholars who criticized Sufi customs were themselves upholders of Sufi practices and beliefs, and some were even members of relatively orthodox Sufi orders, such as the Nāṣiriyya,[52] the Darqāwiyya,[53] the 'Ayaniyya,[54] and the Tijāniyya.[55] Islamic reformists did not deny Sufism (*taṣawwuf*) as such; rather, they dismissed what they perceived as false Sufism, which was practiced in some of the Sufi orders (*ṭuruq*). More specifically, they condemned those Sufi beliefs and practices for which they could not find textual bases in the Qur'ān or the Prophetic traditions.[56] For example, flogging and slashing parts of the body while in a trance, ecstatic dancing and singing, acts of worship to trees and stones, decoration of tombs, and expression of intense veneration of graves were criticized as strictly forbidden.[57] A story about al-Dukkālī recounts his attack against a sacred tree on which branches women would hang amulets, hairs, and pieces of cloth in the hope that it would grant their wishes.[58]

Some reform-oriented 'ulamā' openly expressed opinions that directly associated a number of Sufi practices with moral laxity and social decadence. They argued against reprehensible innovations (*bid'a*) that do not coincide with the normative position of "the righteous ancestors" (*al-salaf al-ṣāliḥ*) and constituted "disregard to the original spirit of *taṣawwuf*," such as extreme acts of worship, the use of musical instruments, and singing and dancing in devotional exercises.[59] This is illustrated in a statement written by al-Nāṣirī, who explicitly condemned the heinous nature of excessive practices of worship and the belief that they render proximity to God:

> Then these common people continued in their despicable [practices] in which each group comes together at known times in a specific place to [carry out] their

> reprehensible innovations [*bid'a*], and [they use] bowls, tambourines, pipes, singing, dancing, and stamping, and maybe they add to this fire or something else for honoring their leaders. They immerse in this for a long time until the time for prayer passes. And if an ignorant person [literally, peasant; in Arabic, *fallāḥ*] seeks to make them aware of their true state while they wander helplessly in a state of confusion, they do not pay attention to him and they do not see the disgrace in their state. Rather they believe that they are closer to God. May God raise them from their ignorance.[60]

Gannūn condemned certain acts and beliefs that came to be permitted in some of the Sufi orders that detracted from the principle of the absolute oneness of God (*tawḥīd*):

> Some [people] invoke almighty powers and claim that it is revealed to them in their state of dance and takes hold of them and that they get to know thoroughly transcendental [*al-ghayb*] matters. . . . Then, they go around and tell in their friends' houses that so-and-so was united [*aḥada*] with seven [divinities], and so-and-so was united with ten [divinities], and so-and-so was united with seventy [divinities], and so-and-so was united with three hundred [divinities], and so forth. Without doubt these are psychological or satanic states because triumph is from God, the Exalted, and He is not concerned with the one who pursues the reprehensible or the forbidden.[61]

Gannūn identified a form of *shirk* (associating someone or something with God) in the belief that a living person can gain access to the knowledge of the transcendental world associated with the thought of God and in the veneration or worship of any entity other than God. For him, these were all impious beliefs and impermissible practices because they contain heresies, and he sought to eradicate them.

Some reformists emphasized the polarization of different Sufi orders that, in their opinion, contributed to the disintegration of the *umma*. For instance, al-Nāṣirī lamented the division between Muslims caused by their affiliation to different *ṭuruq*: "And the matter became critical, and [because of the proliferation of Sufi orders] the *umma* became divided. Therefore, in every town or village there are several factions. This was unknown at the time of the first generation of Muslims [*salaf*] who strengthen those who follow them."[62] As exemplified by al-Nāṣirī's comment, the schism associated with the different Sufi orders was considered to constitute a foreign notion to the first generation of pious Muslims and an innovation (*bid'a*) that violates religious precepts and principles. It causes the disintegration of the Muslim community and as such is a reprehensible practice that must be purged. Mā al-ʿAynayn, as noted earlier, was another scholar who called for the unification of Sufi orders.

In the last decade of the nineteenth century these doctrinal ideas and ideological discussions of what constitutes sharīʿa and *bidʿa* spawned a doctrinal and political conflict between the Makhzan, the ʿulamāʾ, and the leadership of the Kattāniyya *ṭarīqa*. In 1894, Muḥammad al-Kattānī, the Sufi shaykh of the Kattāniyya, was accused by his peers among the ʿulamāʾ in Fez of spreading heretical ideas (*bidʿa*) and of leading prayer rituals of dubious legality.[63] This affair reflects the centrality of Sufism in Moroccan Islamic thought and debate in the pre-Protectorate period.

REVIVAL OF *SUNNA*

The late nineteenth-century Moroccan reformers sought to arrest what they perceived to be growing signs of social and moral decline by ensuring an intellectual, as well as social, revival. They envisioned a revival within the framework of Islam, by restoring and giving new vitality to the intellectual legacy of Islam, thereby recentering society. The guiding principle of many among the reform-minded scholars, such as Gannūn, al-Nāṣirī, Muḥammad b. Jaʿfar al-Kattānī, al-Sanūsī, and al-Dukkālī, was to live a holy and ethical life, conforming to the Prophetic example in every detail. This could be done only by returning to the ideal guide to social behavior and individual piety: the Qurʾān and the *sunna*. Perhaps the clearest elaboration of this vision during the period can be found in Muḥammad b. Jaʿfar al-Kattānī's *Naṣīḥat ahl al-Islām*. In it, al-Kattānī equates the renovation of belief and practice by conformity to the Qurʾān and the *sunna* with the regeneration of Moroccan society.

Echoing al-Kattānī's preference for the revival of the *sunna*, many Moroccan scholars pursued the science of ḥadīth, which, as the guide to the Prophetic *sunna*, became the ultimate authority and the real basis of jurisprudence. Emphasis on the study of ḥadīth was one of the main characteristics of late nineteenth- and early twentieth-century Moroccan revivalism. During the reigns of Mawlāy Ḥasan (r. 1873–94) and Mawlāy ʿAbd al-Ḥafīẓ (r. 1908–12), daily scholarly discussion of ḥadīth in the palace was instituted, and ḥadīth scholars such as al-Sanūsī, al-Kattānī, and al-Dukkālī were cultivated and offered royal patronage.[64] Ḥadīth became the most excellent of all disciplines and the focus of intellectual investigation and reflection. Ḥadīth-oriented scholars at the Qarawiyyīn insisted on the study of, and almost exclusive dependence upon, ḥadīth works, and they urged the derivation of the law exclusively from the Qur'ān and the *sunna*. They argued that greatest certainty of God's will could be obtained therein.

Malika Zeghal has argued that this shift in legal scholarship and knowledge toward ḥadīth sciences constituted, in effect, a serious challenge to the authority of Mālikī *fiqh*, the received legal doctrine.[65] I share Zeghal's view that the scholarly attention to canonical ḥadīth collections and the ḥadīth sciences implies a challenge to the Mālikī interpretative community. A story is narrated about al-Sanūsī, who was appointed by Sultan Mawlāy Ḥasan to the royal council of 'ulamā', where the sultan and leading jurists studied ḥadīth works with each other. It is reported that when discussing with his fellow jurists the *Ṣaḥīḥ* of al-Bukhārī, a canonical collection of ḥadīth, al-Sanūsī angered many of them by his insistence on the study of and exclusive reference to the principal sources—the Qur'ān and the *sunna*—without drawing on later interpretations in understanding the ḥadīth. Some 'ulamā' accused him of introducing innovations and denying sainthood. Evidently, these were serious accusations of unbelief, and shortly thereafter al-Sanūsī left Morocco.[66]

Such an emphasis on the study of the Qur'ān and the canonical ḥadīth collections was in direct opposition to the earlier reliance on legal compilations and expansive commentaries and summaries. In their approach to the *sunna*, these jurists reasserted the centrality and unconditional authority of the Qur'ān and the *sunna* in matters of religion and law over the classical legal compendiums. This approach represented a reevaluation of classical legal scholarship and a generally negative assessment of its sources and methodology. Classical ḥadīth collections were identified as a more reliable and sound corpus of traditions on which to base the law, while *taqlīd* of the teachings of the jurists of the school was broadly criticized.[67] This had direct and significant implications for Mālikī law. The crux of the matter was that, by using the ḥadīth collections, a jurist might derive legal rulings and opinions that would be at odds with those of the Mālikī school.

To be sure, this did not mean that proponents of reformist ideas rejected Mālikī law, since this was the school in which most jurists were trained. Its replacement would pose insurmountable problems and might lead to a situation of severe legal instability.[68] However, the reform-inclined 'ulamā' considered canonical ḥadīth collections to be authoritative in and of themselves without any need to complement them with reference to Mālikī legal manuals. It is also important to realize that the ʿulamāʾ who unequivocally referred to the Mālikī discursive tradition never challenged the canonical status of the Qurʾān and the *sunna*, and many scholars referred to ḥadīth works and based some of their opinions on these while remaining in every sense Mālikīs.[69] Typically, scholars who drew heavily on the Mālikī corpus strove to enlarge the concept of Islamic law to include important matters and texts beyond the Qurʾān and *sunna*.

In his discussion of the Moroccan intellectual scene in the seventeenth century, Houari Touati identifies the *fiqh* corpus with local knowledge (*du savoir local*), a sort of culturally constituted law. Touati argues that the trained muftī who operates within a particular society does not simply quote the teachings of his predecessors but seeks to make sense of the world for his audience. Thus, in effect, a muftī in his fatwās bridges academic doctrines and local norms and practices.[70] To put Touati's concept of *fiqh* as local knowledge another way, I argue that for many reform-oriented Moroccan scholars in the period under discussion, opinions that were established primarily on later Mālikī manuals and commentaries were often viewed as improper. In particular, opinions that promulgated prevailing customs and were textually unfounded were attacked as being deficient.

PROMOTING *IJTIHĀD*

The cornerstone of the legal methodology of ḥadīth-oriented ʿulamāʾ, such as Gannūn, al- Nāṣirī, al-Dukkālī, and al-Ḥajwī, becomes apparent in their discussions of *ijtihād*, the means by which a scholar independently derives his arguments.[71] In principle, in all legal matters these scholars stressed the importance of the practice of *ijtihād* and shunned what they regarded as its opposite, *taqlīd*, the unquestioning adherence to established doctrine. The correct legal opinion must be independently elaborated by the scholar using the principal sources of the Qurʾān, the canonical ḥadīth corpus, and the foundational works of the Mālikī *madhhab*.

For many reform-minded scholars, the acceptance of another person's opinion on a given matter without knowing the texts on which it is based amounts to deviation from the *sunna*, a reprehensible innovation (*bidʿa*). Ideally, the teachings and legal opinions of Mālikī jurists of earlier generations are to be followed only if one fully understands how they were arrived at in the first place.[72] Recognizing that the practice of *taqlīd* was the accepted standard by the muftīs of the time, al-Ḥajwī provides a plan and a curriculum that, if followed, would produce *mujtahids*. He says,

> The student needs to demonstrate a strong determination in the comprehension [of the meaning of the text], to become accustomed to the freedom of his thought, and to occupy himself with reflections on the text of God and the *sunna* of the Prophet. [In addition,] he needs to abandon the practice of pondering the ossified teachings of the later generations of jurists [*muta'akhkhirīn*] and instead to begin training in understanding the Qur'ān and the *sunna* and the original teachings of scholars who had practiced *ijtihād*, such as Mālik and other jurists of his rank who concerned themselves with a deep and thorough understanding of the ḥadīth collections of al-Bukhārī, al-Muslim, *al-Muwaṭṭa'* [of Mālik], and the *fiqh* works of al-Shāfiʿī and Abū Ḥanīfa and their like. If we return to the knowledge of the *mujtahids* and their methods of acquiring it, then we shall become *mujtahids* like them.[73]

Undoubtedly, these reformist ideas, which found their chief expression in a criticism of *taqlīd* and in a revival of ḥadīth through *ijtihād*, represented a serious doctrinal challenge. As clearly articulated in the words of al-Ḥajwī, the proponents of reformist ideas reoriented the sources of law by calling for the direct use of the Qur'ān and the canonical ḥadīth collections and rejecting the practice of adhering to traditional manuals of law. They attacked the prevalent pedagogical theory and curriculum and outlined their path to acquire knowledge and produce jurists. In their religious discourse, they forcefully redefined both the qualifications for attaining the status of religious scholar and the conduct of religious scholarship.

Thus, out of the modern transformation of Moroccan society and polity in the latter part of the nineteenth century, a new discourse of Islamic reform and regeneration emerged. For Moroccan thinkers, the reform of Islam was necessary to revitalize a morally decadent society and to effectively confront European imperialism. They simultaneously challenged the special status and authority of classical Mālikī tradition and asserted the primacy of the authoritative texts. Mohamed El-Mansour observes that over time Mālikism came to represent "an identifying marker" for Moroccans. He argues that Mālikism for Moroccans confirms their specific religious and cultural identity, which distinguishes them from their co-religionists in the Arab East and affirms in them a sense of pride in belonging to a single *madhhab* characterized by its rigor and strict Sunnism.[74] In this sense, the new discourse engaged fundamental questions of authority, belief, and identity; the centrality of Mālikī *fiqh* and the authority of the *fuqahā'* were contested, and a reconfiguration of Moroccan Islam, aiming for a renewed Islam that would secure social revivalism, was formulated. Thus, lurking beneath the polemic over religious scholarship and the tension between sharī'a and *bid'a* were larger and far more complex questions about the very definition of Islamic orthodoxy and religious authority. The answers to what constituted Islamic tradition and who qualified as 'ulamā' were contested.

AL-MAHDĪ AL-WAZZĀNĪ AS A CHAMPION OF A NEW MĀLIKĪ ORTHODOXY

As demonstrated earlier, al-Wazzānī's career as a prominent professor at the Qarawiyyīn and a famous muftī in Fez, and his relationship with the political authorities of the day, placed him at the center of the intellectual and doctrinal debates at the turn of the twentieth century. As described previously, al-Wazzānī maintained a close association with recognized Moroccan thinkers who explicitly criticized the intellectual and legal milieu and subscribed to reformist ideals that called upon the reconfiguration of legal knowledge and the methodology employed by jurists. Moreover, al-Wazzānī was well informed about the teachings of Jamāl al-Dīn al-Afghānī, Muḥmammad 'Abduh, and Rashīd Riḍā, members of the most celebrated circle of religious reformers of the late nineteenth and twentieth centuries. Many newspapers from the wider world of Islam that introduced a wealth of information about varied programs of modernization and agendas of reform in different Islamic centers were available in Morocco. Thus, it is also probable that al-Wazzānī reflected on texts and works of other Muslim critics, reformers, and educators from the Muslim world, especially from the Ḥijāz and the Levant.

In addition, my sketch of al-Wazzānī's work indicates that he engaged the changed world he occupied and the new discourses that emerged in the period. His writings invariably refer to the extensive transformation of Morocco and to revivalist ideals, especially his fatwās and newspaper articles on contemporary concerns and practices as well as those treatises in which he elaborates and promulgates his thoughts pertaining to local Sufi tradition. Surely, al-Wazzānī was concerned with the decisive critique and dissatisfaction with Mālikī scholarship and the reform ideas that emerged in late nineteenth-century Morocco. We can imagine that he contemplated the discourse of the reformist scholars that stressed the reorientation of Islamic thought and legal sciences away from Mālikī manuals and compilations of legal opinions toward the use of the Qur'ān and canonical ḥadīth collections while advocating *ijtihād*. The precise answers he gave remain unknown. All I know for sure is that in 1902 the prominent jurist al-Mahdī al-Wazzānī started writing his monumental Mālikī fatwā compilation, which he completed and printed at the lithographic printing house in Fez eight years later, in 1910, under the patronage of the ruling sultan, ʿAbd al-Ḥafīẓ.[75]

It is my contention that in compiling the *New Miʿyār*, al-Mahdī al-Wazzānī reacted to—or against—these Islamic reformist ideas, which challenged not only the special position and authority of the Mālikī legal tradition but also his own authoritative position within the existing legal system. Geared toward ensuring the revival of the Moroccan Muslim community, the reformist ideas contested existing practices and beliefs and offered new ways of understanding and reacting to the new historical conditions. In particular, by emphasizing the word of the Qur'ān and the Prophetic traditions, reformist ideas depicted Mālikī scholars and most of the corpus of Mālikī *fiqh* as parochial and irrelevant to a modern Muslim existence. For al-Wazzānī, nothing less than the stability of the legal system and the preservation of his interpretative community were at stake. In response, his *New Miʿyār* was an attempt to defend and restore an interpretation of Islam that reinforced the authority of Mālikī *fiqh*. In it, he sought to guarantee the continuing vibrancy and relevance of Mālikī wisdom, his own interpretative authority and social prominence, and the survival of the Moroccan Muslim community in a changed world.

In the preface to the *New Miʿyār*, al-Wazzānī explains his incentive for compiling the book, the method he used, and the content he included:

> Sharīʿa jurisprudence [*fiqh*] is the most exalted knowledge [*ʿilm*] that claims attention, and it is the most valuable [material] to which people of knowledge [*ahl al-dirāya*] aspire, because it is *fiqh*—the knowledge of rules [*aḥkām*] that regulate the actions of the believers [*ʿibād*] and articulate the legal norms [*al-miʿyār al-sharʿī*]—that determines the reward at Judgment Day.
>
> Given that the most excellent [knowledge] is the type around which judicial decision [*qaḍāʾ*] and considered legal opinion [*futyā*] revolve . . . I hastened to compile this book and to commit [this knowledge] to writing. I therefore assembled in it an ample number of responses of the most recent jurists [*mutaʾakhkhirīn*], selecting for inclusion what I deemed as the most excellent discussions of the expert jurists who are firmly rooted [in knowledge]. . . . The foun-

dation of [the book] is the [responses] that are most frequently mentioned by judges [*ḥukkām*] and that are a source of confusion for those who dispense justice among mankind. I supplemented some of the replies with [the necessary expansion], e.g., [by means of] commentary [*sharḥ*] and supplementary remarks [*tatmīm*] [on the fatwās], in the hope that some of those who are deficient [in knowledge] will not rush to advance criticism and doubt, and [I included] similar cases, in an effort to provide the greatest benefit [for the reader,] even if each entry [*tarjama*] exceeds what was necessary [for the particular case]. Despite this, I acknowledge my own weakness and incapability openly and clearly.

. . . In compiling [this book] I seek great reward and much honor from God, for He is the noble one who would not disappoint the hopes of one who pursues Him, and He would not turn down and reject one who pursues His hope. . . . I seek from God—may He be exalted—help in completion of the book and borrowing his reward and honor, for He is all-powerful in granting what is appropriate, and He is my guardian and an excellent master.[76]

In his preface, al-Wazzānī recounts how he conceived the idea of compiling this enormous collection. Certainly, he was inspired by his awareness of the religious and pious dimension associated with the preservation of Islamic law and jurisprudence. But, beyond doubt, his main reason for writing the work was a more practical one. Al-Wazzānī dedicates his work to the preservation and perpetuation of Mālikī *fiqh*. Indeed, he intends it to serve as a reference book for jurists and judges in rendering justice, sustaining the world of Mālikī jurisprudence. It seems that after many years of acting as a muftī, teacher, and writer, al-Wazzānī realized he had accumulated a large collection of fatwās. Motivated by the hope that his work would reassert the authority of Mālikī juristic thought, al-Wazzānī began his project.

First, he examined carefully the fatwās at his disposal. A large number of them were most likely his own replies to questions asked by his contemporaries. Then, concentrating on these fatwās, he added many more that were issued by other distinguished Moroccan scholars. Finally, in order to ensure their usefulness, he pursued his research further and complemented them with his own explanations and comments and incorporated additional fatwās to clarify the meaning of complex responses. The composition of this work surely involved enormous labor; these particular fatwās were not compiled by chance. Al-Wazzānī identified a reliable repository of Mālikī wisdom, singled out specific opinions, and arranged his material. As indicated previously, the guiding principle of the organization of the *New Mi'yār* was collecting and collating opinions central to the qāḍī's work for the purpose of deciding court cases or those that provide jurists and judges with an elaboration of intricate opinions of fundamental importance. It was his expectation that this work would offer solutions for all conceivable cases that a contemporary judge or jurist might encounter. Intending his work to serve as a comprehensive guide—an encyclopedia—al-Wazzānī named it *al-Mi'yār al-jadīd al-jāmi' al-mu'rib 'an fatāwī al-muta'akhkhirīn min 'ulamā' al-Maghrib* (The new comprehensive and clear standard measure of legal opinions of the most recent jurists of Morocco).[77]

Al-Wazzānī's inclusion of fatwās issued by muftīs other than himself should not be taken to indicate that he was merely a copyist who transcribed thousands of fatwās. A fundamental aspect of the *New Mi'yār* is that, despite its collective nature, it is the intellectual output of a single muftī living in a particular time and place. Indeed, the presence of al-Wazzānī can be discerned everywhere in this work. The core of this text is al-Wazzānī's own fatwās. Furthermore, in many cases, he supplemented his texts with fatwās issued by other muftīs to reinforce his argument. In countless cases, al-Wazzānī added his opinion and offered his comments at the end of a fatwā. He himself identified and selected his own fatwā texts and other relevant opinions of muftīs as well as cases addressed by judges that were to be included in the collection. Al-Wazzānī chose particular content, the method of its arrangement, and the extent to which it was explicated. His overriding concern was the incorporation of cases that were the most useful and necessary to contemporary muftīs and judges in light of the particular sociolegal needs and concerns of his community. Thus, in terms of its cultural import, this fatwā collection is an independent work of a highly individualistic nature, which reflects the editorial choices of al-Wazzānī.

With this in mind, I argue that al-Mahdī al-Wazzānī's central concern was to formulate a legal text that would provide a foundation for the revival of Mālikī jurisprudence and a constructive response to the Moroccan discourse of critique and reform of tradition. This radically ambitious work had to address directly the problems and accusations facing *fiqh* and to formulate solutions for solving them. I maintain that in his *New Mi'yār* al-Wazzānī took the significant step of making Mālikī jurisprudence both manageable and relevant to his own time, place, and culture.

From this perspective, the *New Mi'yār* can be seen as an attempt to systematize and standardize *iftā'*. Whereas previously knowledge essential to arriving at a correct ruling had to be painstakingly located in numerous *fiqh* manuals, with his new encyclopedic text al-Wazzānī efficiently brought together the most recent and legally correct opinions in a single text. Furthermore, as he indicates in the preface, his undertaking aimed at updating the legal tradition of the Mālikī school with the latest fatwās deemed to be relevant to contemporary needs and of frequent occurrence.

I want to return to Talal Asad's engagement with the concept of Islamic orthodoxy. His characterization of the construction and reconstruction of Islamic orthodoxy as emerging in conditions of conflict and contestation of interpretations is useful to my thinking. Orthodoxy, he suggests, is the locus of a relationship of power. What interests me in particular is that the definition of orthodoxy involves strong acts of demarcation. Within the process, believers are distinguished from heretics, texts are challenged and reinterpreted, and authoritative arguments are rephrased and articulated. Out of the elaboration of orthodoxy, a corpus of existing beliefs, practices, and institutions is undermined, and a new set of binding norms and standards that are meant to be followed is formed. I argue that precisely such a contest and competition over what constitutes Islamic orthodoxy characterized the period in which al-Mahdī al-Wazzānī operated, and a reconstitution of orthodoxy was his *New Miʿyār*. To put this proposition another way, the Moroccan reformist discourse that scrutinized and reevaluated the Mālikī legal tradition was countered by al-Wazzānī's project, which was committed to defend its preeminent authority and reassert its continuing relevance.

His selection of *New Miʿyār* as the title of the work evinces the role he saw both for his book and for himself as a latter-day al-Wansharīsī. The *New Miʿyār* was intended to replace the *Miʿyār* of al-Wansaharīsī. Four centuries after its composition, the latter became irrelevant. Al-Wazzānī's world and the discursive terrain that he engaged were radically different from those of al-Wansharīsī. Mālikī knowledge had to be imprinted by the new needs and concerns of a modern society. This is where I employ Daniel Brown's insight about the transforming relationships of modernity and tradition. His argument that *all* responses to modernity from a religious tradition, even those of the most conservative defenders of tradition, are at the same time fundamentally shaped by the modern as well as anchored within tradition is crucial to my story of the *New Miʿyār*. His observation that "the most conservative defenders of tradition cannot help but reshape the very tradition that they seek to preserve unchanged" is particularly insightful. In consequence, I argue that, against the reformist critique, al-Wazzānī composed in his *New Miʿyār*, in effect, "a new yet old" Mālikī orthodoxy. As will become clear very quickly, my point is that, although firmly rooted in the Mālikī discursive tradition, al-Wazzānī's project cannot be understood outside the particular context of Moroccan modernity. The options available to him and the course of action he took were bounded and shaped by the historical changes and the discursive break that they created. In the following chapters, I further explore the nature and meaning of the *New Mi'yār*.

4 DELINEATING MUSLIM-CHRISTIAN RELATIONS

IN THE SECOND HALF of the nineteenth century in Morocco, the definition of Islamic orthodoxy became a locus of disagreement and contestation. Interpretations and debates were grounded in key questions of what constitutes Islamic knowledge and conduct of religious scholarship. The corpus of knowledge and the elaboration of sharīʿa jurisprudence were fundamental for the determination of correct norms and practices and ultimately, the rules and procedures that would regulate Muslim society. Al-Mahdī al-Wazzānī, like other jurists of the pre-Protectorate period, engaged the emergent discourse dictated by Moroccan modernity, and his *New Miʿyār* represents an incisive conceptual and ideological response to the epistemological/discursive break. Driven by the desire to restore and reinforce the preeminent authority of the Mālikī legal tradition, al-Wazzānī's project of Islamic reform was intended at the same time to directly confront the reformist critique and address the problems and challenges facing Mālikī *fiqh* in the context of a changing world. When it is considered in this way, I have suggested that in his *New Miʿyār*, al-Wazzānī, in effect, composed a new Mālikī orthodoxy, emphasizing its renewed nature as a response to changing realities.

In an effort to broaden our reading and understanding of the *New Miʿyār*, the next three chapters interrogate the nature and meaning of the entire work. Two questions inform my investigation: What is al-Wazzānī's mode of discourse? What agenda or ideological orientation shapes his legal deliberations? Together the succeeding chapters constitute a detailed analysis of the methods and consciousness of the work and offer an argument about its function and social logic. As noted, I have been particularly inspired by Brinkley Messick's argument for an understanding of the muftīship as an institution of worldly interpretation. Messick suggests that muftīs craft meaning for a society in its own terms by relating an indigenous notion of text to a particular set of circumstances. I endorse and employ this insight. My argument is that al-Wazzānī's juristic discourse invokes a pattern of sophisticated interaction between Mālikī legal doctrine, sources of legal authority, and the rhetoric of legal argumentation, on the one hand, and the new historical conditions, and the new consciousnesses shaped by them, on the other. To put it slightly differently, in his *New Miʿyār*, al-Wazzānī sought to both resist and reconcile the changes in his age from within Mālikī scholarship. His goal was to infuse Mālikī thought with meaning relevant to the world he occupied. In the process, he actively transformed Mālikī knowledge and offered a local and updated interpretation of legal tradition for a particular Muslim society. For al-Wazzānī, reordering Mālikī tradition as informing and regulating beliefs, values, and social practices under the new modern conditions was necessary to restore and guarantee its authority.

In this chapter, I pursue my effort to explore the form and meaning of the *New Miʿyār* in relation to two texts composed by al-Wazzānī. The texts are recorded in the chapter on jihād in which al-Wazzānī addresses questions dealing with the application of Islamic law to various issues pertaining to contact with the non-Muslim world and Moroccan Jewry.[1] As in the case of other Middle Eastern and North African countries, the late nineteenth century coincided with growing European interference in Moroccan affairs and increasing colonial aggression that challenged the sovereignty of the sultan. Contact between Muslims and the Christian world was seen as one of the major causes of the weakness of Islam and the Moroccan state. It is obvious that during this period extensive transformations, both structural and discursive, occurred. Thus, al-Wazzānī's juristic engagement with the challenges of European imperialism seems to offer a fruitful route into the *New Miʿyār*.

A FATWĀ ON SECURING CONSULAR PROTECTION AGAINST THE TYRANNY OF A MUSLIM RULER

The first text discussed here is a fatwā issued by al-Wazzānī on an unspecified date during the latter part of the nineteenth century.[2] This fatwā is of great interest because it takes us into a sociolegal domain—the *ḥimāya*, or protection system—that became increasingly troubled in this period of transition in Moroccan history.[3] *Ḥimāya* refers to the practice whereby, especially from 1860 onward, foreign residents granted extraterritorial rights to their local employees and business agents (known as *ahl al-ḥimāya* or *aṣḥāb al-ḥimāya*) that conferred legal and fiscal immunities on Moroccan subjects under the protection of European consulates.The principle of extraterritorial rights was based on earlier agreements between Morocco and European states that placed foreigners living in Morocco under consular protection.[4] By the late nineteenth century, while foreign commerce grew and the numbers and influence of Christian merchants increased, the system of protection witnessed steady expansion. As growing numbers of both Jews and Muslims (and even prominent Makhzan officials) became protégés of foreign powers, the protection system was seen by the Moroccan power elite and the ʿulamāʾ as one of the major causes of the weakness of the state.[5] The conference of Madrid, convened by the European powers in 1880 in an effort to end the abusive expansion of consular protection, failed to stem the tide. As Mohammed Kenbib aptly described it, "Far from restricting the practice of granting protection and limiting the abuses of the system, numerous articles [signed during the conference], in effect, expanded its scope. Many categories [of locals who received patents of protection] that thus far existed only de facto became official."[6]

A system in which Moroccan subjects became protégés of foreign powers considerably transformed relations between the Moroccan ruler and his subjects and directly challenged Moroccan authority and sovereignty.[7] For instance, historians of Moroccan Jewry have demonstrated how the evasion of taxes by Jewish protégés, especially the refusal to pay the *jizya*, the most important symbol of the superiority of Islam and the responsibility of the Moroccan state for the protection of the Jews, was a consequence of the consular protection.[8] Muslim merchants, prominent state officials, political dissidents, and criminals also recognized that considerable profit and protection could be attained by becoming more and more linked to the foreigners residing in Morocco and the foreign consulates. For instance, in 1906 during the political crisis preceding the Ḥafīẓiyya uprising that dethroned Sultan ʿAbd al-ʿAzīz, both Mawlāy ʿAbd al-Ḥafīẓ, who led the rebellion, and his most important ally, the powerful tribal leader al-Madanī al-Glāwī, solicited French protection.[9]

One of the most important figures who became a protégé of France in the last decades of the nineteenth century was Sīdī ʿAbd al-Salām al-Wazzānī, the sharīf of Wazzān, whose prestige was unparalleled.[10] During his conflict with Mawlāy

Ḥasan, he not only placed himself under French protection but went even further by supporting the French territorial encroachment in the Touat Oasis situated along the Moroccan border with Algeria.[11] The obvious insult to the Moroccan sultan's sovereign rights may be of great value in evaluating the circumstances that gave rise to al-Wazzānī's fatwā. Over the years, al-Mahdī al-Wazzānī maintained close contacts with the city of Wazzān and its prominent sharīfs, especially with ʿAbd al-Salām al-Wazzānī, who initiated him into the Wazzāniyya *ṭarīqa*. It is conceivable that al-Mahdī al-Wazzānī may have been valued by the Makhzan for his political connections and ties with the sharīf of Wazzān and that these connections would have allowed him to intercede on behalf of the Moroccan sultan, Mawlāy Ḥasan.[12] Considered in this way, al-Wazzānī's fatwā can be interpreted as an attack on the sharīf of Wazzān, who placed himself under the protection of the French, asserting the sultan's objections to the expressed offense to his authority and prestige.

Al-Wazzānī's fatwā purports to be a careful legal response to an earlier fatwā issued by a distinguished Tunisian jurist who justified the practice of securing consular protection against injustices perpetrated by a tyrannical ruler. Unfortunately, the full text of the request for a fatwā (*istiftāʾ*) is not included in the *New Miʿyār*, probably because the response (*jawāb*) was sufficiently explicit to demonstrate the matter under discussion. The loss of the *istiftāʾ* means that I do not know the identity of the person who posed the question. It may have come from al-Wazzānī himself, from the Moroccan sultan, or from one of his agents. The tone of the response may provide a clue to the intended audience. The response is written in language that would have been intelligible to a jurist familiar with legal discourse and the art of legal reasoning. It is formulated with the care and precision that characterize al-Wazzānī's style. Significantly, it refers to an array of sources and maintains a detailed level of legal discussion. Although there is no evidence that the Moroccan sultan was directly involved in the case, there is no doubt that he could have followed al-Wazzānī's line of reasoning.[13]

At an unspecified date, during the latter part of the nineteenth century, an unidentified person approached al-Wazzānī, asking his counsel on "the disastrous calamity [*dāhiya*] that had become prevalent [*ʿammat*] throughout the country at that time, namely, seeking the protection of the infidels [*al-iḥtimāʾ bi'l-kuffār*]."[14] Al-Wazzānī begins his discussion by indicating that he does not know anyone who has justified this practice, with the exception of one legal opinion issued by a distinguished Tunisian jurist by the name of Sīdī Ibrāhīm al-Riyāḥī al-Tūnisī (d. 1849), the *shaykh al-jamāʿa* or supreme juridical authority of Tunis, who supervised the activities of the muftīs in the capital city.[15] Conscious of the legal value of a fatwā issued by a jurist and muftī responsible for instructing other muftīs, al-Wazzānī immediately turns to a careful examination of that text.

The Fatwā of al-Riyāḥī

From al-Wazzānī's response the following facts may be reconstructed: At an unspecified date, possibly in the first half of the nineteenth century, a certain chief (*amīr*, pl. *umarāʾ*)[16] kidnapped and forced into service (*khidma*) the two sons of a certain qāḍī al-ʿAnnābī.[17] The qāḍī, presumably desperate to ransom his sons, offered the chief a large sum of money, which he accepted. However, in apparent disregard for his end of the bargain, the chief did not release the qāḍī's sons. The qāḍī then fled to the house of the British consul stationed in Tunis, seeking protection from the injustice (*ẓulm*) that had befallen him. The consul became involved in the case and went to great lengths to secure the release of the qāḍī's two sons and promised their safety, along with that of the qāḍī, in a written document authorized by the Tunisian bey.[18]

Because the case involved a qāḍī, a prominent member of the Muslim community, who sought the protection of non-Muslims (*ghayr ahl al-dīn*) against another Muslim, his disgraceful (*shanʿāʾ*) action became of special importance (*ʿaẓuma*). No doubt acting on the basis of his concern about the possible social and political repercussions of the incident, the bey sent his *istiftāʾ* to the aforementioned chief muftī, al-Riyāḥī. He posed the following question: "Is the persistence of this qāḍī in his position permissible given that what has occurred diminished [his authority] in the eyes of the people?"[19] Details mentioned later in the fatwā suggest that the bey was strongly inclined to dismiss al-ʿAnnābī from his position as a qāḍī, on the grounds that he had defamed Islam, and that he wanted al-Riyāḥī to issue a fatwā corroborating the validity of his decision.

Al-Riyāḥī opened his response by referring to an earlier fatwā he had issued that was relevant to the matter at hand. In that earlier case, he had authorized the seeking of protection from non-Muslims (*al-iḥtimāʾ bi-ghayr ahl al-milla*) because, as he explained, "there is no prohibition against that in the sacred law of Islam." As textual authority for his response, he cited *Rawḍ al-unuf*, a commentary by Suhaylī on the Prophetic biography (*sīra*) edited by Ibn Hishām.[20] In addition, al-Riyāḥī commented that even if in the past the common people (*ʿāmma*) had viewed the seeking of protection from non-Muslims as apostasy (*kufr*), at present they are more mindful and point the blame at the person who causes the Muslim to seek this protection. Thus, he implied, it was the behavior and conduct of the chief that were inappropriate. At this point, al-Riyāḥī made a key reference to the first caliph, Abū Bakr, observing that when he migrated during the time of the Prophet Muḥammad, he placed his family and his property under the protection of polytheists.[21] In other words, to persuade his audience, al-Riyāḥī found support for his position by appealing to the authority of Abū Bakr, an exemplar of the early Islamic *umma*. Note that the legal value of this reference subsequently played an important role in al-Wazzānī's deliberations.

Confident in the direction of his argument, al-Riyāḥī continued by explaining that he could not justify the removal of qāḍī al-ʿAnnābī on the basis of defamation (*tajrīḥ*) of Islam since "he did his duty or what was permitted to him." A Muslim, al-Riyāḥī noted, should not be accused of defaming Islam by such an act "because a man is entrusted with the defense of his life, his family, and his property from injustice, even if it leads to killing, and if he dies in the course of this defense he is counted among the martyrs [*shuhadāʾ*]."[22] Clearly, in his view, there was no ground for a slanderous accusation against qāḍī al-ʿAnnābī.

Al-Riyāḥī next made an overt presumption in his legal strategy and gave an example to emphasize the legitimacy of qāḍī al-ʿAnnābī's act. He explained that "if a man walking on the road encounters a vicious dog, and there is a nearby tavern [*ḥānat khammār*] or other place to which entry is forbidden, it is incumbent upon that man to enter this place in order to protect his own life."[23] By analogy, the chief muftī claimed, seeking protection from infidels was justified in the present case because of the clear danger to al-ʿAnnābī's life.

Having nearly finished his fatwā, al-Riyāḥī argued that he would not renounce his earlier opinion and that it was permissible for qāḍī al-ʿAnnābī to seek protection from non-Muslims, even if the bey chose to dismiss him. He concluded with sincere advice (*naṣīḥa*) to his master, the bey, urging him "to ignore the matter and settle the affair once and for all."[24]

The Response of al-Wazzānī

Ultimately, al-Riyāḥī reasoned, qāḍī al-ʿAnnābī acted in accordance with the standards of Islamic conduct. His fatwā to the bey repeatedly asserts the right to protect oneself from harm and injustice by seeking protection from non-Muslims. Al-Riyāḥī, it will be recalled, was a distinguished jurist, and his fatwā was the only legal precedent available to al-Wazzānī that justified the practice of *ḥimāya*, hence the importance of dealing with it in a systematic manner. Al-Mahdī al-Wazzānī begins the substantive section of his response by univocally rejecting al-Riyāḥī's fatwā, announcing that "evoking difficulty [*ḥaraj*] and abuse [*shaṭaṭ*] [as the basis upon which to permit non-Muslim protection] is entirely wrong [*ghalaṭ*] [since these matters are irrelevant in addressing this legal question at the present time]."[25] It will be remembered that al-Riyāḥī had invoked the authority of Abū Bakr in order to support his legal opinion. Sensitive to the religious significance of this reference, al-Wazzānī raises four specific issues that call into question al-Riyāḥī's juristic reasoning and legal assessment as it pertains to the analogy with Abū Bakr.

1. "Abū Bakr sought protection against polytheists [*al-mushrikūn*], not against [Muslim] rulers who rule over Muslims [*wulāt al-muslimīn*]." The sharīʿa, al-Wazzānī continues, does not stipulate the endurance (*ṣabr*) of ill treatment by polytheists. The reverse, that is, enduring the roughness of Muslim rulers and the prohibition to rebel against them (*al-khurūj ʿanhum*) even if they commit injustice, is prescribed in the law and recorded in many Prophetic traditions. How is it possible, al-Wazzānī asks, to draw an analogy (*kayfa yuqās*) between rebellion against Muslim rulers and seeking the protection of infidels, on the one hand, and seeking the protection of a polytheist against the harm of other polytheists, on the other?[26]

From the outset al-Wazzānī insists on the differences between the particular conditions, which Abū Bakr was compelled to engage and those that impact the Moroccan Muslim community centuries later. He establishes that seeking non-Muslim protection in the context of late nineteenth-century Morocco amounts to rebellion against the Muslim ruler and violation of Islamic norms. Such behavior could not be attributed to Abū Bakr, whose authority is paradigmatic in the eyes of every Muslim.

2. Al-Wazzānī argues: "Seeking the protection of the infidels today means abandoning Islam [*al-khurūj ʿan al-Islām*] and becoming submissive to the infidels. [This act] is equivalent to an infidel's commanding [a Muslim] to do something and he hurries to obey his order, whereas if the greatest of all Muslims commands him to do something, if only to obey, he would neither assist him, nor agree with him, nor consider [his wish], unless the infidel allows him to do so. [Clearly, such conduct] could never proceed from Abū Bakr."[27]

3. Al-Wazzānī asserts that "Abū Bakr sought protection in order to strengthen [*taḥṣīn*] his religion and perfect [*tatmīm*] his belief, not to strengthen his body or property." How is it possible, he asks, to draw an analogy between a

worldly concern (*amr al-dunyā*) and religion (*al-dīn*)? Once again, al-Wazzānī emphasizes the differences in the circumstances that shaped Abū Bakr's choice and those that dominate his world. Cleverly drawing upon Islamic history, al-Wazzānī recalls the notorious Umayyad governor, al-Ḥajjāj b. Yūsuf (d. 714) and other oppressive Muslim leaders who killed thousands of pious followers of the Prophet and other Muslims.[28] Nevertheless, no one from among the Muslim community at the time approved the reprehensible act of seeking protection from the infidels.[29] In speaking about early Islamic history, al-Wazzānī asserts that if the dictate to endure a tyrannical ruler applies to the early *umma*, then it certainly applies to contemporary Muslims.

4. Seeking foreign protection runs counter to the norms of Islamic life, and it could never be ascribed to Abū Bakr. Al-Wazzānī announces, "Those who grant protection [*al-muḥtamūn*] ridicule the Muslims, denigrate their concerns, and wish them shameful things, so that that they will become like them." He quotes Qur'ān 4:89: "They wish you to become disbelievers as they are."[30] Finally, he asserts that infidels who provide protection to Muslims against Muslim sovereigns wish their associates, or protégés, the victory "and other forbidden things of which a Muslim does not approve."[31]

❖

Al-Wazzānī sends a clear message to his audience: Abū Bakr's position differed greatly from that of al-Wazzānī's contemporaries. Any attempt to invoke Abū Bakr and, by implication, the Prophet Muḥammad—whose tradition or practice is the paradigm of Islamic life—as support for seeking protection of infidels against a tyrannical Muslim ruler is invalid and erroneous.

After refuting the validity of al-Riyāḥī's invocation of the authority of Abū Bakr, al-Wazzānī skillfully turns to a point-by-point analysis of al-Riyāḥī's legal opinion and rejects his arguments. He divides his analysis into five parts. Each part opens with al-Riyāḥī's exact words, followed by al-Wazzānī's refutation of his arguments.

1. He begins by quoting al-Riyāḥī's claim: "I issued a fatwā authorizing the seeking of protection from non-Muslims, since there is no prohibition of that in the sacred law of Islam." These words, according to al-Wazzānī, are null and void (*kalām bāṭil*). By issuing this fatwā, al-Riyāḥī neglected the law, for, as al-Wazzānī explains, "it is permitted to write it down [i.e., an authorization to seek foreign protection] only for the purpose of refuting it, as in the case of a fabricated *ḥadīth* [*al-ḥadīth al-mawḍū'*]."[32]

2. Al-Wazzānī next cites al-Riyāḥī's reference to Abū Bakr as support for his argument: "Our master, Abū Bakr, placed his family and his property under polytheist protection." This analogy, notes al-Wazzānī (reiterating the point he made earlier), has no bearing on the present case, because, as should be clear by now, the circumstances faced by Abū Bakr were different from those faced by contemporary society.[33]

3. Al-Wazzānī now focuses his attention and that of his audience on al-Riyāḥī's claim that qāḍī al-ʿAnnābī "did his duty or what was permitted to him." This claim contradicts sharīʿa texts that prescribe the principle of endurance with regard to the actions of Muslim sovereigns. As a proof-text for the illegality of al-Riyāḥī's claim, al-Wazzānī cites a *ḥadīth* reportedly transmitted by Ibn ʿAbbās (d. 687–88). According to this *ḥadīth*, the Prophet said, "Anyone who sees his ruler do that which is loathsome, let him endure and yield, because no one should depart from the community, not even by an inch, and if he [the one who departs] dies, it is a death of religious ignorance [*jāhiliyya*]."[34] The *ḥadīth* underscores the obligation to give unquestioning obedience to the ruler, however unjust he may be. As support for this third assertion, al-Wazzānī cites three legal discussions that corroborate one another on this point.

First, Al-Wazzānī quotes a text written by ʿĪsā al-Sijistānī, the qāḍī of Marrakesh.[35] In his *Nawāzil*, al-Sijistānī noted that the conduct (*sīra*) of the first few generations of Muslims (the "pious forebears," *al-salaf al-ṣāliḥ*) reveals the following:

> If a ruler [*imām*] is tyrannical [*jā'ir*], kills, seizes property unlawfully, and commits sins such as fornication [*zinā*], but deposing him becomes impossible except by murder and by bloodshed, it is forbidden to do so, even if correcting the injustice is mandatory. If he repents, or is left alone, patience is necessary, and there is no way to rebel against him [*al-qiyām ʿalayhi*]. This is demonstrated by the *salaf al-ṣāliḥ*, who had many bad rulers, to whom they offered advice [*naṣīḥa]* to command good and forbid evil as much as possible. However, they were not successful in removing them, nor did they insult them in public or proceed to fight them because the evils of rebellion [*mafāsid al-qiyām*] are stronger and greater than the sins committed by them [the unjust rulers]. The maxim is that if two wrongs occur, the lesser evil should be committed. And in following the *salaf al-ṣāliḥ* there is safety. May God protect us from error and accord us success in doing right. In honor of our Prophet and master, Muḥammad, may God bless him and grant him salvation.[36]

Second, Al-Wazzānī remarks that in his *Nawāzil*, ʿAbd al-ʿAzīz al-Zayyātī (d. 1645)[37] related the following statement cited by qāḍī Abū Sālim al-Kūlālī:[38]

> Ibn al-Khaṭīb [d. 1375] said: "If someone hopes for his [the ruler's] blessing whenever he is subjected to injustice, there is no objection if he swears against the evil doers, secretly and publicly. If he submits to the rule of God, there is no need to go further. However, if the sultan is the oppressor, it is prohibited to swear at him, or at someone who acts wrongly in his name. Because of his [the Prophet Muḥammad's] saying, may God bless him and grant him peace: If [the sultan] acts justly, be thankful, if he oppresses, be patient. Further, the Prophet said: Do that which is required of you, and leave to God that which is required of them [the rulers]. This means that we are required to obey. In addition, the Prophet said: Anyone who curses the sultan, God will impose him [the sultan] as ruler on him. It has been said by some of the 'rightly guided': Our sultan oppresses us. He [the Prophet Muḥammad] responded: I am afraid you will lose him and that someone who is more oppressive than he will come, so the matter is left to God the Supreme."[39]

Third, Al-Wazzānī now addresses the religious obligation that is reflected in the Prophetic *ḥadīth*: "Do not rebel against the sultan [even] if he illegally seizes property and strikes one's back." He cites the opinion of qāḍī Muḥammad b. Sūda:[40]

> Sound Prophetic traditions are explicit in [speaking about] the protest of the rightly guided Muslims [*ahl al-ḥaqq*] against anyone who denied the fatwā of Ibn Manẓūr and directed his protest and blame against him.[41] For [denying Ibn Manẓūr's fatwā] is nothing but alteration of religion, overturning the truth, rejection of the texts [*nuṣūṣ*, i.e., the Qur'ān and ḥadīth], and denial of the *salaf*'s endurance of the pain inflicted by al-Ḥajjāj and people like him from among the oppressors. In their time, one would not find many from among the people of religious knowledge [*ahl al-ʿilm*], such as Companions of the Prophet, Successors, and their Followers. Nonetheless, they did not approve of agitation and rebellion against the sultan. And there is no indication given to their contemporaries from among the people of power and courage [that they approved of that] when they saw the consequences of rebellion, the violation of contract, and infidelity to the act of allegiance to the ruler [*bayʿa*] from the person who issued it. [We might learn from] their action—may God have mercy upon them and may we benefit from them—that they held to the sharīʿa and they did not allow wrong ideas to be forced on them by the common people [*al-ʿawāmm*],

> who complain, advocate their individual opinions, and refuse the principles of religion, namely, the appointment of the ruler and the prohibition of rebelling against him. May God save us from them and from their harm.[42]

According to al-Wazzānī, al-Riyāḥī was entirely wrong in stating that qāḍī al-'Annābī acted in accordance with his Islamic rights and duties. In this long and detailed legal discussion, he not only refutes al-Riyāḥī's specific argument but also, citing three legal opinions, establishes that obedience to the ruler is tantamount to submission to the *sunna* of the Prophet and the *salaf*. Furthermore, obedience is not conditional on the ruler's taking advice from, or consulting with, his subjects, or on his dispensing justice, avoiding sins, or acting upon the religious obligation to "command good and forbid evil." Obedience to the sultan is a religious obligation that may not be forfeited. Disobedience is a sin.[43]

4. Next, al-Wazzānī responds to al-Riyāḥī's statement that qāḍī al-'Annābī acted properly by seeking consular protection: "Because a man is entrusted with the defense of his life, his family, and his property from someone who commits injustice, even if it leads to killing." This statement is an error (*ghalaṭ*), he says, adding, "because it does not apply to the *amīr* who would not be removed." In other words, self-defense against an unjust Muslim ruler is prohibited, as it may result in his killing. The second caliph, 'Umar b. al-Khaṭṭāb, is reported to have said, "If he [the ruler] oppresses you, be patient; if he dispossesses you, be patient; if he strikes you, be patient, and if he commands injustice, say, 'obedience [*ṭā'a*] to my Lord and not to anyone who was created like me.'" To reinforce his point, al-Wazzānī cites the Prophet, who said, "Hear and obey, even if an Ethiopian slave whose head is like a raisin is placed over you."[44]

5. Finally, al-Wazzānī considers al-Riyāḥī's line of reasoning in his hypothetical example of a man who was forced to enter a tavern after encountering a vicious dog. Al-Wazzānī argues that this example is worthless (*sāqiṭ*). He writes:

> Entering a wine shop and the like is not the same as entering the religion of the infidels [*millat al-kuffār*]; it does not glorify them, nor does it reveal an attachment to them, and it is not an insult to Islam [*dīn al-Islām*].

Al-Wazzānī emphasizes that between the example and the present case "there is distance and difference as [great as that] between a lizard and a whale." After citing the words of a poet—"she went East and I went West; what a big difference between East and West"—he completes his deliberations.[45]

Al-Wazzānī signals the end of his response with his characteristic signature, "and God knows best. This is the saying of the author, may God protect him."

Attaching Two Related Opinions

Al-Wazzānī concluded his fatwā, but his juristic effort was far from over. As he was copying the text of his fatwā into what would become the *New Miʿyār*, he shifted from the role of jurist to that of compiler and took the opportunity to complement his fatwā with two legal opinions written over the course of the nineteenth century. I imagine that he, first, considered the authoritative discussions of jurists of the Mālikī school on the issue at hand. Surely, he viewed his legal position in accord with the school's scholarship. But as al-Wazzānī made clear earlier, he did not know *any* legal opinion that permitted seeking protection from non-Muslims. Thus, to further support his claim, he also considered collections of opinions of other schools available to him. Then, he selected two opinions that he found commendable and substantially edited their form and content. Finally, he recombined them in his work to create essentially a new composition, asserting his argument that the practice of seeking the protection of infidels amounts to ethical and legal transgression. The transition from the end of his fatwā to the first legal opinion is marked by a concise comment: "Then I saw [the following discussion] in the *Ajwiba al-Kāmiliyya* that confirms what I have said."[46] Al-Wazzānī now cites a fatwā issued by the Ḥanafī scholar Muḥammad Kāmil bin Muṣṭafā al-Ṭarābulusī (d. 1897).

The Fatwā of al-Ṭarābulusī

Although I do not know the identity of the questioner (*mustaftī*), the request for a legal opinion (*istiftā'*) to which al-Ṭarābulusī responded carefully presents the relevant judicial issues. The question refers to the matter, "which became well-known and frequent at this time, that is, of Muslims seeking the protection of the infidels, thereupon violating the Islamic oath of allegiance [*bayʿa*] in such a manner that the infidels' opinion becomes [for these Muslims] equal to the opinion of their [Islamic] community."[47] The questioner continued delineating the serious violation of Islamic ethical norms by these individuals:

> Whenever a mishap occurs to them, they refer to the infidels and complain to them; whenever the Muslim leaders [*umarā'*] command them [to do something], they refuse, saying: we are protected by so-and-so country; and whenever they are brought before the Islamic court of law [*maḥkama*], a representative of the foreign government attends with them.

For the *mustaftī*, the problem was clear: "Is this [conduct] authorized by the sublime law of Islam?"[48]

The response of al-Ṭarābulusī, as recorded by al-Wazzānī, constitutes an explicit and uncompromising rejection of the practice of Muslims seeking the protection of infidels and was grounded in Qur'ānic quotes. He begins by expressing strong disapproval of this conduct, which he views as a deviation from the straight path: "This repulsive and evil action is not permitted by the sharīʿa. Rather, it is forbidden [ḥarām]." As support for his argument, he invokes the rhetoric of the Qur'ān: "O believers, do not hold Jews and Christians as your allies. They are allies of one another, and anyone who makes them his friends is surely one of them. You will notice that those whose hearts are afflicted with sickness [of doubt] only hasten to join them and say: we fear lest misfortune should surround us" (Q. 5:51–52). For al-Ṭarābulusī, it is improper for Muslims to associate themselves with the infidels, and those who choose to do so are ultimately misled people whose hearts are afflicted with sickness and hypocrisy (*nifāq*).[49]

He then cites Qur'ān 3:28: "And whoever does so should have no [expectations] of God," specifying that this Qur'ānic injunction indicates that those misled Muslims lost God's friendship (*walāya*), because as Qur'ān 2:257 reads, "God is the friend of those who believe." Al- Ṭarābulusī goes on to explain that whoever loses God's friendship is not a believer. Finally, he indicates God's decree for those Muslims who associate themselves with the nonbelievers, citing Qur'ān 4:138–39: "Give tidings to the hypocrites that painful is their doom; do those who take unbelievers as their friends in preference to the faithful seek power from them? But all power belongs to God." Having completed the substantive part of his response, al-Ṭarābulusī indicates that "the Qur'ānic verses and *ḥadīth* reports on this issue are many."[50] Thus, he indicates that the Islamic position on the issue at hand is plain and unequivocal.

At this point, al-Ṭarābulusī, nearly at the end of his response, shifts from sacred history to contemporary reality and seeks to expose the protégés as a threat to the Islamic government and society:

> Those who seek protection bring more harm on the Muslims than the infidels themselves. They are the reason for the interference [*mudākhala*] of the foreigners in the Islamic government and for their meddling [*tashwīsh*] in the [affairs of] the Muslim rulers [*umarā'*] and their ways of life [*maʿāyish*]. In addition, they offer them the innermost secrets of Islam, and they let them know their [the Muslim rulers'] weaknesses. Hence, they serve as spies [*jawāsīs*] for them.

These protégés, in the eyes of al-Ṭarābulusī, offend Islam and Islamic government, and for this offense, they would receive a severe punishment on the Day of Resurrection.[51]

Next, al-Wazzānī refers to a treatise (*risāla*) authored by ʿAli al-Mīlī al-Tūnisī (d. 1832). In his editorial transition, al-Wazzānī briefly informs the reader that in his deliberations, al-Tūnisī "intensified the rejection of anyone who acts in this way."[52]

Al-Tūnisī's Opinion

Al-Wazzānī cites only a brief statement from the *risāla*. He quotes the words of al-Tūnisī: "It is prohibited [for a Muslim to seek the protection of non-Muslims], even if one fears for his property or body, because the protection [*muḥāfaẓa*] of [one's] religion takes precedence over such matters." Apparently, al-Wazzānī felt compelled to clarify al-Tūnisī's opinion, and he indicates that the legal ground for al-Tūnisī's statement lies in the key jurisprudential principle that "if two harms meet, the lesser one is committed." He goes on to explain the principle, invoking a saying that articulates it: "Calamity [*muṣība*] of property [is privileged over] physical calamity; physical calamity [is privileged over] calamity of religion. The chief concern for the believer is his religion, and it precedes anything else." At this point, al-Wazzānī returns to al-Tūnisī's opinion, reporting his saying that "so long as one does not fear for his religion, he is allowed to resort even to an infidel to protect his faith."[53] In essence, al-Tūnisī identifies any Muslim who seeks the protection of the infidels as a nonbeliever.

Notice the process of composition; al-Wazzānī was not satisfied merely with presenting his own legal opinion. Rather, he expanded the scope of his reasoning by creating links to material from earlier times and incorporating it in the new setting. In this way he created a narrative that both assembled multiplicity of voices and consciousnesses of different generations and was particularly relevant to the new historical conditions in his world.

Afterthought

As al-Wazzānī continued his compiling effort, he identified two additional texts pertaining to the present case. Al-Wazzānī rearranged and copied the material as supplemental comments, or an appendix, a full dozen pages after his original fatwā's end.[54] His editorial intervention is clear and felt by the reader. Indeed, it did not stand in my way. It seems that al-Wazzānī allowed himself freedom in the assembly and arrangement of the material within the chapters. For him, the didactic purpose and moralizing function of the chapter lay in the legal opinions and texts compiled into it and were not interrupted by the late expansion of the original composition.

First Text The first text invoked by al-Wazzānī corroborated his argument that Abū Bakr's decision to situate himself under the protection of polytheists is utterly different from the unlawful bchavior of al-Wazzānī's contemporaries. It will be remembered that as support of his assertion that the act of seeking foreign protection is lawful, the Tunisian jurist Ibrāhīm al-Riyāḥī invoked Abū Bakr's exemplary conduct. Al-Wazzānī's editorial intervention is marked briefly: "Later I saw that one of the contemporaries wrote about the Abū Bakr affair, and here is his text." The author of the first text is unfortunately unidentified, but al-Wazzānī quotes his words: "Some of the contemporaries sought information pertaining to this affair [of Abū Bakr] as to the permissibility of seeking protection from the polytheists. However, there is no evidence of that."[55]

The text that follows is short and divided into five reasons in support of the assertion that Abū Bakr's predicaments did not resemble the issue examined in the present case. The author makes the following points: (1) Abū Bakr sought the protection of the polytheists against other nonbelievers and not against the Muslim ruler. (2) Abū Bakr did not embrace the religion of the polytheists, nor did he assist them. (3) Whereas Abū Bakr sought protection of nonbelievers for the purpose of worshipping his God, the people of our own times attain protection for the purpose of disobeying the Muslim ruler. (4) The case of Abū Bakr refers to the legal doctrine, which regards the protection of nonbelievers for the purpose of preserving one's piety as permissible. (5) The case of Abū Bakr occurred prior to the consolidation of legal rules and principles and before the legal duty of Muslims to migrate from non-Muslim territory (*hijra*) had been stipulated.[56]

Although the passage appears long after al-Wazzānī's original fatwā, the legal reasoning and the logic of interpretation remain entirely faithful to it. No consideration should be given to the claim that Abū Bakr's concerns resemble the contemporary state of affairs. Having made this brief statement, al-Wazzānī immediately moves on to the second text.

Second Text Al-Wazzānī signals the transition to the second text with the following brief comment: "After that, I read another reply of one of the contemporaries. Here is the text." The unidentified muftī began his discussion by asserting that "these [Muslims] who attain foreign protection combine disgraceful matters and shameful deeds, some of which are forbidden [*muḥarram*] while others constitute profanity (*kufr*)."[57] That is, the jurist drew a distinction between unlawful and blasphemous acts.

Addressing the first category, he maintains that there are Muslims who disobey and depart from the Muslim community "due to tyranny [*ẓulm*] and [illegal] seizure of property." To validate his argument that such behavior is forbidden, he invokes the authority of two Mālikī jurists. First, he quotes a statement attributed to Ibn ʿArafa (d. 1400): "Ibn Rushd said obedience to him, i.e., the imam, is obligatory even if he was unjust, unless he orders disobedience [to God] [*maʿṣiya*], and many *ḥadīth* reports confirm that."[58] Next, the jurist refers to Shaykh Zarrūq (d. 1493), who reported a saying of the second caliph, ʿUmar b. al-Khaṭṭāb:

> It is incumbent upon you to fear God and to hear and obey the ruler [*amīr*] even if he was a mutilated Ethiopian slave. If he oppresses you, be patient; if he strikes you, be patient; if he dispossesses you, be patient; and if he seeks to lure you away from your religion, say: obedience [*ṭāʿa*] to my God and not to anyone who was created like me, and you would not disobey God.

The jurist adds that the statement attributed to ʿUmar has been corroborated by many *ḥadīth* reports. To illustrate his point, the jurist cites a *ḥadīth* of the Prophet: "Anyone who parts with the [Muslim] community, even if only one inch, died a death in state of religious ignorance [*jāhiliyya*]."[59]

Having dealt with the first category of forbidden acts, the jurist moves on to the second category of blasphemy. At the very outset of the second segment of his deliberations, he explains that although departure from the Muslim community is a severe transgression, "helping and supporting [the nonbelievers] make them more powerful [and thus, constitutes an even greater offense]." He continues to establish that this category comprises Muslims who

> ask them [the infidels] for assistance against the Muslim ruler and call for victory against him. They prefer the rules [*qawānīn*] [of the infidels] over the Islamic principles of law and regard friendship with the enemy of faith as permissible. As an excuse, they say: "I only did that to protect my honor and property."[60]

The jurist determines that these Muslims have seriously violated Islamic norms and rejects the justification they invoke for their position.

Basing his response upon the preponderant judicial presumption (*ghālib*), he argues,

> Surely, for such [conduct] they are [considered] apostates [*murtaddūn*] and deserters [*khārijūn*] from Islam. Their testimony [in court] would not be accepted;

> they would not lead a prayer, and their manumission [of a slave] [*'itq*] would not be effective because the property of an apostate is illegal, and the property of an apostate's slave [procured from] his owner.[61]

Clearly, for the jurist, such Muslims are culpable for subjecting themselves willingly to non-Muslim law and losing their religious conviction.

Having nearly finished his fatwā, the muftī returns to the first category of Muslims, whose acts do not constitute blasphemy even though these Muslims have departed from the Muslim community, arguing,

> They do not wish for the victory [of the infidels] over the Muslims, and they do not brag about their friendship [with infidels], nor do they enjoy it. Rather, they acknowledge the unlawfulness [of their acts]. They strive to protect their property and their honor because of their inability to endure patiently the tyranny [*jaur*] of the rulers and their deputies, and this would not be considered disbelief.[62]

According to the muftī, these Muslims commit a grave offense for their disobedience to the Muslim ruler and their friendship with the enemies of Islam. However, he distinguishes between the latter and sinners who knowingly violate Islam, showing no remorse. Finally, he determines that according to the preferable opinion (*rājiḥ*) of the *madhhab*, although their testimony is unacceptable, it is legally valid to follow them in prayer, and their manumission of slaves, if done correctly, is considered binding.[63]

At this point, al-Wazzānī's appendix ends abruptly. It is likely that he was satisfied with the way he constructed his new comprehensive composition, the material he gathered, and the opinions he juxtaposed in appropriate locations. He must have been especially pleased with the considerable expansion of his original opinion and, in particular, the links he created with other sources. The selected opinions, collected from several earlier works, were not merely gathered together. Al-Wazzānī took a dynamic role in editing and reassembling them into an original composition that unequivocally resisted and rejected a new practice and rationality, shaped by the modern conditions. Now he was ready to proceed with a new discussion.

AN EDITORIAL COMMENT ON MUSLIMS RESIDING UNDER NON-MUSLIM SOVEREIGNTY

For centuries, large Muslim populations lived in the land of unbelief (*dār al-ḥarb* or *dār al-kufr*) and under non-Muslim rule where the sharīʿa was not applied.

The question of how to treat these Muslims and what their ethical and legal duties were was the subject of juristic debate long before the nineteenth century. Scholars of Islamic law have demonstrated that jurists have contemplated these questions since the eighth century and that the diverse juridical discourses on the issue have been shaped by the particularities of the historical contexts in which Muslims have lived.[64] The present text addresses these questions with reference to the world that al-Mahdī al-Wazzānī occupied and engaged.

As will become clear, Mālikī jurists who lived centuries prior to al-Wazzānī's time were compelled to develop responses to the problem of Muslims living in *dār al-ḥarb*.[65] An important example in this connection is the complex and vigorous discourse produced by Moroccan jurists concerned with the status of Muslims living under Christian rule following the loss of Muslim territories to the Spanish and Portuguese in the Iberian Peninsula and Morocco itself in the fifteenth and sixteenth centuries. Mālikī juristic discourse of the day introduced the major concerns of religious scholars in Morocco: voluntary residence among unbelievers, submission to the law of non-Muslims, traveling to non-Muslim territories for purposes of trade, selling weapons to non-Muslims, and the application of Islamic law in *dār al-ḥarb*.[66]

However, this was not al-Wazzānī's world. More than three centuries later, his concerns and interpretations were bounded by the colonial context. During the nineteenth century the wider Muslim world confronted the dominant European colonial structure of power. Vast Muslim populations in central and south Asia, east and west Africa, the Balkans, and parts of the Middle East came under non-Muslim rule. In the Maghrib, by the last decades of the nineteenth century, French imperial hegemony resulted in the complete conquest of Algeria and the occupation of Tunisia. Although Morocco remained independent until 1912, by the last quarter of the nineteenth century, the Muslim community was weakened and overwhelmed by the transforming powers of European imperialism. By the end of the nineteenth century, historical conditions had radically changed, emphasizing the growing disparity in power between Morocco and Europe. Al-Wazzānī's generation was aware of the possibility that Morocco could fall to French control. In other words, the doctrinal challenges raised by Muslims living under non-Muslim sovereignty became an acute ideological problem. The political independence of Morocco was threatened. The challenge for al-Wazzānī was to navigate the reality of overwhelming European hegemony and negotiate a compromise that would preserve his Muslim community.

The text to be discussed here is al-Wazzānī's refutation of a fatwā issued by Aḥmad al-Wansharīsī (d. 1508) during the last quarter of the fifteenth century.[67] The fatwā was most probably written as a response to the Portuguese occupation of territories in northern Morocco and treats the obligation to emigrate from a Muslim territory conquered by non-Muslims and the position of Muslims who voluntarily remain under non-Muslim sovereignty.[68] The record in the *New Mi'yār* contains no information regarding the date on which al-Wazzānī wrote his opinion, nor does it include a text of the *istiftā'*, or question. I suggest that al-Wazzānī did not write his text as an act of *iftā'*, that is, a response to an explicit question posed by a questioner who seeks a muftī's advice. Rather, he wrote it as a discursive strategy and a form of argumentation in the service of his project of revitalizing Mālikī knowledge. In other words, as he was engaged in the elaboration of his legal arguments for the chapter on jihād, reviewing different works authored by his predecessors, assembling and arranging the selected material, al-Wazzānī decided to address this legal issue, which remained problematic and of general concern to the Moroccan Muslim community in his age.

Specifically, al-Wazzānī's text addresses the question of the legality of residence in a Muslim territory conquered by non-Muslims and the validity of legal documents and court testimonies of Muslims residing there. By implication, he delineates the dichotomy between the abode of Islam (*dār al-Islām*) and the abode of unbelief (*dār al-ḥarb*). The admissibility of legal documents and testimonies from Muslim lands conquered by nonbelievers must have been a pressing concern in pre-Protectorate Morocco. By the time al-Wazzānī began writing his chapter on jihād in the first decade of the twentieth century, Moroccan populations had already come under non-Muslim occupation. Inside Morocco in 1900, the Touat Oasis along the Moroccan-Algerian border had been occupied by the French. Furthermore, important Moroccan resident communities prospered in occupied Egypt, Algeria, Tunisia, and the Sudan. A Moroccan presence had been a familiar feature of life in Egypt long before the British occupation in 1882. Moroccan pilgrims crossed Egypt on their way to the Ḥijāz and stayed months in Cairo and Alexandria, scholars visited the celebrated al-Azhar mosque to attend lectures and lessons by leading scholars of the four *madhhabs*, and wealthy Moroccan merchants were an important element in the Egyptian economy.[69] The rural Moroccan population, especially from north-eastern Morocco, found employment on French farms in western Algeria,[70] and merchants and businessmen stayed for long periods in Tunis, a particularly important Maghribi port. Moreover, Moroccan diplomats and special envoys of the sultans resided in Algeria and Tunisia. Finally, in the Sudan throughout the nineteenth century an important Moroccan commercial community consisting mostly of Fāsī merchants involved in the caravan trade flourished.[71]

Besides Moroccans residing under Christian rule, Muslim merchants and emigrants living under non-Muslim rule moved to Morocco. Nineteenth-century Morocco was very much a part of the Mediterranean network of trade and scholarship linking the Maghrib to the eastern Mediterranean, and Muslims traveled to Morocco for the purpose of study, business, or family affairs. Many others were Muslim exiles, dissidents, and refugees. For example, shortly after the French occupation of Algeria, many Algerians poured over the Algerian-Moroccan border and subsequently settled in Morocco.[72]

These Moroccans living in non-Muslim territory and Muslim expatriates living in Morocco must have brought their judicial and administrative affairs before qāḍīs living under Christian rule. It is highly probable that in his role as a muftī al-Wazzānī himself had to consider certified legal transactions and authenticated witness testimonies, qāḍī assessments of personal integrity,[73] and many other documents that were recorded outside the geographical realm of Islam. As new historical conditions emerged, older ways of seeing and arranging the world became irrelevant, and legal opinions that had been relevant to the needs of a particular age became obsolete.

Al-Wazzānī's text starts with a recounting of the fatwā of al-Wansharīsī, which involves some editing and abridgment, a common practice in other fatwās preserved in the *New Mi'yār*.[74]

The Request for a Fatwā

The *istiftā'* to which al-Wansharīsī responded is formulated as follows: "Abū al-'Abbās Sīdī Aḥmad al-Wansharīsī, the guardian of the *madhhab*, was asked about Berber people [*qawm*] who remained in their native territory subjugated to the infidel enemy [*al-'adūw al-kāfir*] despite their having a way to leave it."[75] The question, formulated in general and abstract terms, refers to Berber people voluntarily residing in land that used to be Muslim but was now occupied by non-Muslims, without specifying their location. The *mustaftī* asks two questions. First, "Is their residence there [under these specific circumstances] permissible, or not?" He went on to specify that the relationship between these Muslims and the infidel enemy may be divided into three groupings:

> (1) Some of them reside in their native territory and do not associate with the infidels; (2) others go to the infidels for the purpose of trade and inform them

> about the affairs of the Muslims; (3) yet others fish with the infidels, advise them about Muslim territories, appeal to their judges and legal decisions, and wish them: "May God extend your stay."[76]

In his second question, the *mustaftī* asks for al-Wansharīsī's response "regarding Muslim property seized by the infidel enemy. Is it allowed to buy it from them, or not?" The *mustaftī* then continues to explain that a student has been going to the infidels in order to buy books [previously owned by Muslims] from them. He finished his *istiftā'* with a plea to al-Wansharīsī to determine the legal issues raised by the case: "Clarify it for us, and may you be honored with reward and peace."[77]

The Response of al-Wansharīsī

Al-Wansharīsī opens his response with a careful formulation of the terms and order of the argument, explaining that the case involves several distinct inquiries. He then divided his response into four segments: (1) living in *dār al-ḥarb* subject to non-Muslim (*kufr*) rule; (2) entering *dār al-ḥarb* and associating with the infidels for the purpose of trade and informing them of the weakness (*'awra*) of the Muslims; (3) fishing with them, appealing to their judges and legal decisions, and wishing for their extended stay; and (4) buying from them what they seized from Muslims' property.[78] In his reply, al-Wansharīsī shifts from one topic to the next, signaling the direction of his argument with cues, for example, "as for the first [inquiry]" or repeating verbatim the issue under consideration, common in other fatwās.

First Inquiry Al-Wansharīsī begins his response to the first inquiry with the following argument:

> Subjection to the infidel and residence in *dār al-ḥarb*, despite [the freedom] of migration [*nuqla*] and [the option of] keeping away from it, is forbidden. It is not allowed, not even for a blink of an eye or for one hour of the day. It is absolutely necessary to migrate from the land of unbelief to *dār al-Islām*, where their [infidel] rules [*aḥkām*] are not valid.[79]

As support for his uncompromising insistence that residence in non-Muslim territory should be avoided if the option of migration exists, al-Wansharīsī invokes the authority of the primary sources of the law: "The proof [*dalīl*] of that," he asserts, "is in the Qur'ān, *sunna*, and the consensus of the school [*ijmā'*]."[80]

First, al-Wansharīsī cites Qur'ān 4:97–98:

> As for those whose souls are taken by the angels [at death] while in a state of unbelief, they will be asked by the angels: "What [state] were you in?" They will answer: "We were oppressed in the land." And the angels will say: "Was not God's earth large enough for you to migrate?" Their abode will be Hell, and what an evil destination! But those who are helpless, men, women, and children, who can neither contrive a plan nor do they know the way, may well hope for the mercy of God.[81]

For al-Wansharīsī, the Qur'ānic injunction is clear. Muslims should escape oppression by migrating to *dār al-Islām* unless they have no choice in the matter because either they do not know the way or fear that they will die along the way.

Second, al-Wansharīsī cites a statement attributed to the Prophet Muḥammad: "I am innocent of [that is, I disown] any Muslim who resides with polytheists." Finally, al-Wansharīsī claims that "all the imāms [*a'imma*] agree on this matter."[82] In his view, the two precedents from the Qur'ān and *sunna* establish that it is obligatory for Muslims to migrate from *dār al-ḥarb* to *dār al-Islām*. Once again, he asserts that the main problem is that a Muslim who lives in *dār al-ḥarb* will be subjected to the laws of non-Muslims.

At this point, al-Wansharīsī is prepared to establish that his opinion is grounded in the juristic consensus (*ijmā'*) of the Mālikī school. First, he invokes the authority of the founder of the Mālikī school, Mālik b. Anas, explaining that

> Mālik strongly disliked living in territory in which the Companions of the Prophet are vilified. How much more [was his aversion to living in] territory in which one might become subject to the devil, anger the Merciful, invoke the Trinity, and worship idols! No Muslim would live in such derogation except an individual of flawed and tarnished faith.[83]

Next, al-Wansharīsī draws attention to the imāms, who established that "if one does not find a way to escape the snares of unbelievers [*ḥibāl al-kafara*] other than by sacrificing his wealth, it is his obligation to do that. If he does not do that, his respectability is suspected [*lam takmul ḥurmatuhu*], his testimony [in court] cannot be accepted, and he has no right to [share] in the spoils of war and in the fifth [of the crop as wages]."[84]

As further support for his position, al-Wansharīsī reports that Mālikī jurists debated the issue of the inviolability of the property of Mudéjars, Muslims who remained in the Iberian Peninsula under Christian rule (*amwāl al-dajan*).[85] He explains that the issue raises the following question: "Is the property of Muslims treated according to the jurisdiction of the land, that is to say, is it considered as the property of the enemy, or is it still property of Muslims [and as such protected by Islam]?" Al-Wansharīsī maintains that in addressing this question, one jurist argued that it is not allowed to have any association (*muʿāmala*) with Muslims residing in non-Muslim territory and that it is not permissible to greet them, comparing them to illegitimate sectarians (*ahl al-ahwāʾ*).[86] Thus, using his extensive knowledge of the law, al-Wansharīsī points to another legal debate that confirms his opinion about the illegality of Muslims residing in *dār al-ḥarb*.

Then, al-Wansharīsī cites a distinguished Andalusian jurist, Abū al-Walīd al-Bājī (d. 1081), who stated that "[if] a Muslim who resides in *dār al-ḥarb* despite his ability to migrate is killed by mistake, the payment of blood money [*diya*] is not due [to his relatives] against him."[87] In other words, for al-Bājī, Muslims residing in non-Muslim territory die as if they are unbelievers. Finally, al-Wansharīsī mentions that Mālikī jurists rejected the testimonial authentication (*mukhāṭaba*) of Mudéjar judges, including qāḍīs in Valencia, Tortosa, Pantelleria, and Majurca.[88] He explains that these jurists justified their assertion on the basis of the claim that "the acceptance of a qāḍī's testimonial authentication is conditional upon the legality of his appointment, which is based upon the legality of the one who appointed him."[89] This final legal issue, the disqualification of the testimonial authentications of Muslim judges residing in non-Muslim territory, was categorically rejected by al-Wazzānī, and I will return to it later. However, for the moment, al-Wansharīsī's interpretation appears to be rigorously argued and firmly grounded in authoritative opinions, according it the required Mālikī doctrinal authority for validation.

Second Inquiry Having completed the first segment of his response, al-Wansharīsī now turns to the second inquiry raised by the case. In organizing his deliberations, he divides his discussion into two parts: (1) entering *dār al-ḥarb* and associating with infidels for the purpose of trade and (2) informing them of the weakness of the Muslims.

Focusing on the first part, he argues: "As for entering [*dār al-ḥarb*] for the purpose of trade, seeking worldly possessions and accumulating the ephemeral things of this world, it is forbidden and invalidates a Muslim's credibility [*jurḥa*]." For this reason, such Muslims cannot be allowed to lead prayer, and their testimony in court cannot be accepted. He notes that no one may enter the land of polytheism (*arḍ al-shirk*) except to redeem Muslim captives. He then insists that it is incumbent upon Muslim leaders and communities to prevent Muslims from entering non-Muslim territory for the purpose of trade, even by means of placing checkpoints (*marāṣid*) on the road. This is especially necessary if it is feared that Muslims would sell non-Muslims "that which provides them with strength [*qūwah*] over *ahl al-Islām* when they use it [in war]." As textual authority for his point, al-Wansharīsī refers to Saḥnūn (d. 854), who reported in the *Mudawwana* that Mālik strongly disliked Muslims traveling to the land of war (*arḍ al-ḥarb*) for purposes of trade because they might be subjected to the laws of nonbelievers (*mushrikīn*).[90] Note that al-Wansharīsī's contention that association with non-Muslims for the purpose of trade discredits a Muslim's credibility, and thus the validity of his testimony introduces another point of doctrinal dispute that will subsequently be addressed by al-Wazzānī.

Turning next to the second part of his discussion, al-Wansharīsī writes: "As for entering [*dār al-ḥarb*] for the purpose of guiding the infidels about Muslims and informing them about their weaknesses, if such conduct is established with sufficient evidence against a Muslim, who is a disgrace and an outcast, he may be killed and will not be granted repentance."[91] Al-Wansharīsī clarifies that this uncompromising view is based on opinions attributed to Ibn al-Qāsim (d. 806) and Saḥnūn (d. 854). Interestingly, al-Wansharīsī now presents six opinions, some of which refrained from the imposition of the death penalty indiscriminately, introducing an interesting variation of the school's opinions on the topic.

First, he cites a statement attributed to Saḥnūn, who treated a Muslim who assists non-Muslims as a rebel who may be killed legitimately: "Payment of blood money for his heirs is not due against him, for he is considered an illegitimate rebel [*muḥārib*]." Next, al-Wansharīsī refers to a transmission of Saḥnūn on the authority of a certain distinguished Mālikī jurist (*ṣāḥib*, pl. *aṣḥāb*),[92] which supports the imposition of a lesser punishment: "He [a Muslim who assists non-Muslims] should be flogged for severe punishment, and his imprisonment should last long. After that, he should be removed from *dār al-ḥarb*." Then, al-Wansharīsī cites an opinion transmitted by Ibn Wahb (d. 827): "He should be killed unless he repents."[93]

Al-Wansharīsī now reports an opinion transmitted by Ibn al-Mājishūn (d. 827): "If [this conduct] is [founded on] an error he made or an opinion based on ignorance and weakness, and he is not from among the people who wish to harm Islam, then he should be punished severely and be beaten. If he is accustomed to do it, he should be killed." Next, al-Wansharīsī mentions another opinion: "He should be killed, unless he is forgiven because of his ignorance." Finally al-Wansharīsī asserts that following al-'Utbī (d. 869) and al-Lakhmī (d. 1075), "the imām should formulate an independent judgment in the matter."[94] It should be noted that al-Wansharīsī began his discussion by asserting a strict position that any Muslim who assists non-Muslims should be killed. However, without explicitly saying so, he implies that the Mālikī *madhhab* is divided on the issue and presents a variety of responses from eminent Mālikī jurists.

Third Inquiry Al-Wansharīsī proceeds to the third segment of his argument, dividing his discussion into two parts. He begins as follows: "Fishing with them and appealing to their judges and legal decisions are forbidden and undermine a Muslim's credibility [*jurḥa*]." He maintains that these actions are detestable, indeed, almost prohibited (*taḥrīm*), because they humiliate the glory of Islam and its people and "Islam grows and does not decline, and it dominates and is not dominated by others."[95]

In the second part of his discussion, al-Wansharīsī does not hesitate to criticize Muslims who "wish the cunning infidels—may God banish them—an extended stay." This, he writes, marks their apostasy from Islam (*ridda*), their heresy (*ilḥād*), and the corruption of their conscience and belief because approving unbelief is in itself infidelity. To illustrate his point, al-Wansharīsī cites as a legal precedent a case that occurred during the days of the great Mālikī jurist Shihāb al-Dīn al-Qarāfī (d. 1285). The case is about a man who said to another, "May God make you die as an unbeliever." A certain shaykh issued a fatwā that confirmed the man's blasphemy, because of his hope (*irāda*) for infidelity.[96] For al-Wansharīsī, the case plainly and unequivocally establishes that Muslims who hope for the prolonged stay of the infidels are sinners (*fasaqa*) and infidels themselves and should be beaten and punished harshly until they repent.

As support for his opinion, he cites a case in which the caliph 'Umar b. al-Khaṭṭāb severely flogged a Muslim convert who came under suspicion for his religious belief. It is reported that at one point, the convert who received the painful punishment turned to 'Umar and said to him: "O, Commander of the Faithful [*amīr al-mu'minīn*], if you wish to cure me, then you have healed my illness, and if you wish to kill me, then finish me off." At this point, according to the report, 'Umar released him.[97]

Fourth Inquiry All that remained for al-Wansharīsī was to address the fourth and final segment of his argument: "buying from them [the infidels] what they have from Muslims' property." Al-Wansharīsī begins by citing an opinion from the *Mudawwana* of Saḥnūn, according to which, if a Muslim enters *dār al-ḥarb* under immunity (*amān*) and purchases a slave who belonged to another Muslim from an infidel, the original owner of that slave has the right to buy him back from the buyer for the same amount that he had paid the infidel, if he can establish the nominal nature of the transaction on the basis of evidence. In the absence of such evidence, the slave will be returned to his original owner without compensation to the buyer.[98] For al-Wansharīsī, the opinion establishes that Muslims have the right to buy property in *dār al-ḥarb* that previously had belonged to Muslims. To ensure fair compensation from the original proprietor, the buyer is required to provide a proof that validates the transaction.

Next, he proceeds to argue that the legal ruling pertaining to entering *dār al-ḥarb* for the purpose of either salvaging books or other goods is one and the same. However, he explains that it is imperative for the student who enters *dār al-ḥarb* for the specific purpose of buying books to obtain books of greater importance first. Most important is to rescue the Qur'ān; then collections of Prophetic *ḥadīth*; then law (*fiqh*) and then jurisprudence (*uṣūl al-fiqh*); next, scholarship in the areas of Arabic, linguistics, medical science, Qur'ān commentaries (*tafsīr*), especially the commentary of Ibn 'Aṭiyya, and recitation of the Qur'ān.[99]

This concludes al-Wazzānī's summary of the fatwā of al-Wansharīsī. Writing during the last quarter of the fifteenth century, al-Wansharīsī was acutely aware of infringements on Muslim lands in the western Mediterranean. Christian enemies, especially the Portuguese, were dangerous, but Morocco was still a competing Mediterranean power. Al-Wansharīsī's world could support his unwavering legal opinion and attitude; voluntary residence under non-Muslim rule is prohibited. Muslims should migrate from *dār al-ḥarb* to *dār al-Islām*. By the late nineteenth and early twentieth centuries, European hegemony became the ever-present reality throughout the wider Muslim Mediterranean, and al-Wazzānī had to provide a new interpretation of the Mālikī tradition that responded to the new historical conditions. In the discussion that follows al-Wansharīsī's text, al-Wazzānī categorically revokes his predecessor's opinion. Taking into account the prestige of al-Wansharīsī and the exemplary authority of his fatwās, al-Wazzānī could not simply dismiss the fatwā as peripheral or misguided. In an editorial comment, he presents a lengthy and complex argument that incorporates explicit references to authoritative masters of the school and attests to a careful study of the school's discourse.

Al-Wazzānī's Refutation of al-Wansharīsī's Fatwā

Al-Wazzānī begins his refutation of al-Wansharīsī's fatwā as follows: "In this response, al-Wansharīsī exaggerated [*bālagha*] in renouncing uncompromisingly and under any circumstances [*'alā al-iṭlāq*] the testimony [of such Muslims residing in *dār al-ḥarb*] and the testimonial authentication [*khiṭāb*] of their qāḍīs, and it is necessary for me to carefully examine this."[100] It will be recalled that in his response, al-Wansharīsī argued that voluntary residence in non-Muslim territory is not allowed, and he therefore discredited the testimonial authentications of Muslim judges. In addition, he insisted that entering *dār al-ḥarb* and associating with infidels for purposes of trade are prohibited and corrupt a Muslim's credibility. For this reason, he maintained, the testimony of such a Muslim cannot be accepted in an Islamic court.

It seems to me useful to note that al-Wansharīsī's concerns and preoccupations encompassed other fundamental issues pertaining to the status and obligations of Muslims living in non-Muslim territories. He discussed the question of voluntary residence under non-Muslim sovereignty and the obligation to migrate; he debated the inviolability of Muslim lives and property; he examined opinions relating to the punishment given to a Muslim who assists non-Muslims; and he deliberated on the right to return to a territory controlled by non-Muslims to purchase Muslim property. Nonetheless, al-Wazzānī was principally concerned to challenge al-Wansharīsī's view that the testimony of Muslims ruled by non-Muslims and the testimonial authentication of their judges are invalid. I do not take al-Wazzānī's response to be random. As I have noted, the modern conditions that al-Wazzānī engaged made some questions less worth asking than others. To put it another way, in the age of European imperialism, as Islamic societies deeply entrenched in the struggle against European colonial rule, the old debates about voluntary residence under Christian rule, the duty to migrate, the obligation to protect Muslims residing in non-Muslim territory, or their right to recover confiscated property seem irrelevant. However, for al-Wazzānī, who lived and operated in pre-Protectorate Morocco, the validity of legal documents and testimonies of Muslims living under non-Muslim rule continued to assume relevancy.

Aware of al-Wansharīsī's reputation, al-Wazzānī cleverly sought corroboration for his legal analysis in a fatwā issued by al-Wansharīsī himself at a later date. The fatwā deals with a group of Muslims who migrated from al-Andalus to North Africa after its occupation by the Christians and subsequently encountered serious financial difficulties. As a result, they regretted their emigration, mocked North Africa, and publicly expressed their hopes to return to *dār al-ḥarb*. In a lengthy response, al-Wansharīsī argues that it is prohibited for Muslims to reside under infidel rule and that migration (*hijra*) from non-Muslim land is an absolute duty.[101] It is safe to say that no fatwā has been more closely identified with the juristic activity of al-Wansharīsī and his authoritative contribution to the elaboration of law within the Mālikī school. Al-Wazzānī next cites a relatively long segment from the fatwā.

The Second Fatwā of al-Wansharīsī Al-Wazzānī now focuses his attention on a section of the fatwā that introduces diverse opinions on the question of the credibility of Mudéjar judges, these Iberian Muslims who resided under Christian rule, and the validity of the legal documents they produced. The text begins with a statement by al-Wansharīsī:

> As for the illegitimacy and loss of credibility [*jurḥa*] of someone who lives [in *dār al-ḥarb*], returns [to it] after emigrating [*hijra*], or wishes to return [to it], and as for barring him from [those offices] requiring righteousness such as judging, witnessing, and leading prayer—it is an obvious [case], and no one with the slightest grasp of the applied branches of the law [*al-furū' al-ijtihādīya*] and cases of law [*al-masā'il al-fiqhīya*] doubts that. Their testimony is not accepted, and so is the testimonial authentication [*khiṭāb*] of their judges.[102]

Al-Wansharīsī states categorically that the residence of Muslims in non-Muslim territory is unethical and therefore corrupts the testimonies of such Muslims and the documents certified by their judges. The text continues with an opinion attributed to the Tunisian muftī Ibn 'Arafa (d. 1400):

> [Accepting] the testimonial authentication of a qāḍī is conditional upon the legal validity of his appointment by someone who is entitled to appoint him. Be cautious with the testimonial authentication of Mudéjar judges, including the qāḍīs of the Muslims of Valencia, Tortosa, and Pantelleria, when received by us.[103]

Ibn 'Arafa's opinion reveals that the concern with the validity of documents authorized by Mudéjar judges was linked to a concern with the validity of their appointment to the position of qāḍī.

Next, the text centers on a long fatwā issued by the distinguished Imām Abū 'Abdallāh al-Māzarī (d. 1141) after Sicily fell to the Normans in 1091.[104] In it, al-Māzarī addresses the validity of rulings and documents issued by Muslim judges living in Norman Sicily. The text runs as follows:

> Imām al-Māzarī was asked whether the rulings of the qāḍīs of [Norman] Sicily and [the testimonies] of their professional witnesses ['*udūl*] may be legally

accepted [in a Muslim territory] or not, considering that [the judicial rulings and testimonies] are a practical necessity and that it is unknown whether their residence there under the rule of the infidels is by obligation or choice.

He answered: There are two aspects that may cause [judicial decisions and testimonies] to be denounced [*qādiḥ*]. The first implicates the qāḍī and the evidence [*bayyināt*] that establishes his integrity [*ʿadāla*], because residence in non-Muslim territory under infidel rule is not permitted. The second [aspect] involves the [legality of his] office, namely, if the qāḍī was appointed [to his position] by non-Muslims.[105]

Al-Māzarī's carefully formulated legal opinion explicitly touches upon the two issues. He began by addressing the first topic, launching into a preliminary discourse in which he expounded upon the notion of *ʿadāla*, or integrity of Muslims. Al-Māzarī explained that it is necessary "to think about Muslims positively and to regard their disobedience as unlikely." He continued by making it clear that in his view "one should accept [the credibility of] anyone who appears to be honorable, even though it is possible [for him], in fact, to commit a great sin in secrecy, unless evidence is provided against his virtuousness." He reasoned that "a legal decision [*ḥukm*] [as to one's credibility] is inferred on the basis of what is evident" rather than "false ideas and unfounded suspicions." Al-Māzarī seems to determine that a legal decision on anyone's integrity or credibility must be reached by a consideration of relevant, specific evidence, in accordance with the judicial procedure that involves issuing any ruling.[106]

Having argued that, al-Māzarī proceeded to consider the question of integrity within the specific context of Muslims residing in occupied territories under non-Muslim rule:

As for [a Muslim] residing in a non-Muslim territory out of necessity, there is no doubt that this [residence] does not detract from his credibility. The same holds, if his reason [*taʾwīl*] [for residing there] is correct, such as living in non-Muslim territory in hope of leading the infidels [to Islam] or turning them away from an error. Al-Bāqillānī [d. 1013] indicated this as well for Mālik's associates when permitting [Muslims] to enter [non-Muslim territory] in order to free a prisoner of war.

However, if he resides [in non-Muslim territory] voluntarily, out of ignorance [of the prohibition of living under infidel rule], and offers no reason for this, then this [residence] detracts from his credibility. The [scholars of the] *madhhab* debated the rejection of the testimony of someone who enters [non-

> Muslim territory] voluntarily for trade, and they disagreed in interpreting the *Mudawwana* [on this point].
>
> Otherwise, if he [a Muslim living in non-Muslim territory] appears to be honorable, and the reason for his residence is uncertain, in whatever respect, then the legal principle [*aṣl*] is to excuse him [for his residence].[107]

Although al-Māzarī's opinion confirms the general rule that voluntary residence in *dār al-ḥarb* renders Muslims' testimony and judgments invalid, his deliberations also introduce a leniency toward upright Muslims who reside in occupied territories for valid or uncertain reasons.

Next, al-Māzarī directed his attention to the second issue raised by the present case, the validity of judges appointed by infidels:

> As for the second aspect [which may cause judgment and testimony to be denounced], namely, the infidel's appointment of judges, notaries, and others in order to prevent the people from [wrongdoing]—this is imperative [*wājib*], so much so that a follower of the *madhhab* claimed that it is rationally imperative, even though [this opinion] is invalid [*bāṭil*].
>
> If the infidel's appointment of this qāḍī was in response to a request from the [Muslim] community or for the reason that he helps [the infidel] by holding the post of a judge, then it does not detract from his legal decisions and their enforcement. [Indeed, it] resembles an appointment by a Muslim sultan.[108]

Al-Māzarī sends a clear message to his reader: the appointment of a judge by an infidel is valid, and his judgments and the certified documents he composes must be honored.

At this point, al-Wansharīsī reports different opinions within the *madhhab* pertaining to the validity of the appointments of judges by an unjust ruler. The text begins with a statement by al-Wansharīsī himself: "The scholars of al-Andalus issued a fatwā about those loyal to the apostate, 'Umar b. Ḥafṣūn, arguing that their testimony was not allowed and the testimonial authentications of their qāḍīs should not be accepted."[109] Here, he advocates the position that invalid appointments of judges nullify their documents. However, he maintains, that "there was controversy about accepting the nomination to the judgeship from an unjust ruler [*amīr*]." Drawing on *Riyāḍ al-Nufūs fī ṭabaqāt 'ulamā' [al-Qayrawān] wa-Ifrīqiyā* of Abū Muḥammad b. 'Abd Allāh al-Mālikī (d. 970), he explains:

> Saḥnūn said: "Abū Muḥammad 'Abd Allāh b. Farrūkh [d. 792–93] and Ibn Ghānim [d. 806], the qāḍī of Ifrīqiyā, both[of whom] transmitted the teachings

> of Mālik, disagreed. Ibn Farrūkh said: A qāḍī should not accept the judgeship if an unjust ruler nominated him. Abū Ghānim said: It is permissible [for him] to take office, even if the ruler is unjust. Then, he wrote with this [issue] to Mālik, who said: The Persian, i.e., Ibn Farrūkh, is correct."[110]

Mālik resolved the disagreement by supporting the opinion that judges should not accept appointments from rulers who are not upright. The text concludes with a second opinion of Ibn ʿArafa: "They [early Mālikī jurists] did not consider [the qāḍī's] acceptance of an appointment from a successful contender who fights against the rightful imam to be a morally wrong act that invalidates his credibility [*jurḥa*] because of [their] fear [that the absence of a judge may lead to] the obstruction of rulings."[111]

With the second opinion of Ibn ʿArafa, al-Wazzānī completes his presentation of the fatwā of al-Wansharīsī: "This is the saying of the *Miʿyār*. Consider this." From al-Wazzānī's point of view, the question of the integrity of Muslims residing under the rule of nonbelievers and the validity of documents certified by their judges had been a subject of debate among Mālikī jurists long before his time. It is also significant that al-Wansharīsī, an eminent legal scholar both during his lifetime and centuries thereafter, explicitly engaged authoritative Mālikī opinions that inverted his uncompromising position and incorporated them into his later, highly authoritative fatwā, which he included in his *Miʿyār*.

Six Supplementary Opinions Al-Wazzānī's refutation of al-Wansharīsī's position, however, is far from over. Next to his examination of the section from al-Wansharīsī's *Asnā al-matājir*, al-Wazzānī juxtaposes six additional opinions that contradict al-Wansharīsī's first fatwā. He marks the transition from the end of the text of the *Miʿyār* to his text by the word *qultu*, "I say."

First, he refers to a transmission of al-Mawwāq (d. 1492), a commentator on the *Mukhtaṣar* of Khalīl, on the authority of Ibn ʿAllāl, who said: "[As for an occasion] when nonbelievers occupy a certain area and then appoint a judge for the Muslim population [residing there], I do not recall any text [that disallows this] by the jurists of the *madhhab*." Second, he mentions ʿIzz al-Dīn Ibn ʿAbd al-Salām, who said: "If they nominate a judge, he will enforce [court rulings] as necessary in order to protect public welfare [*maṣālīḥ*] and prevent complete corruption [*mafāsid*]." Third, al-Wazzānī cites an opinion mentioned in the *Sharḥ al-Tuḥfa* of Ibn Nāẓim: "[As for] the qāḍīs in a Christian land, who for whatever reason were appointed by the Christian infidel, the office of the judgeship makes their judgments legally valid and their appointments correct."

Fourth, al-Wazzānī quotes an opinion mentioned in the *Nawāzil* of the famous Tunisian jurist al-Burzulī (d. 1437 or 1440):[112] "If the infidel nominated him [the qāḍī], either as a result of the [Muslim] community's request or for the reason that he helps [the infidel] by holding the post of a judge, this does not detract from the credibility of his ruling, because the people of a locality take the place of the sultan in his absence." Fifth, he reports an opinion attributed to Muṭarrif (d. 835) and Ibn al-Mājishūn: "If a tyrant disobeys the [legitimate] ruler and conquers [a part of] his territory and then nominates an upright qāḍī, his judgments are legally valid."[113]

Finally, al-Wazzānī incorporates an edited and abridged version of a fatwā issued by ʿAbd Allāh b. Muḥammad b. Mūsā al-ʿAbdūsī (d. 1442 or 1445), mentioned in the *Nawāzil* of ibn Tarakāt.[114] As he was copying the fatwā into the *New Miʿyār*, al-Wazzānī omitted details he deemed irrelevant to his discourse. The modified *istiftā'* is concerned with "a document coming from a Christian territory, [verified] by the testimony of Muslim witnesses residing there."[115] The remainder of al-Wazzānī's text comprises the muftī's response.

Al-ʿAbdūsī begins his response by addressing three different scenarios relating to Muslims residing in non-Muslim territories. First, he concedes that "if their residence there is a matter of choice, there is no doubt that this is a great sin, which requires the rejection of their testimony, because residing amid the infidels with the ability to migrate from them is prohibited by juristic consensus [*ijmāʿ*]." To support his assertion, he invokes the authority of the Prophet Muḥammad, who said: "I am innocent of any Muslim who resides in the midst of the polytheists." Next, al-ʿAbdūsī refers to a second scenario: "If, however, they have been prevented from leaving, unless they relinquish their property without fearing for their lives and their families, then it is their duty to leave, turning over their property, on the condition that [the infidels] will spare them enough to reach a Muslim territory." Finally, introducing the third scenario, al-ʿAbdūsī observes, "If, however, they fear for their lives or for their families, it is permitted to them to live amid them, and this will not discredit their testimony."[116] Al-ʿAbdūsī clearly recognized some historical realities that justified the residence of Muslims in non-Muslim territory. He reasoned that it is not always unethical and thus does not necessarily undermine a Muslim's credibility.

Turning next to the appointment of Muslim judges,[117] al-ʿAbdūsī asserts,

> As for the qāḍī who [resides] there, if appointed by the local community of Muslims, then his legal decision is lawful, as is the judicial practice based on

> his testimonial authentication, provided it is confirmed that they [the Muslim members of the community] appointed him and that it is his signature [on the legal decision or testimonial authentication], because the community takes the place of the sultan whenever he is away on any issue.
>
> If, [on the other hand,] the Christian ruler appointed him, neither his appointment nor his court ruling is lawful. [If, however,] the community of Muslims approves of it voluntarily, and not under duress, then his legal decision is lawful, just as if he were appointed in the first place by them voluntarily, and this makes it their [the Muslims'] appointment and not his [the Christian ruler's]. Subsequently, if his appointment is valid, and he nominates [morally] superior witnesses [*'udūl mubarrizīn*] to testify for the people, their testimony is accepted on the basis of their signatures, on the condition that resorting to the testimony is permitted.[118]

Here, al-'Abdūsī focuses on the validity of the appointment of judges. He concedes that even if appointed by non-Muslims, a Muslim judge preserves his credibility because his position is justified by the approval of the Muslim community. With this final statement, al-Wazzānī concludes his summary of the fatwā of al-'Abdūsī.[119]

Having nearly finished his refutation of al-Wansharīsī's interpretation, al-Wazzānī concludes with the following:

> This [the previous discussion] is better than the response of the author of the *Mi'yār* about the unlawfulness of the testimony of their witnesses and the illegality of the testimonial authentication issued by their judges under any circumstances, mentioned before, because of the opinion held by some scholars that *bilād al-Islām* does not become *dār al-ḥarb* at the very moment when [*bi-mujarrad*] the infidels capture it. Rather, with the rupture [*inqiṭā'*] of Islamic rites [*sha'ā'ir al-Islām*] and as long as the Islamic rites or most of them continue, it does not become *dār al-ḥarb*. And God knows best.[120]

For al-Wazzānī, occupied Muslim territory remains Muslim so long as Muslims are allowed to practice their religion and live under the laws of Islam. Consequently, Muslims residing in such territory remain ethical. Unfortunately, al-Wazzānī does not specify what he considers to be the ability to practice religion or "rupture of Islamic rites." In my view, this was probably a conscious decision not to determine the specific conditions that must be fulfilled but rather to actively construct answers as new historical conditions emerged.

DISCUSSION

The two cases examined in this chapter shed light on the nature and meaning of the *New Miʿyār*. The point I particularly seek to illustrate about al-Wazzānī's discursive style and consciousness is that his legal interpretations serve to "bring Islamic-legal knowledge into the world and the world into knowledge." In both cases, al-Wazzānī was compelled to engage historical change dictated by Moroccan modernity from within Mālikī legal doctrine and discursive tradition. In other words, his deliberations are at the same time grounded in crucial Moroccan concerns in the context of European colonial aggression and expansion and composed in the technical legal idiom intelligible to jurists well versed in Mālikī legal doctrine. In my view, this is the crucial aspect of al-Wazzānī's project of revival and reform because it is this approach that infuses Mālikī thought with relevant meaning and guarantees its impact as the guiding framework for contemporary ethical Muslim life.

The first text is a mosaic of juristic opinions collected by al-Wazzānī from varied sources that were composed throughout generations of Mālikī legal creativity. A fatwā issued by al-Wazzānī himself in response to an *istiftāʾ* lies at the center of the text. In it, al-Wazzānī confronted the question of growing numbers of Muslims who came under foreign consular protection that became particularly acute in the last decades of the nineteenth century. Al-Wazzānī's opinion contested both the new practice and the discourse that were shaped by the new historical conditions. His statement is an unequivocal condemnation of the Muslim protégés and a rejection of an earlier fatwā that authorized the practice. Al-Wazzānī determines that Muslims seeking the protection of infidels commit rebellion against the Muslim ruler and thereby violate Islamic norms. Al-Riyāḥī was, in the eyes of al-Wazzānī, a misguided jurist who neglected the law, and his fatwā was "entirely wrong" and should be nullified.

But there was more at stake for al-Wazzānī. In his fatwā, he expresses unconditional support for the ruler, however insufferable, tyrannical, and despotic he might be. Al-Wazzānī demands that subjects manifest absolute and unlimited obedience to the sovereign; criticism, opposition, and rebellion against the sultan are illegitimate. It may be argued that al-Wazzānī conceived of the sultan's governance and relationship to society as autocracy. Al-Wazzānī posits conformity with the ideal of submission to the ruler no matter how oppressive he may be; it is noteworthy that there is no plea to the sultan, not even in implicit terms, to respect Islamic legal norms and to conduct himself in accordance with justice. Nowhere in his fatwā does al-Wazzānī remind the ruler that he must avoid sin and rule justly or that his authority or the obedience of his subjects is bound by and contingent upon his subservience to the religious law and the *sunna*. Even more striking is al-Wazzānī's failure to offer any advice that would help the sultan conform to just conduct. Indeed, his fatwā implies that the appropriate implementation of the law is not relevant. It appears that al-Wazzānī's aim in writing his fatwā was not only to prohibit the practice of *ḥimāya* but also to provide the doctrinal underpinnings for a Makhzan in need of legitimation. Though al-Wazzānī's deliberations were constituted by modern concepts and institutions, they were at the same time grounded in the Mālikī legal tradition. In his response, al-Wazzānī invoked the opinions of earlier Mālikī authorities, and his discursive strategies, such as raising rhetorical questions and constructing hypothetical arguments, adhere to the juristic style of constructing fatwās.

But al-Wazzānī was a dynamic and creative compiler with a pressing agenda. As he indicates in the preface to the *New Miʿyār*, the work aimed at assembling as much material as he could find on each individual topic, well beyond the requirements of a comprehensive discussion. Next to his fatwā, al-Wazzānī juxtaposed two legal opinions issued by the Ḥanafī al-Ṭarābulusī and the Mālikī al-Tūnisī and later added an appendix. The material he selected and compiled focuses on the sinfulness of the practice of Muslims seeking the protection of infidels and the dangers that it poses to the larger Muslim society. The tone and the rhetoric of the opinions do not differ from those of al-Wazzānī's fatwā. The inclusion of the additional material was designed to expand the scope of the *New Miʿyār* from the narrow perspective of the juristic position of a single muftī to a repository of the heritage of Mālikī wisdom. We may suppose that by citing the Ḥanafī opinion, al-Wazzānī maintained that his opinion was not confined to Mālikī law or to any particular school. This reorganization of opinions and their arrangement into a single text, in effect, fashioned a "new yet old" juristic composition. In this way, al-Wazzānī connected older narratives with the new historical conditions and restored a dialogue between an age-old legal tradition and his own world.

The second case, al-Wazzānī's refutation of al-Wansharīsī's fatwā, was also deeply grounded in the context of European imperialism. By the beginning of the twentieth century, the residence of Moroccan subjects in European-controlled areas of the Maghrib and the Middle East and the growing community of Muslim expatriates in Morocco demanded al-Wazzānī's contemplation of the prohibition for Muslims to live voluntarily under non-Muslim rule and the insistence on the corrupted credibility of such Muslims. Modern conditions demanded the construction of new distinctions and concepts. Al-Wansharīsī's view that the voluntary residence of Muslims in non-Muslim territory and their subjection to non-Muslim law is unethical had to be marginalized, and a new interpretation that was not necessarily intelligible as an Islamic norm in the world he occupied had to be approved. The definition of *dār al-Islām* had to exhibit less rigidity and allow for negotiation with the modern transformations. In this case, al-Wazzānī contested older ways of interpreting the world and accommodated the changes created by the new historical conditions.

But al-Wansharīsī was the greatest scholar of his age, and his opinion simply could not be dismissed and mocked. For al-Wazzānī, the key issue was how to accommodate change without undermining al-Wansharīsī's juristic reputation. For this reason, al-Wazzānī anchored his composition within a carefully thought out and arranged presentation of a doctrinal dispute within the Mālikī school. He cites a lengthy series of opinions of outstanding Mālikī jurists, such as al-Mawwāq, al-Burzulī, and al-ʿAbdūsī. Most important, he opens his refutation with an opinion issued by al-Māzarī and cited by al-Wansharīsī himself at a later date. In this way, al-Wazzānī crafted a new composition in which he established his own point of view through the voices of al-Wansharīsī and other Mālikī authorities. By seeking the output of earlier generations, al-Wazzānī formulated a response that was faithful to the past (and to al-Wansharīsī) and appropriate for the present.

5 REFASHIONING NOTIONS OF GENDER AND FAMILY

IN THIS CHAPTER, my interrogation of al-Mahdī al-Wazzānī's *New Mi'yār* takes us into a sociolegal domain—kinship and domestic life—that was exposed to conflicts and pressures in the period under discussion, the late nineteenth and early twentieth centuries. Specifically, I focus on the detailed reconstruction of two fatwās, issued by al-Wazzānī, that highlight the method and consciousness of al-Wazzānī's entire work. The significance of the family as a major legal category in the *New Mi'yār* is noteworthy. Many of its chapters address aspects of domestic life, kinship relationships, and gender distinctions. Al-Wazzānī engaged questions that concern familial property devolution, the rights and duties of husbands and wives, and the limits of patriarchal power. He elaborated on parental support and spousal control, practices pertaining to marriage, and the conditions for divorce.

That al-Wazzānī opted to discuss at considerable length issues that had a shaping influence on family life no doubt springs from the significance of family law in religious doctrine and practice. Yet my understanding of al-Wazzānī and his *New Mi'yār* and my own reading of the source suggest that his interest in the family was not merely occasional. Al-Wazzānī was convinced that domestic issues were significant enough during this period to demand his attention and consideration. The distinctive contours of Moroccan modernity systematically transformed the conditions in which Moroccans lived. Al-Wazzānī's response was to prove that Mālikī legal tradition was compatible with the new conditions of the Muslim community, and his concern was to rearrange it to accommodate Morocco's modernity.

It is obvious that during the late nineteenth century, the Moroccan state and society experienced an accelerated phase of reforms and change that had significant repercussions on the family unit. My concern here is with two spheres of change that require special attention: the European economic expansion and the Makhzan's economic reforms. One of the most powerful factors that triggered socioeconomic structural changes during the second half of the nineteenth century was the increasingly growing European economic intervention. The commercial treaty with Great Britain in 1856 (later extended to include all European states engaged in trade with Morocco), which eliminated most of the monopolies held by the sultan and fixed customs duties on imports at extremely low rates, was designed to assure freedom of trade. Effectively, it signaled the incorporation of Morocco into a relationship of inequitable exchange with the world economy.[1]

The provisions of the treaty, according to Mohammed Kenbib, seriously transformed the Moroccan state. The era of protective trade came to an end, and Morocco plunged into a pattern of European domination:

> The beginning of a process of distortion of the Moroccan economy and the appearance of new structural imbalances coincided with the loss of the sultan's control over customs and the abolition of the different monopolies. . . . Subjected to the draconian articles of unequal commercial treaties that were extended to all the great powers by means of the article pertaining to the most favored nation, the Makhzan was no longer able to respect its own decrees prohibiting certain products over which it had previously held commercial monopoly.[2]

The treaty of 1856 facilitated a surge in foreign trade that the Makhzan soon was no longer able to benefit from or control. In the decades preceding the establishment of the French Protectorate, foreign trade had grown in volume and value at unprecedented rates. The import/export balance and the composition of commodities changed considerably, encouraging structural changes. Beginning in the 1880s, European imports into Morocco increased steadily while Moroccan exports dwindled.[3] The growing demand for certain agricultural products on the world market depleted local supply, with the result that prices soared for principal commodities, such as grain, olive oil, almonds, hides, wool, and leather. Imported manufactured goods competed with local crafts, plunging artisans into a severe crisis.[4]

In addition to substantial losses for the royal treasury caused by the prohibition of taxes and tolls on imported goods and the abolition of royal monopolies, Morocco suffered from mounting debts to European powers. After the disastrous war against Spain in 1859–60, Morocco was forced to pay a large indemnity. Payments to Spain and to the British, who loaned the Makhzan money to pay the Spanish, continued for years.[5] This depletion of the Moroccan treasury came at a time when the expenses of the state were rising. Following the war with Spain, the Moroccan government undertook financial and administrative reforms in order to defend itself against the European powers and to collect enough revenue.[6] Numerous reforms were adopted, but the cost of running the state apparatus and its expanding administration combined to bankrupt the treasury.

Seeking to increase its revenues from customs duties on the growing trade with Europe, the Moroccan government was forced to encourage the presence of foreign merchants who were protégés of European consulates. According to Miège, in 1858 there were 611 Europeans living in Morocco; by 1864 there were 1,350. In 1885 the number grew to 3,500.[7] The abusive expansion of the system of consular protection made it possible for these Europeans and their local brokers and business agents to evade taxes. This significantly reduced the Makhzan's revenues derived from foreign trade and taxes and seriously impaired the finances of the state. The abuses of the system became a direct challenge to the efforts of the Makhzan to collect taxes, especially since it was used by many local merchants who attached themselves to protégés and demanded to be exempt from taxes.[8]

The Madrid conference of 1880 determined that foreigners could own land in Morocco. By the 1880s the system of protection followed European commerce into the rural countryside and facilitated the establishment of European businesses in the interior. European merchants set up agricultural partnerships with Moroccans, who also claimed the protection of one foreign state or another and were avoiding tolls and taxes.[9] During this period, Morocco witnessed a substantial growth of speculators in the agricultural sector, who made large profits amid widespread hardship.[10]

Pressed for cash, the Makhzan levied taxes on urban merchants and rural peddlers who brought their goods to urban markets. This meant, in effect, that the Makhzan increased pressure on the masses to generate more tax revenue, while foreigners and their protégés were exempt from payment. This met with considerable social resistance, as when the tanners of Fez protested the imposition of the market tax known as the *mukūs* in 1873.[11] In 1901 the Makhzan attempted to introduce a new tax, the *tartīb*, which imposed a fixed tariff on agricultural produce and livestock and eliminated corruption and tax exemptions, including those of protégés, government officials, and *shurafā'*. French protests and opposition from the 'ulamā' obstructed the efforts of the government to collect this tax.[12]

Economic difficulties were compounded during this period by frequent, lethal droughts and famines. For instance, in the hundred-year period from 1795 to 1895, there were forty years of scarcity or drought in southern Morocco.[13] The drought and famine of 1878–79 was particularly devastating, inaugurating seven years of environmental crisis.[14] Hunger and starvation were followed by epidemics and deaths, and many villages were depopulated or totally decimated.[15] Scores of refugees from the desolated countryside moved to coastal towns, but there were many in the rural population who went bankrupt. Hungry peasants in the rural countryside were forced to get loans for which the collateral included the debtor's property and future harvests. Failure to meet the payments demanded by money lenders led to the expropriation of rural lands and the increasing alienation of peasants from land.[16] From the mid-nineteenth century onward, expanding European economic intervention, new kinds of taxes imposed by the Moroccan government, and natural calamities played a major role in the impoverishment and displacement of rural society. The last decades of the nineteenth century were marked by a rapid rise of rural migration toward the coastal urban centers, especially to Tangier, Essaouira, and Casablanca.

As in the case of other Middle Eastern and North African economies, the social disruption caused by the influx of European cash and goods, increased taxation and inflation, displacement of rural markets, and rural migration to port cities inadvertently introduced changes in forms of households and family life.[17] During the second half of the nineteenth century pressures on family life and structures in the countryside intensified. As foreign merchants, money lenders, and speculators, working through local agents, increasingly pressed their claims in the rural countryside, families had to struggle to make ends meet. Many families found themselves impoverished by their dealings with European merchants and their middlemen, backed by consular protection.[18] Specifically, my concern is with the impact of the expanding foreign economic penetration, coupled with famines and droughts, on the composition of households and kinship ties in the countryside. Desperately seeking employment, large numbers of peasants, women as well as men, found employment opportunities in towns and port cities. Entire families were uprooted, leaving behind extended households and joining the migrant labor force, which came into towns from the countryside.[19] In addition, western Algeria, notably the province of Oran, provided employment for migrants from northeastern Morocco and the Rif Mountains.[20] This migrant labor force was employed on French farms when labor was in demand, but dependent on seasonal changes, many returned to their homes in the Moroccan countryside. Thus, much of the male population in northeastern Morocco was transient. Some sources suggest that particularly women and children who stayed behind or were abandoned found themselves having to survive by all means necessary.[21]

Rural migration and urban growth triggered changes in household structures, family networks, and gender relations. For instance, it is estimated that during the drought and famine of 1878–79 large numbers of refugees, particularly from the Sous, settled in Essaouira, inflating the town's normal population from about sixteen thousand to about twenty-seven thousand. The large influx of rural migrants worsened conditions of poverty and aggravated problems of housing and sanitation. New immigrants would join households of relatives, resulting in whole families living on rooftops and in courtyards. Seeking to maximize gains, some merchants were able to profit greatly by renting out smaller properties and charging exorbitant sums.[22] Women and men had to adjust to a new environment, involving smaller households and physical proximity among nonkin.

In the latter half of the nineteenth century, foreign economic penetration, in particular foreign trade, greatly strained the artisan sector of the urban population. It has been established that after the 1856 commercial treaty, large quantities of raw cotton, cotton cloth, and manufactured cotton goods were imported into Morocco and eventually caused the abandonment of cotton farming and manufacture in and around Salé.[23] In 1858 there were fifty-three workshops for weaving cloth and wool in Rabat and Salé; by 1885 cloth weaving had disappeared in the two cities.[24] Demand for certain resources on the international market, such as leather, wax, and wheat, inflated prices of primary material on which local artisans depended.[25] From around 1865 until 1900, the artisans who formed the majority of Salé's labor force became increasingly impoverished.[26] Both Slawi women and men depended for their livelihood on farming, crafts, and trade in locally produced goods. As local crafts continued to decline during the last decades of the nineteenth century, many women, like men, lost their main source of income and economic security with no hope for support and protection from their husbands or male relatives, who were equally left with no resources. Nevertheless, some crafts prospered during the pre-Protectorate period. Wool blankets, rugs, and carpets became lucrative commodities and were exported to Europe. Women bought and sold wool and yarn and were employed in menial jobs, such as the processing of wool—washing and dyeing it and making it into yarn. The growing demand for carpets provided numerous women with labor. Many women worked at home, but others worked in factories owned by women.[27]

It is clear that at the turn of the nineteenth century, the family as a basic social unit experienced new pressures and arrangements generated by the new circumstances and changing conditions. These structural transformations progressively introduced changes in household structures, family relations, and gender roles. This historical context may be of great value in investigating al-Wazzānī's fatwās. As new historical conditions in late nineteenth-century Morocco emerged, older gender practices and attitudes were undergoing a change. New arrangements and expectations were opened up, and for the Mālikī legal tradition to become more effective as a regulator of Moroccan lives, it was necessary for the legal opinions to relate to the new conditions and needs. Recognizing the changes in family life and household structure, al-Wazzānī insisted on interpretations aimed at the material improvement of Moroccan women as the means toward their more efficient participation in society and advocated the rearrangement of patriarchy. His arguments depicted older cultural attitudes toward women and forms of patriarchy as ignorant and misguided, which were detached from the foundations of Mālikī thought.

A FATWĀ ON THE IDENTITY OF THE LEGITIMATE BENEFICIARIES OF A FAMILY ENDOWMENT

The fatwā that serves as a starting point for the investigation of al-Wazzānī's discursive style and orientation in this chapter is a case of a family dispute over an endowment (known in the Maghrib as *ḥubus*, pl. *aḥbās*). Since the early centuries of Islam, a large and complex inheritance system had been carefully developed and articulated by professional jurists as a body of specialized jurisprudential scholarship. The sharī'a inheritance law, known as the *'ilm al-farā'iḍ*, or "the science of shares," constitutes a vital legal instrument of the Islamic system of property transmission that dictates the compulsory division of wealth after death.[28]

However, passing on the family patrimony to the next generation during the lifetime of property holders assumed a number of more flexible forms, such as family endowments, dowry, property sales, and gifts of cash and valuable goods. Thus, while the Islamic inheritance law is fixed, the implementation of this law frequently constitutes only one alternative for families and individuals.[29]

The family endowment is probably the most important strategy for transmitting property between generations.[30] A founder who wishes to create an endowment sequesters immovable property belonging to him, usually real estate or land, in perpetuity. The income generated by the property is distributed among the beneficiaries of the endowment according to a strategy defined by the founder in an endowment deed (*rasm al-taḥbīs*). This strategy stipulates the usufructory rights of the beneficiaries within the first generation of beneficiaries and from the first generation to the second and all subsequent generations. The property thereafter may not be bought, sold, or inherited. If the line of designated beneficiaries dies out, the revenues revert to a religious or charitable purpose specified by the founder. In this manner, the founder controls the devolution of the endowment revenues for many generations after his or her death.[31]

The opening fatwā examines the story of a woman whose claim to the family endowment revenues triggered court litigation. The fatwā is particularly revealing of the way al-Wazzānī's discourse invokes a pattern of sophisticated interaction between Mālikī doctrine, sources of legal authority, and the rhetoric of legal argumentation, on the one hand, and the new historical conditions, practices, and needs that emerged in the context of Moroccan modernity, on the other. I demonstrate that in constructing his response, al-Wazzānī argues against a contemporary legal interpretation that sanctions practices of resources allocation within the family that unequivocally intend to exclude women's descendants and reinforce gender inequality. Recognizing the effects of the social and economic restructuring of Moroccan society in the latter half of the nineteenth century, al-Wazzānī invokes an interpretation that promotes women's empowerment, authorized by Mālikī discourse.

My interest in this fatwā is as a provocative instance of the agenda and temperament of the *New Miʿyār*. Al-Wazzānī's Morocco was undergoing extensive transformation, which created both discursive and structural changes. Older social arrangements, norms, and ways of interpreting the world had to be discredited and replaced with new ones shaped by the new historical conditions. In elaborating his response, al-Wazzānī deliberately contested an older interpretation, which in his view was incompatible with new sensibilities and embraced practices that guaranteed the material improvement of women in accordance with fundamental Islamic values and forms of thought. In this way, al-Wazzānī reinforced and enhanced Mālikī tradition and thought as an effective regulator of contemporary social relations and Islamic morality.

The case under examination here most likely took place in Fez at an unspecified date during the late nineteenth century. It focuses upon a woman whose name and age are not specified in the fatwā. We do, however, know the name of her father, the scholar Idrīs Ṣafīra. For convenience, I refer to the woman as Bint Idrīs.[32] On an unspecified date, prior to the events that are unraveled here, Idrīs Ṣafīra drafted an endowment deed. The fatwā commences with its recounting.

Creation of the Family Endowment

In his deed, Idrīs designated certain properties belonging to him as an endowment for his currently living children, sons and daughters, and for any children who might be born to him in the future, sons and daughters, and for his grandchildren, and his great-grandchildren, males and females, until the line comes to an end.[33] Idrīs subsequently stipulated the manner in which the revenues of the endowment were to be divided among the designated beneficiaries.

First, he specified that the males (*dhukūr*) may use the endowment revenues without restriction (*muṭlaq*, that is, regardless of their marital status), whereas the females (*ināth*) may do so only so long as they are not married. That is, Idrīs restricted the entitlement of females to the endowment revenues in every generation for as long as they were related to another male who provided for them. Upon the termination of the females' affiliation to their providers, Idrīs brought them back into the pool of the beneficiaries.[34] He added that "a son [*ibn*] is not included [as beneficiary of the family endowment] with his father [*wālid*], but his paternal uncle [*'amm*] does not prevent him [from receiving his legitimate share in it]."[35] By means of this formulation, Idrīs determined that a son is not entitled to enjoy the revenues of the endowment together with his father and becomes a qualified beneficiary only upon the death of his father. However, a son and his paternal uncle may exercise usufructory rights simultaneously.[36] This clause and the choice of language were significant in connection with the family dispute, and I shall return to it later.

To ensure the perpetuity of the endowment, Idrīs most likely designated a religious institution whose nature is not identified in the source as the pious and charitable ultimate beneficiary to which the endowment revenues would revert if the line of beneficiaries came to an end. After drafting the deed, Idrīs is reported to have summoned two notary witnesses (*ʿudūl*) to attest to a legal ceremony known in Mālikī law as *ḥiyāza* (handing over, or *qabḍ* in Islamic legal doctrine), in which the terms of the endowment were read aloud and its creation was formally declared.[37] It is with the *ḥiyāza* that Idrīs Ṣafīra created a valid family endowment.

From the content of the fatwā we learn that following the creation of the endowment, Bint Idrīs married and gave birth to a daughter but was subsequently widowed. On an unspecified date, in all likelihood after Idrīs died, a dispute over the revenues of the family endowment emerged among members of the family. Bint Idrīs, now a widow and a mother, demanded her share of the endowment revenues, together with her daughter's share. Evidently she had not remarried, and, according to one possible reading of the endowment deed, she and her daughter qualified as beneficiaries of the endowment.

It was at this critical moment that one or more of the beneficiaries, presumably Bint Idrīs's brothers or their descendants, intervened to challenge her claim. They insisted that Bint Idrīs's daughter did not yet qualify as an endowment beneficiary and sought to prevent her from sharing the endowment revenues. Although the fatwā does not contain direct information regarding subsequent events, it appears that Bint Idrīs's claim triggered the family dispute that resulted in court litigation. As it seems, Bint Idrīs's brothers filed a complaint with an unnamed qāḍī. To buttress their claim, the defendants presented the qāḍī with a fatwā they had solicited from a muftī whose name is not specified in the source but who is identified as one of al-Wazzānī's contemporaries.

The Fatwā of the Unnamed Muftī

A trained jurist, the unnamed muftī began his response with a close reading of the endowment deed. He identified a key clause in the deed that specifies the manner in which the endowment revenues were to be divided among the beneficiaries. As summarized by al-Wazzānī, the muftī declared that the founder's stipulation that "the son is not included [as beneficiary of the family endowment] with his father" also applies to children of daughters [*awlād al-banāt*]. That is, the muftī understood that the conditions set by the founder concerning fathers and sons should also be extended to the case of mothers and their children. He proceeded to determine that "any child [male or female] whose mother is a widow does not qualify [as a beneficiary of the family endowment] with her." In order to substantiate his position, the muftī now drew an analogy between a daughter and a son, and between a mother and a father, arguing that "a daughter [*bint*] is just like a son [*ibn*]; indeed, [the application of the conditional clause in her case] is even more appropriate. Also, a mother [*wālida*] is just like a father [*wālid*]; indeed, [the application of the conditional clause in her case] is even more appropriate."[38] That is, the muftī arrived at the determination that whereas Bint Idrīs, who was widowed, does qualify as a beneficiary of the endowment, her child, male or female, is not entitled to share the endowment revenues with her.

In his response, the muftī implicitly refers to the principle of agnation (manifested in his emphasis that the application of the clause is more appropriate in the case of a mother and her daughter). According to this principle, females may qualify as beneficiaries in every generation, but they do not transmit this status to their descendants, either sons or daughters. This restriction results from the cultural assumption that a woman's descendants belong to her husband's agnatic group, not her father's. Thus, if a founder creates a family endowment for his son and his lineal descendants, the principle of agnation gradually will exclude both female and male descendants who are not related to the founder through a male link.[39] From the muftī's point of view, the case appears conclusive. The clause that restricts the entitlement of a son's lineal descendants must be understood as also restricting the descendants of a daughter.

Bint Idrīs's case, however, was not resolved with the issuance of this juridical opinion. If it were to end here with the muftī's definitive fatwā, it probably would not have made it into al-Wazzānī's collection. It is the later twists and turns in Bint Idrīs's story that attracted al-Wazzānī's attention and, if only a century later, my curiosity. The case, and the fatwā issued, echoed outside the walls of the courtroom. The presiding qāḍī apparently was reluctant to accept the fatwā, presumably because the muftī based his argument upon his independent legal reasoning and failed to support it with an authoritative text.[40] Therefore, before rendering his decision, the qāḍī decided to request a fatwā from the eminent muftī al-Mahdī al-Wazzānī. In accordance with the conventions relating to a request for a fatwā from an expert jurist, the qāḍī no doubt sent a transcription of the endowment deed, a summary of the facts of the case, and the fatwā of the anonymous muftī to al-Wazzānī, to whom he posed the following question: "Is it [legally] correct to rely on this fatwā in [issuing] a judgment [*ḥukm*], or not?"[41]

As will become clear to the reader, al-Wazzānī's response demonstrates the error in the muftī's interpretation that extended the conditional clause to include a mother and her children. I am going to suggest that al-Wazzānī rejected unequivocally the muftī's reasoning and understanding, which were founded on conceptions and premises he understood to be completely incompatible with the modern social and economic arrangements, and prescribed a new social order that provided an Islamic resolution to contemporary social problems.

The Fatwā of al-Wazzānī

Al-Wazzānī's response was addressed specifically to the qāḍī and written in the formal language of legal discourse, characterized by linguistic concision and references to Mālikī sources of legal authority. Noteworthy are the sophistication of legal reasoning and the straightforward organization of the response, as reflected in the explicit shifts from one topic to the next. Al-Wazzānī begins his response by asserting that the earlier fatwā was erroneous and should therefore be nullified. He goes on to declare that "not even two young boys would express disagreement [regarding its nullification],"[42] thereby diminishing the muftī's professional reputation.

After rejecting the fatwā, al-Wazzānī continues to formulate carefully his analysis of the precise intention of Idrīs at the time of the endowment's creation and the meaning of his endowment deed. According to al-Wazzānī, the wording of the founder is explicit, and thus his intention is accessible. The founder's stipulation "[an endowment] for his children, sons and daughters, and for their children, males and females, until the line comes to an end" is clear in its generality. It qualifies *all* his children and grandchildren, regardless of their gender, as beneficiaries of the endowment. Al-Wazzānī proceeds to observe that the founder disqualified "only a son [*ibn*] from [receiving the endowment revenues] with his father [*wālid*]. However, a daughter [*bint*] is designated [as a beneficiary] with her father, and any child [*walad*] is designated [as a beneficiary] with his mother in an unrestricted manner [that is, independent of gender]." Thus, al-Wazzānī refers to the obvious and apparent meaning (*lafẓ*) of the words used in the endowment deed and declares that the opinion of the muftī constitutes "a clear error that does not allow silence in any way because it is a modification of the words of the founder."[43]

In his response, the unnamed muftī did not make any reference to legal precedents or textual statements. It was for this reason, presumably, that the qāḍī consulted with al-Wazzānī before issuing his judgment. Seeking to substantiate his insistence on the fulfillment of the exact words of the founder and to make his answer as convincing as possible, al-Wazzānī adduces textual authority for his line of reasoning. He invokes the authority of two distinguished Mālikī jurists who stipulated that the words used by the founder of an endowment must be treated as final and immutable. First, al-Wazzānī cites a statement attributed to Khalīl b. Isḥāq (d. 1374): "The formulations [*alfāẓ*] of the founder [of an endowment] must be carefully upheld, like the words of the Divine Lawgiver [*al-shāriʿ*]." Al-Wazzānī also cites an opinion attributed to Abū ʿAli Ibn Raḥḥāl (d. 1728), who said, "If a founder drafts a legally valid endowment deed, one must uphold [its terms]. Any violation of his words is legally void, for his words should be upheld."[44] By citing these two legal opinions, al-Wazzānī supports his contention that the exact words of the founder should prevail and underscores the gross error of the unnamed muftī who misinterpreted the founder's wording. Because the earlier fatwā was based on an erroneous interpretation of the founder's intention, al-Wazzānī demands its immediate nullification.

Having argued that the unnamed muftī had failed to discover the founder's intention and thus had reached a wrong conclusion, al-Wazzānī devotes the remainder of his response to a close reading of several key phrases in the fatwā. Drawing upon his knowledge of the rhetoric of legal discourse, al-Wazzānī observes that in determining the identity of the beneficiaries, the muftī ignored several verbal and circumstantial signifiers (*qarā'in*, sing. *qarīna*) of great import to any determination of the founder's intent.[45]

Specifically, attention to the technical language of the endowment and the social practice, he contends, serves to clarify the intent of the founder. Al-Wazzānī finds textual authority for his argument in the statement of an unidentified jurist from the chapter on *ḥubus* in the *Kitāb al-Miʿyār* of Aḥmad al-Wansharīsī (d. 1508): "Consider [first] the words used by the founder [in the endowment deed], if they exist. If there is a linguistic or a circumstantial qualifier [*qarīna lafẓiyya aw ḥāliyya*], then these are comparable to the actual words [in indicating] the founder's intent. If no such [words] exist, then consider the customary purpose [*maqṣid ʿurfī*], and act accordingly."[46] This statement supports al-Wazzānī's contention that in determining the identity of the beneficiaries, the unnamed muftī should have referred to the formal language and the underlying social purpose of the endowment. Al-Wazzānī now turns to discuss two problems with the fatwā issued by the unnamed muftī.

First, he sharply criticizes the muftī's failure to identify two apparent linguistic signs used by the founder in the endowment deed to clearly indicate the designated beneficiaries. To demonstrate this, al-Wazzānī isolates the muftī's conclusion that "any child [male or female] whose mother is a widow does not qualify [as a beneficiary of the family endowment] with her." Presumably, the muftī extrapolated this conclusion from the founder's words that "a son [*ibn*] is not included [as beneficiary of the family endowment] with his father [*wālid*]." This conclusion, al-Wazzānī asserts, "is one of the greatest wonders one hears, for the founder expressed the exact opposite, namely, that a child [*walad*] qualifies [as a beneficiary] together with his mother [*umm*]." The founder, al-Wazzānī continues, specifically disqualified only a son from sharing in the endowment revenues with his father. It follows, then, that the founder intended to include a son as a beneficiary with his mother.[47]

In other words, whereas the unnamed muftī drew an analogy between a mother and a father, al-Wazzānī unequivocally rejected it and interpreted the founder's specification as applying exclusively to a son and his father. In further support of his argument, al-Wazzānī determines that "believing that [the word] 'father' [*wālid*] stands for a father and a mother contradicts custom [*'urf*] and language [*lugha*], which plainly distinguish a father [*ab*] [from a mother]."[48] It follows that the plain meaning of the Arabic word "father" (*wālid*) is clear and should not be extended to include a mother.

Likewise, al-Wazzānī contends that in drafting the family endowment deed, the founder designated "his children, male and female, and their children, male and female, until the line comes to an end." That is, the founder inserted the particle "and" (*wāw*) between the first and second generations of beneficiaries. By creating such an endowment, al-Wazzānī asserts, the founder designated "the children of his children [*awlād al-awlād*] [as beneficiaries of the endowment], and certainly [the children] with their mother."[49] Thus, the transparent language of the deed, according to al-Wazzānī, indicates that the founder intended that any child (*walad*), regardless of gender, qualifies as a beneficiary of the family endowment together with a mother. On the basis of this literal interpretation of the text, al-Wazzānī concludes that the analogical reading exercised by the unnamed muftī was misconceived.

Second, having dealt with the issues pertaining to the linguistic qualifiers, al-Wazzānī moves on to examine the social function of the endowment. He first explains that the muftī's analogy between a daughter and a son is preposterous (*ghayr ma'qūl al-ma'nā*). He argues:

> It is established that a daughter [*bint*] is weaker [*aḍ'af*] than a son [*ibn*] and that he is stronger [*aqwā*] than she is, and there is no equality [*musāwāh*] between them. Precisely for this reason, the founder restricted the entitlement of a son [*ibn*] together with his father [*wālid*] but not that of a daughter, for she is weaker than he is, and an endowment [*ḥubus*] is a pious gift [*ṣadaqa*], to which she has a greater need than he does.[50]

Whereas the unnamed muftī insisted upon interpreting Idrīs's words as implying equal treatment of sons and daughters, al-Wazzānī argued the contrary. To support his conclusion, he made another direct appeal to a distinguished Mālikī authority, reporting that "it is said by al-Zurqānī [d. 1710]: a woman is poor by nature."[51] Thus, he concludes that Idrīs intended to employ the terms "son" and "father" literally as gendered terms (i.e., the categories of "son" and "father" by no means subsume the categories of "daughter" and "mother").

Al-Wazzānī turns to examine the muftī's analogy that "a mother [*wālida*] is like a father [*wālid*]." "This saying," he declares, "is meaningless, for she is not like him and it is not more appropriate [to apply the clause in her case]. Rather, this statement is null and void and the reversal of truth."[52] He concedes that such an analogy would be needed only if the founder of the endowment had not specifically identified a mother and her daughter as beneficiaries. In this case, however, the founder clearly qualified "his children and their children, male or female, together [as beneficiaries of the endowment] and thus included the daughter and the mother in his words."[53]

Having nearly finished his analysis, al-Wazzānī asserts that the analogy drawn by the muftī between a mother and a daughter and a father and a son, despite the founder's clear reference to them and to their entitlement to the endowment, "is among the facts [*umūr*] that nature [*ṭabʿ*] rejects, and reason [*ʿaql*] and revelation [*sharʿ*] refute." This conclusion leads to the final resolution of al-Wazzānī's legal deliberation and to the completion of the fatwā. Al-Wazzānī completes his response with his characteristic signature: "God knows best. It was said and written by al-Mahdī, may God be kind to him."[54]

Presumably, al-Wazzānī sent the fatwā to the unnamed qāḍī, who, after studying it, issued his judgment. Unfortunately, the aftermath of this court case is unrecoverable. Many questions remain unanswered: Did the qāḍī accept al-Wazzānī's fatwā and award Bint Idrīs's daughter her share? Did Bint Idrīs's relatives comply with the court decision? Or did the familial drama perhaps become more entangled following this decision? Al-Mahdī al-Wazzānī did not leave behind sufficient information to allow the historian to suggest a plausible resolution to this story. However, for the purpose of my present investigation of al-Wazzānī's *New Miʿyār*, the story of Bint Idrīs, as preserved by al-Wazzānī, offers important insights into his discursive dynamics and the social logic of his work, to which I return later.

For now, a salient feature of al-Wazzānī's deliberations that bears preliminary consideration here is his explicit call for change in cultural attitudes and practices toward women. In his fatwā, al-Wazzānī refutes an argument that justified the exclusion of females and their offspring from enjoying the revenues of the family endowment and promotes a view that guaranteed their material improvement. As I have already suggested, the social disruption caused by foreign economic penetration, the administrative expansion of the central government, imposition of new taxes, rural immigration, urban growth, and natural calamities accelerated considerably in the last decades of the nineteenth century. During this period, women often lost income and economic security, had to fend for themselves, and adjust to new family arrangements and expectations. Al-Wazzānī engaged the Mālikī legal tradition to make an argument for an Islamic resolution to a contemporary social problem. To put it differently, an inherently oppressive attitude toward women needed to be replaced by a new family arrangement that enabled women to address and navigate modern Morocco. Now, I turn to amplify the fine details of my observations.

A FATWĀ ON A MISMANAGEMENT OF A WOMAN'S MAINTENANCE

The second fatwā to be analyzed in this chapter records a family dispute over maintenance (*nafaqa*). Islamic law holds the husband solely responsible for the material support of his wife, regardless of her own resources. Once the marriage has been consummated, and for as long as he is married to her, a husband is required to provide his wife with her basic necessities—food, clothing, and housing. *Nafaqa* is the sum of money paid by the husband to his wife for buying these necessities. Support money is not fixed as a lump sum. The obligation of the husband to support his wife entails provision at a level and quality appropriate to her social background.[55] If a husband neglects his duty to provide maintenance, he may be imprisoned until he does, and his wife has the choice of divorcing him if she wishes to take her case to court. In addition, if a husband abandons his wife without providing her material support, or cannot be found or reached, the woman may initiate a lawsuit to reclaim her *nafaqa*.[56]

Al-Wazzānī's fatwā examines the story of an abandoned wife whose claim for her lawful *nafaqa* triggered a dispute with her brother-in-law. Al-Wazzānī's discourse is another instance in which a disputation of an older interpretation of the world is constructed, and new interpretation, based on both contemporary consciousness and Mālikī discursive tradition, is authorized. In it, referring to Islamic norms and concepts, methods of rhetoric, and modes of reasoning, al-Wazzānī explores the scope and nature of the patriarchal order of the family. As modern socioeconomic forces reshaped family life and inspired the emergence of new practices and needs, older forms of family relations and arrangements lost their pertinence. I suggest that within the context of the historical change that altered the conditions and the awareness of the Moroccan Muslim community, al-Wazzānī carefully constructed a legal interpretation that emphasizes legal constraints and limitations on patriarchal authority.

The Facts of the Case

One of the first fatwās to capture my attention as I read through al-Mahdī al-Wazzānī's chapter on maintenance was issued with regard to a family dispute that took place in Fez at an unspecified date during the late nineteenth century.[57] It centers on a married woman and her brother-in-law, whose names are not mentioned in the source. For convenience, I call the woman 'Ā'isha. 'Ā'isha was married to a man who abandoned her but designated his brother as his legal representative or a proxy (*wakīl*) to provide her with maintenance on a monthly basis.[58] The arrangement between 'Ā'isha's husband and his brother suggests that the brother was expected to pay 'Ā'isha her maintenance in one payment every month. Although the fatwā does not contain direct information regarding her dwelling arrangement, it may be reconstructed from the remainder of the text that throughout her husband's absence, 'Ā'isha was not staying in her brother-in-law's house. Most likely, she was living with one of her male relatives, such as her father or brother. The source does not specify the reason for the husband's absence. Instead, it is clear that initially he probably intended to return, as suggested by the fact that he authorized his brother to provide for 'Ā'isha.

But six months after her husband's departure, 'Ā'isha was informed by her brother-in-law that her husband had divorced her. It appears that upon learning of her divorce, 'Ā'isha or her legal guardian (a man from her patrilineage) approached her brother-in-law and demanded her accumulated maintenance for the six-month period that elapsed between her husband's departure and her divorce, during which time her marriage was still in force.[59] There is good reason to believe that 'Ā'isha had the support of her natal kin, who, aware of her predicament, probably encouraged her to protect her rights and demand what was owed to her.

The brother-in-law refused to pay this, claiming that he had already paid for 'Ā'isha's provision. The dispute was now brought before a qāḍī. I do not know the identity of the person who initiated the complaint, but it may have been one of 'Ā'isha's male relatives. Her natal family no doubt had a stake in protecting her claim for material support. In the absence of such support, her male kin guardian would pay all her expenses. After examining the case, the qāḍī accepted 'Ā'isha's claim and ordered her brother-in-law to pay her maintenance, unless he could produce testimonial evidence (*bayyina*) that might establish proof of payment.[60] In practice, the qāḍī instructed 'Ā'isha's brother-in-law to summon two reliable witnesses who could testify to the transaction.[61]

First Fatwā

Discontent with the qāḍī's decision, the brother-in-law sought to have the judgment nullified.[62] He presented the facts of the case to an unnamed muftī, a contemporary of al-Wazzānī, and asked him to reexamine the judgment. The muftī issued a fatwā that directly contradicted the qāḍī's ruling. In compiling his *New Mi'yār*, al-Wazzānī chose to present only a brief summary of the unnamed muftī's fatwā, exclusively focusing on the legal ground upon which the muftī supported his argument. In his fatwā, the muftī accepted the claim of the brother-in-law on the grounds of analogy (*qiyās*) between a missing husband and his present legal representative.[63] He argued that a claim made by the husband's legal representative is analogous to a claim made by the husband himself. According to Mālikī doctrine, a husband's statement that he has left provision for his wife, if validated by an oath, cannot be challenged by the wife. In other words, the muftī argued that in this case, the brother-in-law's statement that he indeed paid 'Ā'isha her maintenance is equal to a claim made by a husband, and therefore, should be accepted.

At this point, the case was presented to al-Mahdī al-Wazzānī. Although the source does not specify who approached al-Wazzānī and for what purpose, there are two likely scenarios. One is that 'Ā'isha's brother-in-law took the fatwā to the qāḍī who issued the judicial decision (or to one of his contemporaries) and asked him to overturn his ruling. In all likelihood, the qāḍī found himself in a dilemma after the brother-in-law returned to him with a fatwā that contradicted the earlier judgment. Not sure how to proceed, he asked al-Wazzānī for help. The second scenario is that 'Ā'isha or her legal guardian approached al-Wazzānī, hoping to get a fatwā that would buttress her case and corroborate the soundness of the judicial decision that required her brother-in-law to correct the injustice he caused her and pay her maintenance.

The Fatwā of al-Wazzānī After studying the case, al-Wazzānī wrote a legal opinion that was short and to the point. No doubt it was addressed specifically to the qāḍī, as suggested by the technical style of the discussion and the extensive use of sources of legal authority of the Mālikī school. Al-Wazzānī begins his response by declaring that the fatwā issued by the unnamed muftī was a mistake (*ghalaṭ*).[64] At issue was the juridical methodology by means of which he reached a legal conclusion. According to al-Wazzānī, the unnamed muftī had analogized legal issues that were in fact distinct. The muftī's legal reasoning, al-Wazzānī argues, provides doctrinal support for a case of controversy between two spouses, whereas in the present case, the disagreement is between a wife and the legal representative of her absent husband. As the law clearly states, the statement of an agent cannot be accepted unless it is accompanied by testimonial evidence.[65] Thus, in the case under examination, al-Wazzānī maintains, the brother-in-law's statement that he, in fact, paid 'Ā'isha's maintenance can be accepted only with the testimony of two witnesses who could confirm the transaction.

To persuade his audience, al-Wazzānī now invokes doctrinal authority as support for his position. He cites Khalīl b. Isḥāq (d. 1374), who established in his *Mukhtaṣar* that "the legal representative is liable, [even] if he fulfills the obligation but did not summon witnesses." He next cites six additional opinions of earlier distinguished Mālikī jurists who corroborated the view espoused by Khalīl: the opinions attributed to Shaykh Aḥmad (d. 803), Ibn Qāsim (d. 806), al-Qayrawānī (d. 996), Ibn Yūnus (d. 1059), al-Qalshānī (d. 1458), and al-Zurqānī (d. 1710).[66] Al-Wazzānī chose to interpret these opinions as broadly as possible. For him, *in any case of uncertainty*, the burden of proof is imposed on the legal representative, and it is his obligation to produce witnesses who could testify to a prompt transaction. Apparently, al-Wazzānī's proper representation of these opinions will be questioned by his contemporaries.

Having established textual authority for his response, al-Wazzānī is now ready to conclude his discussion. Again, he dismisses the fatwā of the unnamed muftī on the grounds of flawed analogy and confirms the initial ruling of the qāḍī. He asserts,

> Many [more] texts attest to this legal position [established previously], and they all indicate that the [qāḍī's earlier] ruling that imposed the burden of proof on the [husband's] legal representative is justified and that what was written in the fatwā, namely, the analogy [between the husband and his brother], is incorrect and deserves no attention.[67]

Finally, al-Wazzānī signals the end of his response with his characteristic signature: "God knows best. It was said and written by al-Mahdī al-Wazzānī. May

God be kind toward him." Presumably, al-Wazzānī sent the fatwā to the qāḍī, who, after studying it issued his judgment.

Refutation of al-Wazzānī's Response At this point al-Wazzānī shifts from the role of jurist to that of compiler, explaining that subsequent to the issuance of his fatwā, no fewer than eight fatwās addressed his reply.[68] Al-Wazzānī's opinion had been seriously challenged. It is precisely this context of argumentation and, therefore, of cultural intervention and re-creation that bears consideration here. The identity of the muftīs who issued the fatwās is unspecified. They nevertheless were al-Wazzānī's contemporaries, and it is likely that they were familiar with one another. Al-Wazzānī's editorial intervention takes up less than one line in the text, which unfortunately does not allow me to determine who brought the case to the attention of the muftīs and for what reason.

It is possible that the presiding qāḍī, now confronted with two contradicting fatwās—one issued by the unnamed muftī and the other by al-Wazzānī—consulted with other jurists and asked them to examine the content of the texts. Perhaps, as experts in legal knowledge responsible to sustain a society that adheres to the highest standards of Islamic conduct, the jurists were compelled to comment on their colleagues' discussion. Whatever the case, there is no doubt that al-Wazzānī's opinion was highly controversial. Here is an interesting example of why the material that al-Wazzānī selected for his work is an ideological subject. His cultural creativity and innovation are evident in his approach to the rearrangement of the content of Mālikī knowledge. By choosing to preserve and transmit this legal discussion, al-Wazzānī used his *New Mi'yār* as a medium for canonization and authorization of certain opinions and marginalization of others.

Al-Wazzānī does not provide us with the full texts of the eight fatwās, perhaps because, in his view, the law is unequivocal and does not require further elaboration, as he indicates several times in his ensuing reply. Nevertheless, it is clear beyond doubt that the eight fatwās refuted al-Wazzānī's opinion. From al-Wazzānī's response, we learn that the muftīs advanced the following three arguments to express their disagreement: First, the muftīs confirmed the analogy between the husband and his legal representative, established in the first opinion issued by the unnamed muftī. They explained that the agent in the present case is analogous to a husband who returns home after being absent and claims he has been sending his wife's maintenance while he was away. They proceeded to state that just as in the case of a husband, the brother-in-law's claim that he indeed provided ʿĀʾisha with her maintenance should be accepted if he would take an oath.

Second, the muftīs criticized the specific texts invoked by al-Wazzānī. It will be recalled that in support of his opinion that the burden of proof lies upon the agent, al-Wazzānī invoked six statements attributed to leading authorities of the Mālikī school. The muftīs argued that the subject of the cited texts is a controversy between the legal representative and the person who designated him, thereby asserting that al-Wazzānī in fact abandoned the true subject of the case and invoked an irrelevant issue. Finally, the muftīs questioned the sincerity of ʿĀʾisha's claim. They maintained that the fact that ʿĀʾisha demanded her maintenance from her brother-in-law only after she was informed about the dissolution of her marriage weakens her claim.

The Second Fatwā of al-Wazzānī

In a point-by-point analysis of the muftīs' opinions, al-Wazzānī refutes their arguments. From the nature of his response, it is clear that he had in front of him the original opinions issued by them or a copy thereof. At the outset of his reply to these muftīs, al-Wazzānī establishes that "there is nothing [new] to add to the case on what was already written." According to al-Wazzānī, the case is clear; the analogy between a husband and his proxy constitutes a plain error. Confident in his reasoning, al-Wazzānī specifies that there are two distinct legal issues to be considered in cases of maintenance: (1) a controversy over the payment of *nafaqa* between a husband and a wife or (2) a controversy that occurs between the proxy of the absent husband and the wife.[69]

In the first case, al-Wazzānī explains,

> He [the husband] is absolutely taken at his word if he claims that he paid her, whether he claims that he paid her indirectly [through an agent] or directly, because he is her legal guardian [*li-annahu amīn ʿalayhā*].[70] In the second case, he [the legal representative of the absent husband] is not taken at his word, because he is a stranger with respect to her, not a guardian with relation to her [*li-annahu ajnabī minhā ghair amīn biʾl-nisba ilayhā*].[71]

As support for his assertion about the husband, al-Wazzānī next cites two statements. First, he invokes the following saying from the *Mudawwana* of Saḥnūn:

> If someone remains with his wife for several years after consummating the marriage, and he is wealthy, and she subsequently claims that he didn't provide her with maintenance, she may receive it [her rightful *nafaqa*] from him, if he con-

firms her claim; if, however, he rejects her claim, then the presumption lies with him, and he takes an oath. Likewise, in the case of an absent husband who appears and claims: I have been sending her the *nafaqa*, but she accuses him of lying, his word is accepted together with an oath.[72]

Next, al-Wazzānī quotes an opinion attributed to al-Burzulī (d. 1437 or 1440):

> His [the husband's] word is accepted [without proof] whether he is present or absent, and she [the wife] cannot challenge his claim, because she is in his possession [*li-annahā fī ḥauzihi*], and the claim of the person who possesses [the property] is accepted. However, if she was not in his house and in his possession because she has not reached physical maturity [*bulūgh*], then her word is accepted.[73]

For al-Wazzānī, the cited opinions illustrate that the legal representative is not like a husband. The clear statement of the law asserts that a husband's claim for the payment of his wife's maintenance, if supported by an oath, is accepted and does not require further testimony because a wife is in the possession of her husband and in his household. But this was in contrast to the present case because "the wife in this case was neither in the house of the legal representative nor in his possession." Thus, al-Wazzānī reasoned, "It is her word that is accepted."[74]

Having completed his discussion of the first legal issue, a controversy between a husband and a wife over the payment of *nafaqa*, al-Wazzānī now turns to discuss his assertion about the proxy of a missing husband. For him, the law was clear and unequivocal, and although he had established the saying of the law in his first fatwā, he now offers an additional view. Al-Wazzānī cites an opinion related on the authority of al-Mawwāq (d. 1492): "If he [a missing husband] designates a proxy to pay his debt on his behalf, or if he [designates a proxy to] sell something on his behalf, he [the proxy] may not pay that without testimonial evidence. If he does pay without testimonial evidence, then he is liable." Al-Wazzānī notes, "The texts that support this opinion are numerous, and there is no need to elaborate on this, and that which we transmitted in the first fatwā is sufficient."[75]

Al-Wazzānī concludes this section of his argument, openly attacking the juridical methodology of the muftīs:

> What right do these muftīs—may God protect them—have to employ analogy [*qiyās*] and rational arguments [*al-ḥijāj al-ʿaqliyya*] and neglect the legal texts [*al-nuṣūṣ al-sharʿiyya*]? The present case is a controversy between the wife and the legal representative, and many texts indicate that the agent's word should not

> be accepted with regard to the payment unless he has testimonial evidence. They [the muftīs] neglected those texts and treated the statement of the legal representative with regard to the payment as acceptable without testimonial evidence, by analogy to a husband who returns from a journey and claims he had been sending her *nafaqa* while he was away. Thus, they abandoned the clear text of the case itself, and they ended up using irrelevant analogy, and this is not acceptable, because one may not apply analogy when there are texts that contradict it.[76]

According to al-Wazzānī, the muftīs failed to address the facts of the case, employed a misguided analogy, and neglected the existing texts.

Next, al-Wazzānī turns to discuss the muftīs' accusation that he invoked irrelevant texts that referred to "a controversy between the legal representative and the person who designated him." This, al-Wazzānī notes, is also incorrect because the texts address two legal possibilities, a controversy between a husband and his agent as well as between a legal representative and a wife, without considering them separately.[77] Thus, al-Wazzānī justifies unequivocally his reference to the opinions of these Mālikī jurists.

At this point in his argument, al-Wazzānī considers the muftīs' specific analogy between a legal representative and a husband who returns home after a journey and claims he has been sending his wife's maintenance while he was away. No doubt sensitive to the accusations that his legal conclusion was a mistake, al-Wazzānī wanted to address every aspect of their arguments. Thus, despite the fact that he already addressed the analogy between a husband and a legal representative, al-Wazzānī here addresses the analogy again. He explains, "Their saying: Were he [the husband] to appear, and she claims that the legal representative did not pay her anything, [her statement] is not accepted, and the husband must do no more than take an oath," is invalid (*bāṭil*). "Because," according to al-Wazzānī, "the legal representative, unlike the husband, is not reliable [*muṣaddaq*] with regard to paying her, as we have established already. For he [the husband] is her guardian [*amīn*], whereas his legal representative is not. Thus, the analogy between one who is not a guardian and one who is a guardian is wrong and must be nullified."[78] In undermining the analogy, al-Wazzānī rejects the underlying presumption that the legal position of a husband and his brother-in-law with respect to the wife is equal.

Finally, al-Wazzānī challenges the muftīs' argument that ʿĀʾisha's extended silence throughout the six-month period during which her husband was absent, before demanding her maintenance, weakens her claim. In refuting their argument, al-Wazzānī argues that ʿĀʾisha employed plain wisdom (*mujarrad ta'aqqul*) in delaying her claim upon her brother-in-law either because she waited to get the entire sum at once or because she felt shame and was reluctant to inconvenience her brother-in-law. However, following the dissolution of her marriage, 'Ā'isha felt that she could demand her maintenance. This temporary delay is insignificant and does not harm 'Ā'isha's claim of her maintenance.[79]

As support for this assertion, al-Wazzānī next cites an analogous fatwā issued by Abū Sa'īd Ibn Lubb (d. 1380). The *istiftā'*, or request for a fatwā, refers to a minor girl whose mother remarried. The mother and her husband had provided for the girl "from the time of nursing to her marriage and the consummation of her marriage." Sometime after her marriage, the girl died and her legacy was divided. The girl's mother and her husband demanded a share in the girl's legacy for the period during which they provided her maintenance. Although the text does not contain the question, it is clear from the muftī's response that the questioner raised the issue of legality of the couple's request many years after the fact.

In his reply, the muftī explained that "the share of the mother and her husband is not canceled because of the delay in their demand until she got married, if the delay was out of pity and the wish to grant respite."[80] Ibn Lubb then found textual authority for his response by citing a fatwā on the issue of deferred *nafaqa* issued by an unnamed muftī and transmitted by Ibn 'Āt (d. 1212). The fatwā refers to a minor child in her father's custody, who inherited considerable wealth from her mother. The father took it upon himself to pay her provision, although according to the law, if she had the capacity to provide for herself, all the expenditure may be taken from her property and the father should not be obligated to his daughter's maintenance. Years later, after her marriage, the father demanded from his now affluent and married daughter to pay him for her maintenance for the period she was a minor in his custody. The muftī confirmed that the father's deferred claim is legally correct.[81]

For al-Wazzānī, Ibn Lubb's fatwā provided the final support to his argument that the muftīs' position had no basis in Mālikī doctrine. It follows that his recommendation that 'Ā'isha's brother-in-law was required by law to produce witnesses to the payment of her *nafaqa* should be accepted. At this point, al-Wazzānī's fatwā ends with his characteristic signature: "And God knows best. It was said and written by al-Mahdī al-Wazzānī. May God be kind toward him."

'Ā'isha's story is a microexample that provides me with an opportunity to make contact with al-Wazzānī's vision of the relationship of women to their maintenance. Unfortunately, al-Wazzānī's fatwā gives us only one scene from the drama of ʿĀʾisha and her husband's family. How did the story end? Did ʿĀʾisha achieve her goal? Whose legal opinion and interpretation was finally authorized by the judge? I must leave these questions unanswered. We do not know whether the first judicial decision that required ʿĀʾisha's brother-in-law to pay her accumulated maintenance was enforced and implemented or rejected and reversed. Notwithstanding, ʿĀʾisha's story allows us to penetrate al-Wazzānī's discourse and juristic argumentation and investigate the function and meaning of his *New Miʿyār*.

DISCUSSION

My argument in this book is that al-Wazzānī's deliberations are firmly rooted in both the Mālikī discursive tradition and the new historical conditions that actively shaped new consciousness and awareness. It is this feature of the *New Miʿyār* that in my view is the most significant in al-Wazzānī's project of Islamic reform; this is how the *New Miʿyār* functions both as a medium for preservation of tradition and an instrument for its innovation and re-creation. As we have seen, in the two cases examined in this chapter al-Wazzānī took issue with contemporary religious authority and rejected legal opinions that he identified as fundamentally incompatible with Islamic reasoning, concepts of morality, and the logic of norms and social roles shaped by the modern age.

Al-Wazzānī saw himself as a reformer with a duty to address directly the problems and accusations facing *fiqh*. The very survival of the Muslim community was at stake, and he had to revitalize what was viewed by many of his contemporaries as a decadent and stagnant legal tradition that was out of touch with the dramatic changes in society that marked Moroccan modernity. From his perspective, uninformed jurists perpetuated ignorance and oppression, and in order to retrieve and restore the true meaning of Islam, their interpretations would have to be discarded and replaced by concepts, beliefs, and practices that promoted Islamic morality and guaranteed the survival of the Muslim community in the modern world.

It will be recalled that the first text I examined consists of a fatwā issued by al-Wazzānī in response to a request from a qāḍī. In it, al-Wazzānī disputes the legal interpretation proposed by the unnamed muftī, who endorsed a social order founded on older concepts and beliefs, and formulates a new opinion through the prism of the social and structural changes produced within Moroccan modernity. In constructing his legal interpretation, al-Wazzānī employs complex interplay between legal discourse and hermeneutical tools, on the one hand, and the new rationalities and consciousnesses shaped by the modern world, on the other. An expert jurist, he draws upon textual analysis and rhetorical strategies, focusing attention on literal meaning of words, particles, and conjunctions and their signification. His juristic opinion adheres to established Mālikī doctrine, cites earlier legal precedents, and relates opinions issued by Mālikī jurists as specific support for his opinion. Moreover, al-Wazzānī criticizes older arrangements of transmission of wealth within the family that perpetuate the inferior status of women and their descendants. Al-Wazzānī's careful argumentation and the language he employs are especially revealing in this context. Let us reexamine this fatwā text.

Idrīs Ṣafīra created an endowment for his currently living children, male and female, and for the future children he might have as well as for their descendants, male and female. In his deed he specified that males were entitled to exercise their rights freely and regardless of their marital status. The females, he stipulated, would exercise their rights so long as they were not married, that is, only when and if they were unmarried, divorced, or widowed. In addition, he stipulated that "a son is not included [as beneficiary of the family endowment] with his father." As we have seen, al-Wazzānī took issue with the unnamed muftī, who determined that the phrase restricting sons from becoming beneficiaries of the endowment with their fathers must be understood as also including mothers and their children. According to the unnamed muftī, "a daughter is just like a son; indeed, [the application of the conditional clause in her case] is even more appropriate. Also, a mother is just like a father; indeed, [the application of the conditional clause in her case] is even more appropriate."

When we examine the unnamed muftī's interpretation, we find that he implicitly associates the process by which material wealth flows from one generation to the next with cultural constructs. Without doubt, he links patterns of property transmission with the concern for the preservation of the integrity of the family patrimony. Accordingly, the need or desire to protect the integrity of the family wealth is embedded in the notion that patrimonial continuity took place in the relationship between fathers and sons. As for women, the institution of marriage is viewed as an important factor in explaining this cultural presupposition. A daughter is likely to leave her natal household upon marriage. From the point of view of the natal family, the marriage of a daughter threatens the integrity of the family patrimony because her personal property is transferred to her new marital family. Note that this concern is consistent with Idrīs

Ṣafīra's stipulation that conditioned a female's entitlement on her being unmarried, divorced, or widowed. The children of a daughter, according to this cultural logic, belong to their father's agnatic group, not their mother's. This notion of agnation stems from the patriarchal social order. The family in this social order is explicitly a male's family. Females join it as wives, and the children born to them belong to their father. With regard to property, ties through female relatives fluctuate and disrupt the indivisibility of the family patrimony. This point is amplified in the interpretation of the unnamed muftī, who insists on the exclusion of the children of daughters from the family endowment.

My point here is that the fatwā of the unnamed muftī highlights practices and values that promoted the prominence of the founder's direct lineal male descendants and enforced sharp gender hierarchies. Endorsing the principle of agnation, the muftī advocated an understanding that progressively removed the rights of females and their descendants to the family patrimony. For al-Wazzānī, this fatwā represented an uninformed opinion issued by an ignorant muftī that perpetuated the crisis of Mālikī jurisprudence and abandoned Islamic morality. Reflecting on the unnamed muftī's argument, al-Wazzānī strongly objected to his attitude, which "is among the facts that nature rejects, and reason and revelation refute."

As new historical conditions emerged in late nineteenth-century Morocco, older gender norms and practices were undergoing change. New possibilities and rationalities were opened up, and for the Mālikī legal tradition to become more effective, it was necessary to establish it as responding to and regulating the needs of a modern Muslim community. In his endeavor to determine what exactly Idrīs had intended at the time of the endowment's creation, al-Wazzānī asserts that "it is established that a daughter is weaker than a son, and that he is stronger than she is, and there is no equality between them. Precisely for this reason, the founder restricted the entitlement of a son with his father but not that of a daughter, for she is weaker than he is, and an endowment is a pious gift, to which she has a greater need than he does." After commenting on the asymmetry between daughters and sons, al-Wazzānī reiterates his opinion with regard to the inherent vulnerability of women, citing the words of a highly respected Mālikī jurist asserting that "a woman is poor by nature." Finally, to emphasize the magnitude of the error committed by the unnamed muftī, al-Wazzānī states that the analogy between a mother and a father "is meaningless, for she is not like him, and it is not more appropriate [to apply the clause in her case]. Rather, this statement is null and void, and the reversal of truth."

Recognizing the changes in family life and household structure, al-Wazzānī advocates norms and attitudes that fit into a new understanding of women's status in society. In his deliberations, he, in effect, urges fathers to cease discriminating against female members of the family and their descendants. He explicitly calls on fathers to grant women and their children preferred access to family property, thereby guaranteeing their socioeconomic position. Although Islamic law grants women rights, widespread customs and conventions, sanctioned by misguided jurists, enforce women's economic oppression and dependence upon parents, male kin, or husbands. Regulating men's access to family property would improve women's status in society and allow their participation more fully in the new social order.

The socioeconomic disruption that marked the last decades of the nineteenth century compelled women to fend for themselves. Rural women, leaving their families and homes behind, flocked into Moroccan towns and port cities, seeking jobs. Numerous others were abandoned by their male relatives often with no resources and without the people and social networks to rely on. In the cities, rural migration worsened conditions of poverty, and the effects of international trade and capitalist penetration combined with high taxation exacerbated lowered living standards. Stiff international competition led to decline in domestic manufacturing and crafts. Merchants and craftsmen were unable to sustain their business activities, and many women lost their jobs. Mothers found themselves managing the household and in charge of providing for their children. Modern forces reshaped the conceptual conditions and the possibilities of action. For al-Wazzānī, the Mālikī legal tradition had to accommodate the material improvement of Moroccan women as productive members of society and their needs for self-reliance.

The second text I examined includes multiple elements, intentionally collected and arranged by al-Wazzānī into a single, original composition. In it, once again, al-Wazzānī engages a legal interpretation proposed by his contemporaries that he deemed irrelevant. Like the first fatwā, the second case presented an interpretation that threatened to overwhelm Islamic morality and therefore was dismissed as incorrect. Al-Wazzānī contests older arguments, concepts, and meanings and proffers new understandings, orientations, and arrangements. For al-Wazzānī, the muftīs' responses were unequivocally wrong because they were based on a false analogy (*qiyās*) between a husband and his legal representative (*wakīl*), depended upon free reasoning, and systematically neglected the legal doctrine of the Mālikī school. In constructing his legal opinion, al-Wazzānī employs complex interplay between Mālikī legal doctrine and the new rationalities and needs, shaped by Moroccan modernity. He explains the major thrust of the dispute, invokes Mālikī texts to rebut the muftīs' false *qiyās*, and clarifies the semantics of the words "husband" and "legal representative." It is evident that he explicitly associates the law of *nafaqa* with gender asymmetry and illustrates the principle of male dominance and female dependence within the family. In al-Wazzānī's view, however, the law placed legal constraints and real limitations on patriarchy, and he wanted to make sure that the law was actively upheld. Al-Wazzānī's juristic argumentation and interpretation are suggestive in this context. Let us reexamine the fatwā.

It is clear that a strong, gendered vision that buttresses a patriarchal social and familial order underlies al-Wazzānī's legal discourse. Gender plays a large role in defining rights and responsibilities. The husband's role is that of provider, and the wife is the recipient of support. Material support is legally required and expected only from men. Women are not expected to support anyone, not even themselves, and their material support comes from property owned and controlled by men. Furthermore, an absent husband is required to assign his wife her *nafaqa*, and as indicated by al-Wazzānī, this situation has to be carefully defined.

Al-Wazzānī's responses underscore that the authority and responsibility of a husband are different from those of his legal representative in relation to his wife. Both the qāḍī and al-Wazzānī placed the brother-in-law and the husband in two different legal roles in regard to 'Ā'isha. The legal representative is not like the husband, the uncontested head of the family, the provider. The obligation to provide *nafaqa* lies with the husband, and the husband's brother was called to perform this duty as a substitute. But there is no attempt by either the judge or al-Wazzānī to ignore the brother's relationship with 'Ā'isha. He may be a substitute, but he does not assume the role, position, obligations, and rights of the husband. Most important, the brother does not attain the full legal rights of the husband. Notice al-Wazzānī's formulation that "he [the husband] is absolutely taken at his word if he claims that he paid her, whether he claims that he paid her indirectly [through a legal representative] or directly, because he is her legal guardian. In the second case, he [the legal representative of the absent husband] is not taken at his word, because he is a stranger with respect to her, not a guardian with relation to her." Drawing upon an opinion attributed to al-Burzulī, al-Wazzānī proceeds to explain the logic of his argument, saying that because a wife is in the possession of her husband

and in his household, his word is accepted. However, in a case of a legal representative, the wife is neither in his house nor in his possession, and therefore, her word is accepted.

We have seen that al-Wazzānī's salient conceptualization that the positions of the husband and his legal representative in regard to 'Ā'isha are not analogous was very much challenged. In determining that a claim made by the husband's legal representative in the context of *nafaqa* restitution is analogous to a claim made by the husband himself, al-Wazzānī's contemporaries extended the authority of the husband to his legal representative and further enhanced the patriarchal social order. For al-Wazzānī, the law was clear and unequivocal, and the muftīs' arguments were without a doubt incorrect. It seems to me that al-Wazzānī's responses suggest a reordering of the patriarchal structure. Against contemporary pressures, especially, the steady impoverishment and displacement of rural society and the essential changes they brought about in family arrangements and norms and household composition, al-Wazzānī viewed the restructuring of patriarchy as required. Informed by modern conditions and ideas and aware of changing practices and attitudes, he sanctioned a patriarchal order that guaranteed the enforcement of legal limits on the impact of male dominance and limited the role of patriarchal power. My point here is that in his reasoning, al-Wazzānī engaged existing discourses and approaches that advocated an older form of patriarchy he deemed tyrannical and replaced it with a new interpretation that aimed at protecting women's rights and regulating men's coercive authority.

Al-Wazzānī's consideration of the modern conditions and consciousnesses, of course, should not be interpreted to deny the patriarchal tone of his legal discourse. Without doubt, al-Wazzānī lived in a patriarchal culture that encompassed familial structure and principles, and his legal opinions underscore this family form. His arguments were not rooted in claims about equal relations between two individuals or the abrogation of patriarchy. In his legal discourse, he reproduces a patriarchal ideology, structures, and practices, as well as the constraints on women's choices and women's subordination to males in important symbolic and actual ways. There is ample evidence in his fatwās to confirm that he viewed the experience of women as more restricted than that of men. Thus, it is not my intent to deny evidence of patriarchal values and norms in al-Wazzānī's discourse. Rather, my argument is that he insisted, within the scope of his knowledge and mode of thinking, that patriarchy was limited in significant ways.

6 REDEFINING PATTERNS OF CONSUMPTION

IN THIS CHAPTER, my investigation of the *New Mi'yār* of al-Wazzānī addresses a sociolegal domain—food, beverages, and patterns of consumption—that was directly linked to the transformations that characterized the late nineteenth century and the beginning of the twentieth century and the concrete anxieties they generated. I situate my inquiry in the wider context of change that occurred in the period under discussion: the expansion of the import of manufactured goods from Europe and changes in Moroccan consumption and taste. In the previous chapter, I sketched out some of the socioeconomic changes that Morocco experienced from the mid-nineteenth century onward as a result of increasingly aggressive European economic pressures and a series of state-designed reforms. As I have mentioned, the commercial treaty concluded between Great Britain and Morocco in 1856 (which later served as the model for arrangements with other European states) secured the integration of Morocco into the capitalist world economy on terms favorable to European economies. The treaty that lowered customs duties on European imports altered the Moroccan economy in significant and unprecedented ways.

One of the direct impacts of the Anglo-Moroccan treaty on the precolonial Moroccan economy was the opening of the Moroccan market to cheaply manufactured European products and the steady erosion of domestic artisanry.[1] For instance, the production of cotton cloth and manufactured goods, which constituted the backbone of the economy of Salé until midcentury, steadily declined as cotton imports from Britain and France grew rapidly in the 1860s (by

65 percent) and 1870s (by 34 percent).[2] In Salé from the late 1860s onward, the gradual abandonment of cotton farming and the decline in the manufacture of cloth forced large numbers of artisans, who were the most important sector of the city's labor force, out of business.[3] Other crafts associated with the preparation of cloth and clothing, such as dyeing, weaving, and embroidering, all declined. By 1885 the trade of weaving cloth had almost entirely disappeared.[4]

However, the high commercial competition and changing economic conditions did not bring hardship for all Moroccans. The last quarter of the nineteenth century witnessed the development of a new social class of merchant elite that depended for its wealth on trade with Europe.[5] The industry of weaving wool blankets, rugs, and carpets in Salé remained prosperous during the pre-Protectorate period. Slawi carpets were exported to Europe, and after the French occupation, various circumstances encouraged export expansion.[6] Numerous merchants in Fez made large fortunes from foreign trade. Many of them settled and established prosperous businesses in the most active Mediterranean ports and other commercial centers of this era. Foreign trade stimulated the economic expansion of the city, and some traditional crafts continued to prosper because of foreign trade.[7] This meant that some rich merchants profited from the growing demand for foreign imports and became principal supporters of increased trade with Europe.

In the commercial expansion that came after 1860, the balance of trade shifted in Europe's favor; Moroccan imports sharply increased as exports were declining. The last quarter of the nineteenth century witnessed a decrease in European demand for the major products in Morocco's trade, such as wool, animal skins, and grains. Miège suggests that some of the causes for the shift in trade included the opening of the Suez Canal, improved transportation and navigation technology, and the modification of export trade laws and regulations. As he demonstrates, especially after 1878 new suppliers and products were available to European markets for better quality at reduced prices, such as Indian and Australian wool and animal skins and American grains. At the same time, European commercial expansion into Morocco greatly increased. By 1870 imported tea, sugar, cotton fabric, candles, oil, matches, glassware, pottery, and tableware spread throughout the country, spurred by falling prices due to cheaper production and transportation costs.[8]

Trade with Christian Europe had posed an ideological problem for the Moroccan sultanate long before the late nineteenth and early twentieth centuries.[9] In the last quarter of the nineteenth century, however, as foreign interference in internal affairs grew, the intermingling of Muslims with European advisers, diplomats, and businessmen increased, and demand for European goods spread widely. Many ʿulamāʾ were opposed to contact with foreigners and viewed foreign trade and the development of new tastes for European commodities as the root of vice and immorality. Muḥammad b. al-Madanī Gannūn (d. 1885), a prominent legal scholar and one of al-Wazzānī's teachers, was strictly opposed to Moroccan merchants traveling to Europe for the purpose of trade and considered such travel an act of treason.[10] For Aḥmad al-Nāṣirī (d. 1897), the new currents of change, especially the European economic penetration and the widespread adoption of European habits, marked a sharp break with the experience of previous generations. Protesting the change, he wrote:

> Know that the circumstances of this generation in which we live differ greatly from those of the generation before it. People's habits [*ʿawāʾid*] transformed considerably. The general state of affairs for merchants and other businessmen changed a great deal; not in the currency they use, the prices they set, or their expenditures, but in that people are anguished. It became difficult for them to earn a living. If we compare the conditions of previous and current generations, we find that they are opposites. The most significant reason for this situation is the close relations with the Europeans. Their intermingling with Muslims has increased, and they have spread throughout the Islamic lands. Their ways and habits supersede those of the current generation, and they are very attractive to Muslims.[11]

The Moroccan sultan himself, Mawlāy Ḥasan (r. 1873–94), was alarmed by both the growing trade in illicit drugs (*al-aʿshāb al-muraqqida waʾl-mufsida*) imported from Europe in large quantities and drug addiction. In 1886, searching for new revenues, he asked the ʿulamāʾ of Fez to issue a fatwā that would legitimize the trade in order to allow the imposition of the standard 10 percent custom duty on imports. In justifying his request, Sultan Mawlāy Ḥasan raised the point that with the fall of prices, drugs had become available to both the powerful and the weak and had become an excuse to permit forbidden behavior.[12] Coffee consumption, although it predated Morocco's incorporation into the capitalist world economy, grew considerably during the late nineteenth century. As a result of this growth in consumption, the number of coffeehouses increased. Cafés attracted not only Moroccans but also newly arrived foreigners. In these cafés, clients socialized, played cards, listened to music, and smoked, thereby engaging in intercommunal connections as well as transgressions.[13] Many among the 'ulamā' viewed this form of amusement as contaminating both society and religion. By the last decades of the nineteenth century, possibly because wine and alcoholic beverages were also consumed there, Moroccan authorities became hostile to cafés and ordered their closure.[14]

The widespread adoption of new tastes that greatly reinforced the demand for imported products is another important aspect of the transformations that occurred in this period. A case in point is the spread of the consumption of imported tea and sugar. Tea was introduced into Morocco by European merchants in the seventeenth century and was considered a drink of luxury and a symbol of social status until the mid-nineteenth century.[15] By the 1870s tea drinking spread beyond the wealthy classes and was broadly consumed throughout society, quickly becoming an important item in the Moroccan diet and social life.[16] Moroccans put sugar in their tea, and the widespread adoption of tea reinforced demand for both products.[17] Miège indicates that as result of the proliferation in the consumption of sugar in the last decade of the nineteenth century, it sometimes served as a medium of exchange or as money in trading. In 1874 around 76,000 kilograms of tea were imported; in 1884 the figure was 275,000 kilograms, representing 264 percent growth, or 14 percent compound annual growth rate (CAGR). By 1890 tea was the third-largest imported item and accounted for 5 percent of the total value of foreign trade. In the six-year period between 1871 and 1877, the import of sugar increased by 73 percent, or 10 percent CAGR. By 1890 sugar was the second-largest item of import and made up 20 percent of all imports. By 1894 it accounted for 25 percent of all Moroccan imports, representing 25 percent growth in four years.[18]

The diffusion of new items imported from Europe certainly countered the interests of artisans, craftsmen, and merchants who suffered from competition with European goods and prices. Moreover, these changes were regarded by some Moroccan 'ulamā' among the causes of the weakness of Islam. For example, Shaykh Muḥammad al-Kattānī forbade his disciples of the Kattāniyya Sufi order to consume tea and sugar. According to his biographer, he perceived the importation and consumption of these commodities as a threat to the Moroccan economy and sovereignty.[19] Opposition and resistance by the population found expression in social unrest and outbursts of xenophobic feelings and anti-European protests. In the last quarter of the nineteenth century, rumors circulated that European sugar was refined with the aid of pig's blood, and fatwās against imported sugar were issued in Fez.[20] These rumors and fatwās, which attest to Moroccan anxieties over the power of Europe and the weakness of Islam, gave rise to the text assembled and arranged by al-Wazzānī, which forms the subject of this chapter.

The text comprises five independent legal discussions, and its special value lies in its juridical content as well as in the creative consciousness of its author-editor. The locus of al-Wazzānī's composition is a lengthy treatise written by a prominent Moroccan jurist in the first half of the nineteenth century, sanctioning the consumption of foreign sugar. Next to it, al-Wazzānī carefully juxtaposed four separate discussions (three of them written by al-Wazzānī himself) that authorize the consumption of three beverages: tea, a strong intoxicating drink made of fruits, and coffee. Al-Wazzānī bolsters his legal opinions by expanding upon the argument made by the earlier jurist. In transforming the multiple literary elements into a single, integral composition, al-Wazzānī fashioned a complex dialogue between the world he occupied, on the one hand, and an age-old legal tradition, on the other. It is this feature of the *New Miʿyār* that restores Mālikī thought and knowledge as a living tradition.

A TREATISE ON THE PERMISSIBILITY OF SUGAR IMPORTED FROM EUROPE

Sugar cane reached North Africa following the Arab expansion to the region in the second half of the seventh century.[21] In Morocco, a commercial sugar industry emerged in the late ninth and tenth centuries, mainly in the south around Marrakesh and the Sous region, and flourished for several hundred years. During that period, due to the scarcity and high cost of timber required for fuel, sugar remained a luxury item. By the beginning of the seventeenth century, the sugar industry in Morocco ceased to exist.[22] One of the primary causes of its disappearance in Morocco, as elsewhere in the Mediterranean, was the development of new markets and suppliers in the new European colonies in the Atlantic and America at the beginning of the fifteenth century.[23] In the sixteenth and seventeenth centuries, sugar refining was increasingly transferred into western Europe, and Morocco imported its sugar from European refineries.[24] Until the late nineteenth century, refined sugar was imported into Morocco mainly in the form of a loaf (in Arabic, *sukkar al-qālab* or *sukkar al-qālab al-muṣaffā*; in French, *pain de sucre*) and was broken up into lumps or pounded into powder. In 1864 Sultan Ḥasan, with the help of an English engineer, built a sugar refinery in Marrakesh. From its inception, the project encountered serious difficulties, including ineffective technology, poor socioeconomic infrastructure, and dependence on foreign engineers and technicians.[25]

The last quarter of the nineteenth century was not the first time that rumors addressing the issue of imported sugar had circulated in Morocco. At the beginning of the nineteenth century, this issue was as explosive as it was during al-Wazzānī's times. The principal text I explore here is a long, detailed, and complex treatise written in response to rumors circulated in Morocco about imported sugar in the first half of the nineteenth century.[26] The treatise was written by Muḥammad al-ʿArabī al-Zarhūnī, a Mālikī jurist who had a distinguished career. He studied with Muḥammad al-Ṭayyib b. Kīrān (d. 1812), an accomplished jurist whose knowledge of Mālik's doctrine as well as the methods of legal reasoning qualified him to practice *ijtihād*,[27] and Muḥammad b. ʿAbd al-Salām al-Nāṣirī (d. 1823), a prominent scholar and Sufi. Al-Zarhūnī was a qāḍī and muftī in Fez, where he lived for a good part of his life until his death in Essaouira in 1844.[28]

From details mentioned in the text, it is most likely that al-Zarhūnī wrote the treatise sometime between the death of the Moroccan sultan Sulaymān in 1822 and his own death in 1844. The treatise takes the form of an extended fatwā and contains a skillfully crafted legal thesis, involving sophisticated argumentation. In it, al-Zarhūnī assembled material from diverse sources and many generations and demonstrated his extensive knowledge of Mālikī law and the science of disagreement (*khilāf*). It was addressed specifically to professional jurists familiar with the methods of legal reasoning, the founding doctrines of the Mālikī school, and the opinions of the Companions, the Followers, and jurists who came after them.

As al-Wazzānī was copying the text into what would become the *New Miʿyār*, he added a short introductory comment in which he expressed his approval of its content as a normative source for instruction: "Sīdī al-ʿArabī al-Zarhūnī, the most erudite scholar, has an excellent reply [*jawāb ḥasan*] about sugarloaf [*sukkar al-qālab*]."[29]

The Treatise of al-Zarhūnī

The treatise begins with the customary pious invocations: "In the name of God, most benevolent, ever-merciful. May God's blessing and peace be upon Muḥammad and his Companions." It continues with a preliminary formulation that frames the text:

> Praise be to God who endowed religious scholars with the traits of the true religion, prevented ignorant opinions from [being included in] their healing sayings

> [*al-aqwāl al-shāfiya*] and their judicious texts, and wisely brought a group of them to the right path so that His command is fully achieved. May God's blessing and peace be upon Muḥammad, who clearly defined that which is permissible [*ḥalāl*] and that which is forbidden [*ḥarām*], nullified doubt [*ḥukm al-shakk*] regarding the proscription of food [*taḥrīm al-ṭaʿām*], and explicated the characteristic traits of the right way to his noble people in order to leave them with a clear and truthful dawn. May God's blessing and salvation be upon him, his family, his Companions, those who follow the clear law of Islam, which rejects uninformed opinion [*al-raʾy al-mujarrad*] and free reasoning bound by no text [*mustaḥsanāt al-ʿuqūl*], and anyone who adheres to them in doing good until the Day of Judgment.[30]

At the very outset of his treatise, al-Zarhūnī explicitly invokes the authority of earlier generations of jurists and their writings and the authoritative statements of the Prophet Muḥammad, situating the work within established discourse and knowledge and anchoring it in the standard opinions and shared doctrines of his predecessors. From the beginning, al-Zarhūnī identifies himself as a follower of tradition, who by definition adheres to the opinions of other distinguished jurists, thereby emphasizing his subordination to the doctrine of the Mālikī school. As we shall see, al-Zarhūnī consciously sought to frame his discussion in terms of affiliation and loyalty to the school's doctrine, suggesting that his legal opinion was not merely his personal opinion but was in agreement with opinions of earlier authorities and grounded in the canonical texts. Finally, al-Zarhūnī expresses his hope for God's patronage and compassion in his present undertaking, asking "God to protect him with His grace and enclose him with His qualities and attributes."

At this point, al-Zarhūnī explains the historical context that led him to write his treatise:

> More than twenty years prior to the present day, a controversy about refined sugar [*sukkar al-qālab al-muṣaffā*] had occurred. It was prompted by a report [*qawl*] of one of the merchants who frequently visited the countries of the Christians [*bilād al-naṣārā*] for trade. He saw that the Christians in one of the countries put blood into the cooking of [raw] sugar for refining [*taṣfiya*] it, until it finally became white and hard, the form in which it arrives in Muslim countries.[31] The news reached the Commander of the Believers [*amīr al-muʾminīn*], Mawlāy Sulaymān [r. 1792–1822], who referred the matter, as was his custom, to the people of knowledge. They all responded [to the issue] with permission [*ibāḥa*] [to use European-manufactured sugar], based on a legal

> presumption regarding the state of affairs [*al-aṣl fī al-ashyā'*] and the nullification of doubt, as established in a legal case.[32] Some of them, however, refrained [from giving immediate permission]. They reexamined the matter, clarified the approach [to the subject] for those who sought advice, and conveyed [an opinion] that heals illness and removes obstacles of doubt and imagination.[33]

In support of his point, al-Zarhūnī now mentions three prominent Fāsī scholars and legal specialists (two of them were his teachers) who wrote on the subject: Sīdī Muḥammad b. 'Abd al-Salām al-Nāṣirī (d. 1823), Sīdī Muḥammad b. Aḥmad al-Rahūnī (d. 1815), and Sīdī Muḥammad al-Ṭayyib b. Kīrān (d. 1812). Furthermore, he is careful to note that other eminent legal specialists and knowledgeable scholars of the time had engaged the issue. In other words, al-Zarhūnī emphasizes that the issue of sugar manufactured in Europe and imported into Morocco had already been discussed by the most qualified people and that the legal authorization to use it had been categorically accepted. Al-Zarhūnī concludes by dismissing the controversy and determining that "a dispute with anybody who disagrees about the present case, based merely on his uninformed [*mujarrad*] opinion, deserves no attention." He finally invokes the authority of Mālik b. Anas, the founder of the school, who was careful to decide on any course of action based on clear and indisputable evidence, adding that to this day, there are righteous people who adhere to Mālik's approach and authorize the use of sugar, in food or beverage, voluntarily or as medication, at any given time, night or day.[34]

Al-Zarhūnī referred to a controversy that occurred twenty years before the composition of his treatise. The controversy about imported sugar, he reports, had resurfaced at the present time. Once again, it was instigated by a report of a merchant who claimed that "he heard from some of the Christians and Jews that it [sugar] is refined with the bones of a dead animal that is impure and cannot be eaten ['*iẓām al-mayta*]."[35] Al-Zarhūnī describes the upheaval that ensued as follows:

> The turmoil over it and gossip about it increased; arguments and insults occurred among people, until suspicion and misgiving set in the hearts of the common people ['*awāmm al-mu'minīn*], members of the community of believers. [Consequently,] requests to clarify its juridical status [*ḥukm*] and explain the true conduct [*ḥaqq*] for every believer increased.[36]

It was at this point that al-Zarhūnī was asked "to stipulate that which satisfies a burning thirst and cures a sick person." He assembled and arranged his material and named the lengthy work *Tuḥfat al-sā'il al-rāghib fī bayān al-ḥukm fī sukkar al-qālab* (A precious gift for the interested questioner: Clarification of the juridical status of sugarloaf). Again, he invokes his subordination to God: "I seek God's help and I rely on him, for He is the most powerful supporter."[37]

Introduction

In the introduction to the treatise, al-Zarhūnī defines a fundamental theme of his analysis and deliberations. He opens with a verse of a poem that serves as the thrust of his statement: "Those who passed did not leave with those who remained [distinction in knowledge] // apart from adhering to knowledge obtained through transmission."[38] Al-Zarhūnī specifically identifies the opinions and doctrines laid down by earlier generations as authoritative statements from which he derives his ruling and his juristic epistemology. In a self-conscious manner, he situates his undertaking within an authoritative and binding tradition. He explicitly insists on inferring his methods and ways from knowledge based on authoritative texts in contrast to uninformed opinions formulated without textual support.

Reflecting on the task at hand, al-Zarhūnī explains the role he assigned to the treatise:

> Given that knowledge [*'ilm*], as it is said, was already ground, refined, and consumed, there is nothing left but to consider the sayings of the people and set them down. For there is no calamity [*muṣība*] in lack of knowledge, but there is calamity in not correcting it to make it right, as was said by the founding master of our school, Mālik.[39]

Al-Zarhūnī promises to reveal the rules that govern the use of imported refined sugar. The real issue for him is to replace incorrect, uninformed opinions with correct ones constructed on the basis of clear and unequivocal evidence sanctioned by tradition. In an attempt to accentuate the challenge that he faced, al-Zarhūnī cites a statement attributed to the Mālikī jurist Qāḍī 'Iyāḍ (d. 1149), who held that "setting ahead that which God postponed and setting back that which God set ahead [trigger] great strife [*fitna*] and corruption [*fasād*] on earth."[40] Thus, establishing the correct opinion and removing the incorrect ones are imperative.

Having stated his immediate concern, al-Zarhūnī appeals to those Moroccans who had debated this critical case and claimed to possess knowledge that qualified them to establish proper Islamic ethics and values. He maintains that it is incumbent upon the people who became absorbed in this affair to fill their time realizing their responsibilities. Al-Zarhūnī warns these Moroccans that abandoning their responsibilities and devoting themselves to other things, such as pursuing whim (*hawā*), leads to the abyss (*huwā*).[41]

He explains that false belief in the divinity (*rubūbīya*) or prophecy (*nubūwa*) of anyone who does not have sufficient knowledge leads humankind to great harm in its faith, knowledge, and conviction. In support of his analysis, al-Zarhūnī interjects a discussion attributed to Aḥmad b. ʿAbdallāh al-Sijilmāsī, also known as Abū Maḥallī (d. 1613), who held that the two practices that led to the condemned circumstances during his time were (1) negligence in devotion and dedication to duties and obligations and (2) studying law and religion from false doctrine and stagnant opinions, based on the ignorance of many deceived and misled men.[42] Al-Zarhūnī's message is clear: people should focus on fulfilling their responsibilities and stay away from misinformed opinions that lead them away from the straight path and the imperatives of the religion.

His recommendation is immediately followed by a rhetorical question: "What gives those who have become absorbed in this affair [of the imported refined sugar] the right to spend uselessly their lives in [nothing more than] idle talk about their [insubstantial] opinions?" Al-Zarhūnī obviously rejects the rumor as an ignorant and unfounded opinion that leads to preoccupation with unsound banalities. To support his position, he cites three statements attributed to ʿAbdallāh Ibn ʿUmar (d. 693), the son of the second caliph and a prominent authority in law. First, al-Zarhūnī invokes Ibn ʿUmar's response to those who asked him whether the blood of fleas is pure or impure. Before responding, Ibn ʿUmar asked his questioners: "Who are you? They said: The people of Kūfa. He then said: How astonishing! You shed the blood of your prophet's son, Ḥusayn [b. ʿAlī], and here you are asking about the blood of fleas." The second statement attributed to Ibn ʿUmar cited by al-Zarhūnī: "You avoid [eating] lizard because it is small, but you eat a pig with his hair and droppings."[43] Finally, al-Zarhūnī notes Ibn ʿUmar's "excellent saying: A characteristic symptom of pursuing whim is the rush toward the good things that are easily gained [*nawāfil al-khayrāt*] and negligence in fulfilling one's duties."[44] Al-Zarhūnī invokes Ibn ʿUmar's statements to the effect that pursuing unfounded trivialities distracts from fulfilling the imperatives of religion. Al-Zarhūnī concludes this section of the introduction by invoking divine sovereignty and human subordination to God, who "leads to that which is right and guides to the true answer."

Having declared that those Moroccans who debated this highly sensitive case should promote the goals and aims of Islam by fulfilling their duties and avoiding unfounded opinions that threaten the moral fabric of Muslim society, al-Zarhūnī now introduces his argument. In line with the legal precedent that was set earlier in connection with the first rumor, he states: "Know that the rumor [*khabar*] that was spread by these people does not have any effect on the permission [to consume] sugar, which is [based on] a legal presumption regarding the state of affairs."[45] In other words, for al-Zarhūnī, the present rumor spreads confusion and deception. Clearly, for him, the legal determination regarding the status of sugar must be based upon Mālikī doctrine and a legal presumption that authorizes the consumption of sugar.

Let us suppose for the sake of argument, al-Zarhūnī suggests, that the rumor has a basis (*aṣl*):

> It is possible that the rumor [originated in] a fallacious or suspicious report, or [is based on] a sight that cannot be determined because of distance, or an attack [*ṣawla*] by someone who is feared. If we assume that the rumor is true, it is possible that it occurred in a particular territory at a particular time for a particular purpose, and there is no rule [*ḥukm*] suitable for a rare case [*nādir*]. Clearly, [this is not useful and] it benefits only the doubt, which does not supersede an established legal presumption in matters of rejection [*ṭarḥ*] of food.[46]

This segment of al-Zarhūnī's analysis concludes the introduction of his treatise.

In the substantive part of his discussion, al-Zarhūnī focuses on five jurisprudential issues that refute the rumor: (1) the consumption of food manufactured by Christians is lawful; (2) the manufacture of sugar is achieved through the removal of impurities, thereby purifying it; (3) determining a legal case based on sheer probabilities is forbidden; (4) a view that is based upon a rare opinion may take precedence over the preponderant state of affairs; and (5) attributing the red color to blood results from insufficient understanding.

The Refutation of the Rumor

1. It is permitted (ḥalāl) to eat the food of ahl al-kitāb[47] At this critical juncture in his argument, al-Zarhūnī invokes the authority of Mālik, who on one occasion was asked about the juridical status of cheese (*jubn*) manufactured by Christians and found in their homes. It was said that it contains the gastric juice of the stomach (in Arabic, *nafḥa*; literally, odor) of a pig.[48] Mālik responded to the query as follows: "I do not like to forbid that which is allowed, but if a person considers it reprehensible, I do not see harm in it."[49] Mālik's statement provided al-Zarhūnī with textual authority demonstrating that the founder of the school considered food manufactured by Christians lawful despite the offense that may be committed in its production. He writes, "Here is the leader of all leaders and a scholar of Medina in the best of times, who did not forbid the consumption of cheese manufactured by Christians despite the allegations against it and who considered it among their food that is permitted by God. And sugar, which is allegedly refined with blood, is the first and most important food that is permitted."[50]

As further support for his claim that food produced by Christians is permitted, al-Zarhūnī turns now to discuss Mālikī legal doctrine. Confident in his audience's familiarity with Mālikī law, he determines that the legal presumption (*aṣl*) may take precedence over the preponderant state of affairs (*ghālib*), out of necessity. He argues that although the preponderant state of affairs regarding food produced by infidels maintains that it is associated with [the legal category of] impurities (*najāsāt*), the legal presumption upholds the permissibility of their food, due to necessity.[51] Thus, al-Zarhūnī states, it is necessary to disregard the issue of impurity (in order to avert undue) distress (*ḥaraj*) and harm (*ḍarar*) and to adhere to the legal presumption.

To persuade his audience, al-Zarhūnī finds textual authority for this point in an opinion attributed to Abū al-Ḥasan al-Abyārī (d. 1219), who asserted that, according to the Mālikī legal practice, an opinion must be based upon the preponderant state of affairs, except if that would lead to great difficulty or entail useless spending of a considerable amount of money. However, out of necessity or due to considerations of social need, it is permissible to adhere to the legal presumption. Under such circumstances, he argued, the latter applies and we avoid the preponderant state of affairs. Al-Zarhūnī immediately adds that a similar statement was made by the distinguished Mālikī jurist Shihāb al-Dīn al-Qarāfī (d. 1285).[52]

Al-Zarhūnī continues to mention four earlier cases that treat the juridical status of goods manufactured by Christians. First, he invokes a saying attributed to Ibn ʿUmar, who related that the Prophet Muḥammad was offered cheese produced by Christians in the Tabūk Oasis in the Ḥijāz. Upon accepting it, "he asked for a knife, invoked the name of God, cut through it, and ate it." Second, al-Zarhūnī cites a statement from the *ʿUtbiyya* of the Cordovan jurist Muḥammad al-ʿUtbī (d. 868 or 869): When Mālik b. Anas was told that the People of Protection (*ahl al-dhimma*) were in the habit of wetting yarn with their hands while preparing woven fabric, his response was to declare that there is no objection to this.[53] Third, al-Zarhūnī argues that commentators on the *Mukhtaṣar*[54] held that all goods manufactured by infidels conform to the Islamic prescriptions of purity and, therefore, are permitted. They explain that the infidels uphold the various religious prohibitions to some extent; otherwise, people would avoid buying their products. Finally, al-Zarhūnī asserted that al-Burzulī (d. 1437 or 1440) espoused a similar juridical position.[55] In all four instances, products manufactured by the infidels were considered permissible.

Having nearly finished this section of the treatise, al-Zarhūnī now makes a hypothetical presumption. Suppose that, for the sake of argument, the contamination (*tanjīs*) of sugar by Christians was established thoroughly and repeatedly in the past. Yet eating it was not declared forbidden, and buying it was not declared prohibited. Indeed, he suggests, many religious scholars are ready to excuse what has become with time a general necessity and a common judicial practice (*ʿamal*) in all countries, without exception.[56] He finds textual authority for this position in Mālik's unequivocal approval of woven fabric manufactured by infidels. He also cites a statement from *Tuḥfat al-Ḥukkām*, the celebrated work of Ibn ʿĀṣim (d. 1427) on Andalusian *ʿamal*: "They authorized dung [*zibl*] in cases of necessity." Put differently, al-Zarhūnī argues that the legal presumption, that is, permission to consume food manufactured by Christians in general, and sugar in particular, is justified on the basis of necessity and was never disputed in the past. Expressing his confidence in his line of reasoning, he concludes: "No one ignores that, except someone who is not committed to learning from the legal rulings of the school [*furūʿ al-madhhab*]."[57]

2. The production of sugar involves the removal of impurities (najāsāt) in a manner that restores its purity[58] Al-Zarhūnī next defends his position by addressing the question of sugar purity. He argues that the different processes used to prepare sugar render it permissible (*ṣalāḥ*). He compares sugar to musk, a perfume extracted from the gland of the male musk deer, used in medicine and cooking.[59] Musk is the end product of a considerable processing that, al-Zarhūnī explains, transforms a part of an animal into permissible perfume. As support for this point, al-Zarhūnī refers to al-Ḥaṭṭāb (d. 1547), who said that the permission to consume musk is on the basis of necessity and that statements by religious scholars permitting a pilgrim (*muḥrim*) the consumption of food dipped in musk is the proof of this.[60]

Now, al-Zarhūnī invokes five legal precedents that consider the legal question of how to treat objects defiled by impurities. First, he notes that al-Burzulī confirmed the permission to use what was stained by blood or urine upon turning the substance of impurity into a permissible one. Second, he mentions that Abū al-Ḥasan al-Zarwīlī, known as al-Ṣughayyir (d. 1319), said: "It is stipulated that blood becomes pure (*ṭāhir*) if it is not removed after washing." Third, al-Zarhūnī reports that in his *Nawāzil*, Ibn al-Ḥājj (d. 1139) transmitted a *ḥadīth* from the *Muṣannaf* of ʿAbd al-Razzāq (d. 827) attributed to ʿUmar b. al-Khaṭṭāb, saying that when ʿUmar considered forbidding wearing clothes stained by urine, a man asked him if he did not see the Prophet himself wearing them. To this ʿUmar replied: Correct. The man then insisted, asking if God did not command: "You have indeed a noble paradigm in the apostate of God" (Q 33:21)? In turn, ʿUmar decided to leave the matter unchanged. Next, al-Zarhūnī cites a statement attributed to ʿAbd al-Razzāq: I saw Abū ʿAbdallāh al-Zuhrī wearing clothes that were dipped in urine. Finally, al- Zarhūnī claims that a similar report was related by al-Bukhārī about Maʿmar.[61] The message is clear: Objects that are defiled by impurities may become pure and thereupon are lawful.

Next, al- Zarhūnī applies this conclusion to sugar:

> Sugar is transformed into pure food by many processes [*aʿmāl*], such as a series of repeated boiling, pouring into different molds according to the stages of cooking, and other processes that are mentioned in the *Tadhkira*.[62] First, you see it as deep red liquid, then it becomes shining white, solid as a stone or even harder, and there is no trace of the substance [*ʿayn*] of impure blood in it at all: no color, no taste, no smell. And if it is determined that the substance of the impurity is gone, then there is no meaning to prohibit what remains.[63]

As further support for his position, al-Zarhūnī examines a second case that is similar to the case of sugar. The case, which is mentioned in *al-Riḥla al-ʿAyyāshiyya* of Abū Sālim ʿAbdāllah al-ʿAyyāshī al-Fāsī (d. 1679–80), deals with a blanket (*millaf*) made in Christian countries from wool sheared from live sheep. In this instance, al-Zarhūnī explains, "The impurity does not remain after the numerous processes that turn the wool into an intensely processed blanket, such as washing, pounding, inflating, cutting, spinning, and weaving. Indeed, the impurity disappears entirely, and therefore, it is not forbidden to wear it because it was established that the substance of the impurity had been removed."[64] These processes, which prevail in the manufacturing of sugar and wool blankets, al-Zarhūnī continues, are commonly used in the manufacture of many other products, such as olive oil (*zayt*). He mentions a fatwā issued by Abū ʿAbdallāh al-Māzarī (d. 1141), who even permitted the use of impure olive oil, drawing on the authoritative opinions of the school. Finally, al-Zarhūnī argues that the practices of purging the impure substance through numerous refining processes are more evident in the manufacture of sugar and oil than in that of food cooked with mouse droppings. Yet Ibn ʿArafa issued a fatwā permitting eating such food.[65]

3. *Making a legal determination based upon mere probabilities is forbidden* Al-Zarhūnī now suggests that it cannot conceivably be argued that European-manufactured sugar has any residue of the impure blood, because of the extensive processing, as well as for another reason. He explains:

> We understand this probability [*iḥtimāl*] as one among many reasonable presumptions [*al-tajwīzāt al-ʿaqliyya*], which are not considered in judicial cases [*aḥkām al-fiqhiyya*], because probability always reasonably exists in many things. There is no food, beverage, garment, or anything else for which it is not reasonable to conceive that it has something impure in it, and this probability is never refuted due to the repetition of the refining processes.

Consequently, in the case under consideration, a legal determination should be based upon the customary legal norm (*ḥukm al-ʿāda*), not upon a sheer presumption.[66]

He continues his analysis, reasoning that even if the sheer presumption is plausible, based upon the assumption that imperfection in the refining process results in blood residue in refined sugar, there is still no reason to deny its purity. In determining the purity of all impure things, we follow a clear practice according to which a series of refining processes and repeated procedures transforms anything and makes it into a product that is incomparable in every way with what it was initially.[67] In other words, al-Zarhūnī argues that even if one follows the reasonable presumption that some blood remains in refined sugar, it is still against school doctrine to nullify its purity because of the understanding that defiled things can be purified.

Focusing his attention on the probability that blood residue is found in sugar, al-Zarhūnī argues that "this is the essence of the futile thought [*waswasa*], [and heeding it] is forbidden."[68] He cites opinions and earlier authorities to support his assertion that consideration of *waswasa*, by definition, is impermissible. He writes, "It was said that *waswasa* is a confusion of the mind and ignorance in the *sunna* of the Prophet. We seek the protection of God against the futile thought of the pious, who stray from the right path of understanding the teachings of religion." He invokes Qur'ān 5:87: "O believers, do not forbid the good things God has made lawful for you; and do not transgress. God does not love transgressors."[69]

Next, he draws on two *ḥadīth* reports of the Prophet. First, it is reported that Muḥammad said,

> God prescribed religious duties [*farā'iḍ*]; do not neglect them. And He fixed *ḥudūd* punishments [sing. *ḥadd*]; do not transgress them.[70] And He prohibited things; do not violate them. And He was silent about certain things, out of compassion to you, not forgetfulness; do not question them.

According to the second *ḥadīth*,

> When a man told the Prophet, "I refrain from eating some of the food [produced by Christians]," he said, "Do not fill your heart [with futile ideas] about anything coming from Christianity."[71]

Al-Zarhūnī's invocation of the two *ḥadīth* reports offers proof of the illicitness of heeding vain thoughts.

As further proof that making presumptions about the possible impurity of imported sugar contradicts the precepts of religion, al-Zarhūnī addresses the ethical example of the Companions. He notes that according to the *Iḥyā' 'ulūm al-dīn* of Abū Ḥāmid al-Ghazālī (d. 1111), "the Companions were concerned with the purity of hearts and were tolerant in matters relating to impurity. They walked barefoot on the soil of streets and sat in it; they prayed on the ground in mosques; they ate flour made from wheat and barley that had been threshed by animals that urinated and dropped dung on it; and they were not careful of the sweat of camels and horses, even though they rolled in impurities. In addition, it has not been reported that they asked any question about the particular details of impurities." This demonstrates their tolerance thereof.[72]

Further, al-Ghazālī claimed:

> The thrust of the case [*nawba*] today amounts to a group of people who consider foolishness [*ru'ūna*] as cleanliness and say that the latter is the foundation of our religion. They spend most of their time beautifying themselves externally, the way a lady's maid [*māshiṭa*] treats her bride, while the inward lies in ruins, loaded with evil ideas, pride, ignorance, insincerity, and hypocrisy, and they neither reject it nor are amazed by it. If anyone allows a thing that the Companions [permitted] out of tolerance, they become upset with him, reject him intensely,

> label him a *Qadarī*,[73] expel him from their group, and reject eating and associating with him. They deem untidiness that is accepted by the Islamic faith as impurity, and foolishness as purity.

"Consider," al-Ghazālī writes, "how the forbidden [*munkar*] became generally accepted [*ma'rūf*], and the generally accepted became forbidden, and how the contour [*rasm*] of the Islamic religion was obliterated, just like its execution [*taḥqīq*] and wisdom."[74] For al-Zarhūnī, al-Ghazālī's passage illustrates the fraud and phoniness in the contemporary preoccupation with the purity of sugar. The Companions, who carry the highest authority, displayed toleration toward impurities, whereas the scrutiny and agitation during al-Ghazālī's time amounted to bigotry.

Al-Zarhūnī concludes this section of his argument as follows: It is clear from what is mentioned above that despite the probability of impurity, the community of legal specialists permitted the consumption of food manufactured by People of the Book, in accordance with the Qur'ānic verse.[75] He refers to a fatwā issued by the Andalusian jurist Abū Bakr Muḥammad Ibn al-'Arabī (d. 1148), which appears in his *Aḥkām al-Qur'ān*. In it, he authorized the consumption of the meat of animals slaughtered by infidels in a manner inconsistent with the ritual prescribed by Islamic law (known as *dhakāt*).[76] The fatwā, al-Zarhūnī notes, was confirmed by later generations based on the rationale that meat is part of the food of the infidels, which is permissible. Al-Zarhūnī continues his line of reasoning:

> It is well known that the described sugar is the first and foremost among their foodstuff that is permissible. It is also known that the Christians purify sugar with substances other than blood in many places in their countries; some refine it with eggs and others with lime, depending on what is known and familiar. Consequently, the imported sugar sold here is probably refined without blood and should be valued for its basic quality, its sweetness. This was carefully stipulated about all products imported from Christian countries, in accordance with the principles of the *madhhab*.[77]

Finally, al-Zarhūnī invokes the authority of the Cordovan jurist Ibn Rushd (d. 1126). In his *al-Bayān*, a commentary on the *'Utbiyya*, he said, "It is not forbidden for anyone who has a sister he does not know in a certain country to marry from that country. The matter is analogous to a case about lice that fell into flour that was then kneaded [to make dough]."[78] Ibn Rushd clearly recognized the invalidity of unqualified probabilities. By citing his position, al-Zarhūnī supports his opinion that in making a legal determination, one should not follow a mere probability.

4. In making a legal determination, a view that is based upon a rare opinion may take precedence over the preponderant state of affairs Al-Zarhūnī next defends his position by invoking the authority of the great thirteenth-century jurist Shihāb al-Dīn al-Qarāfī (d. 1285). Al-Zarhūnī reports that in *al-Furūq*, al-Qarāfī mentions cases in which the law gives precedence to a view based upon a rare opinion (*nādir*) over the preponderant state of affairs (*ghālib*), out of compassion to mankind. The people, however, disregarded the authorized opinions and were possessed by futile thoughts (*waswās*); they firmly believed that they should follow the school's foundational principle, according to which the *ghālib* must be applied, even though the law of Islam rendered it invalid. Al-Zarhūnī notes that al-Qarāfī's discussion contains twenty cases, examples of instances in which the law asserts the precedence of a rare opinion over a preponderant state of affairs. Among these cases, al-Qarāfī specifically addresses the question of food manufactured by Muslims who do not wash with water and are not careful against impurities. According to al-Zarhūnī, al-Qarāfī's analysis reveals that while the preponderant state of affairs holds that such food is impure, the rare opinion regards it as safe and sound, and the doctrine confirms the authoritative status of the rare opinion as a respite to mankind.[79]

Al-Zarhūnī continues his analysis, focusing his attention on an additional case in which a rare opinion takes precedence over a preponderant state of affairs. He examines the question of *ṣāmit*, a certain beverage made of grapes, which comes from the Ghumāra Mountains in northern Morocco and is sold in the markets of Tetuan and other cities, despite the well-known circumstances of its producers, especially their excessive consumption and catering (*munāwala*) of wine, and the preponderant state of affairs, according to which their utensils and dishes are used for the handling of wine. The question regarding the legality of *ṣāmit*, al-Zarhūnī writes, was mentioned in *al-Ajwiba al-Fāsiyya* of ʿAbd al-Qādir al-Fāsī (d. 1680), who argued that the rule for the case authorizes its consumption, according to a rare opinion. Al-Fāsī further explained that the opinion is justified on the principle of avoiding distress and difficulty, conforming to the principles of the *madhhab*.[80] Al-Zarhūnī approves al-Fāsī's conclusion that authorizes the rare opinion in the case of *ṣāmit* and advises his reader to consider the original text.[81] For al-Zarhūnī, the previous discussion provides "a clear proof that when it comes to probability [*iḥtimāl*], the legal presumption, even if it is [based on] a rare opinion, takes precedence over the preponderant state of affairs. It is evident that the question of [European-manufactured] sugar is among matters of probability and its juridical status is pure and permitted."[82]

He returns to an issue discussed earlier, noting that the cause of impurity is removed by a series of processes that refine the sugar. He emphasizes that sugar manufacturing is similar to the production of musk and vinegar, which also involves the removal of impurities and the transformation of tainted products into pure and permissible food. As the coagulated blood in the case of musk and the intoxicants in the wine are dried, both products become permissible. He adds that sugar is distinct from cheese manufactured by Christians, "for it is well known that the gastric juice of an impure dead animal [*mayta*] is mixed in it, noticeable, and does not leave it," yet Mālik did not declare it unlawful. As for sugar, "assuming that it is refined with blood, there is no noticeable blood residue in it."[83]

Al-Zarhūnī next cites an opinion attributed to Ibn Juzayy al-Gharnāṭī (d. 1340–41) in which he addressed God's statement in the Qur'ān, "and made lawful for you is the food of the people of the Book" (Q. 5:5):

> As for food [of the *ahl al-kitāb*], it is divided into three categories: First, ritually slaughtered animals [*ḍabā'iḥ*]. The religious scholars agreed that this category of food is permissible according to the Qur'ānic verse. Second, food such as wheat and fruit that does not involve processes of manufacturing [*muḥāwala*]. This category of food is permitted unanimously. Third, food that involves processes of manufacturing, such as baking bread, pressing olive oil, and making cheese. The food in this category involves processes that might instill impurity in it. Ibn 'Abbās [d. 687–88] prohibited the food of this category, because he held that [the category of] permitted food refers exclusively to the slaughtered animal and because the third category of food might be impure. However, the majority of jurists permitted [the consumption of food of the third category] because they were of the opinion that this category belongs to permitted food.[84]

Obviously, al-Zarhūnī asserts, sugar pertains to the third food category. According to the majority opinion, food in this category is permissible based on a legal presumption regarding the state of affairs. It follows, he declares, from all the opinions we conveyed and the school's foundational principles to which we referred, that the variety of refined sugar imported from Christian countries, molded or not, is legally permitted for sweetening, based on adherence to the legal presumption and despite the probability that it may be refined with blood.[85]

Furthermore, al-Zarhūnī argues that "there are no uncertainties [*shubuhāt*] that require refraining from using it [sugar] on the basis of piety [*wara'*]." The term *shubuhāt* [sing. *shubha*] signifies a "likeness" or "resemblance." As a legal notion, it refers to uncertainties or doubts resulting from a resemblance between an illicit action and a licit one. Because of the resemblance between the two actions, Islamic law averts the prescribed punishment while continuing to view the action as unlawful.[86] In the present case, al-Zarhūnī avers, there are no uncertainties or doubts.

To persuade his audience, al-Zarhūnī cites an opinion attributed to Abū al-Ḥasan al-Abyārī that clarifies the issue of *shubuhāt*. In his text, al-Abyārī explains that the legal category of *shubuhāt* is applied to things or actions that are prohibited due to doubt (*iltibās*). *Shubha* is designated to anything "that is not real [*lā ḥaqīqa lahu*] and belongs to the category of imagination [*min jins al-awhām*] . . . and is used in opposition to proof [*muqābala al-dalīl*], that is, it resembles another thing to the extent that something that is not proved is imagined to be proved." As further support for his point, al-Abyārī invokes a *ḥadīth* of the Prophet, who said, "That which is lawful is clear, and that which is prohibited is clear, and between them matters that are uncertain [*mushtabihāt*]." The problem, al-Abyārī explains, is with the middle group, that is, the *shubha*:

> Lawful without exception is that from which the forbidden quality [*ṣifa*] and the reasons for its flaws [*khalāl*] were banished; prohibited is that which has in it a forbidden quality, such as alcohol, or was produced for a reason that is unlawful, such as coercion and usury. Both categories are clear, and everything pertaining to them follows the rule [for the case in question]. However, if it is conceivable that something different occurred without any proof or sign to indicate this probability, this is not a form of *shubuhāt*, because *shubha* springs from doubt [*shakk*]. Be mindful of the difference between doubt and probability. [Considering something as unlawful and refraining from using it] on the basis of piety should be restricted to cases of doubt and not to mere probabilities.[87]

In his analysis, al-Abyārī identifies *shubha* as a legal category applied in cases that emanate from doubt or uncertainty in contrast to the consideration of a mere probability that is speculative. According to al-Zarhūnī, this opinion supports his argument. The rumor that European sugar reaching Morocco had been refined with blood cannot be classified as *shubha* but rather as hypothetical probability (*iḥtimāl*), which means that its consumption must not be viewed as unlawful.

Al-Zarhūnī now turns to consider al-Abyārī's discourse on the operation of social need and necessity as grounds for abandoning the preponderant state of affairs. Al-Abyārī held that "whenever necessity requires adherence to the legal presumption and avoidance of the preponderant state of affairs, we apply that. The evidence for this is found in the Qur'ān and the practice [*'amal*] of the Companions and the Followers." As support for his assertion, al-Abyārī first invoked the Qur'ān: "And made lawful for you is the food of the People of the Book" (Q. 5:5). It is well known, he declared, that the People of the Book do not protect against impurities and are less concerned with the use of running water for purification than Muslims, and therefore, their food is associated with impurities. Nevertheless, according to the authorized norms, it is necessary to disregard the issue of impurity because of difficulty (*ḥaraj*) and harm (*ḍarar*). Next, al-Abyārī reported that the Companions of the Prophet Muḥammad plunged into wet soil, performed the prayer, and did not wash [the dirt] out. Likewise, they performed the prayer, prostrating on fabric that was woven by *ahl al-dhimma*. By drawing on these reports, al-Abyārī revealed that the legacy of the Companions sanctioned his position that considerations of social necessity justify departure from the preponderant state of affairs. Finally, al-Abyārī discussed the practice of the *madhhab*. He claimed that Mālik disapproved the leftover water (*su'r*) of Christians, but he excused the use of it out of consideration for the scarcity of water and the ease and comfort of using it.[88] Al-Abyārī maintained that by permitting Christians' food and beverage leftovers, Mālik may have taken into consideration the general need and did not neglect it on the basis of piety.

For al-Abyārī, the proper Islamic conduct was established by drawing upon the Qur'ān, the authority of the Companions, and Mālik's teachings. This, he concluded, is a significant element in the elaboration of Islamic law. He argues,

> Legal cases [*aḥkām*] should not be determined upon mere imagination and association of that which is allowed with that which is prohibited. It is necessary to determine legal cases on evidence [*adilla*], correct understanding of the different parts of the issue at hand, and knowledge of the spirit [*nafs*] of the sharī'a as it pertains to every principle. Let it be known that the Companions of the Prophet Muḥammad, who were most knowledgeable in the sharī'a and effective in piety, did not care for this kind of restriction [*taḍyīq*] and did not establish their concerns upon imaginations. If a man, a follower of the doctrine of Mālik, refrains from drinking milk and eating food, which unconfined chickens have touched, he is incorrect in doing it, because Mālik did not object to that. There-

> fore, it is not permitted to [determine legal norms] on account of piety in cases based upon mere imaginations that are not derived from evidence.[89]

Al-Abyārī's text explicitly demonstrated within the context of the bindingness of the Qur'ān and the opinions of the Companions and Followers that the principle of necessity was used to justify departure from a preponderant state of affairs and reinforcement of the legal presumption.

Now, al-Zarhūnī was ready to conclude this segment of his analysis: "From the foregoing it must have become clear to you that [European-manufactured] sugar is permissible. It is one of the good things [*ṭayyibāt*] that are permitted, and it is not necessary to refrain from consuming it on the basis of piety because it is not from the category of *shubuhāt*, as was already demonstrated." To support his assertion, he invokes God's question in the Qur'ān, "Who forbids you attire that God has given to his creatures and the good things that he has provided?" (Q 7:32). He determines that this is the truth from which no one deviates except for a weak person, content with himself, whose transgression was presented to him in a favorable light and he saw it as obedience, or who did not learn "that forbidding that which God allows and permitting that which God forbids are one and the same. Because one gets close to God not through reason [*'uqūl*] but rather through the transmitted law of Islam. We are adherents of tradition [*muqallidūn*], and we deem it important to follow what is required by the texts of the *madhhab*."[90]

5. Attributing the red color to blood stems from inadequate perception Al-Zarhūnī next argues that the suspicion that "the red color at the initial cooking of the sugar comes from blood mixed in it is an error [*ghalaṭ*] that originates from insufficient understanding and lack of acuteness. This red color is the substance of sugar [*'ayn al-sukkar*]." It is like the red color in a brazilwood tree (*'andam*), he writes, which comes from purity of origin (*aṣāla*), not from blood. Perhaps traces of red color returned to the juice following the cooking processes when it encountered heat or cooling humidity. He claims,

> This is the truth we learned from people who observe and hear. It was mentioned to us by the most important ambassadors of the Moroccan state to Europe, who do not fail to see clearly and do not get things mixed up, because of their high degree of knowledge, culture, and vigilant research of everything they see and hear, especially strange things [*gharā'ib*] that we do not have. Similarly, this was mentioned to us by the most successful merchants who travel to many Islamic and Christian states.

In support of the reliability of knowledge shared by merchants, al-Zarhūnī explains that sugar is abundant in Islamic states like other sweet extracts that are red, such as honey, the juice of sugar cane, licorice, grape, and date.[91]

Al-Zarhūnī now suggests that jurists have presented in detailed works, in the past and more recently, authoritative statements about the types of sugar and the variety of its uses. All of them, he asserts, mentioned that it is red at the initial cooking, but no one mentioned that it is contaminated with blood or other impurities. To illustrate his point, al-Zarhūnī cites a summary of a discussion attributed to Dā'ūd al-Anṭākī, author of the *Tadhkira*. In it, he described the processes involved in manufacturing (*ṣan'a*) and cooking (*ṭabkha*) the different types of sugar:

> Sugar manufacturing involves peeling, threshing, and pressing [to extract juice], using well-known tools. It is cooked until it becomes thick, whereupon it is poured into a large and wide clay pot whose upper part narrows gradually. It is left in this pot, covered with sugar cane leaves in a place inclined to warmth for approximately a week. This type of sugar is called *aḥmar*. Then, it is broken into pieces and cooked for a second time, poured into funnels, and suctioned from the upper part to remove any dirt. This sugar is called the *sulaymānī*. Then, it is cooked for a third time: If it is poured into an elongated mold without being cooked thoroughly, it is called *fānīd*; if its cooking continued and it is poured into a pinelike funnel, known as *ildaj*, or a rectangular one, it is called *qalam*. If it is cooked for a fourth time, poured into glass pots to which peels of sugar cane were woven, this type of sugar is called *qizāzī*. The latter is known in Syria. It is of excellent [quality] and is called today *ḥamawī*.[92]

In al-Zarhūnī's eyes, al-Anṭākī's classification confirms his argument that distinguished members of the community of jurists who examined the processes of sugar manufacturing did not refer to blood in their writings.

At this point, al-Zarhūnī notes that al-Anṭākī also mentions a list of countries that grow sugar cane and specifies that Egypt is currently the most important among them and that the Nile ensures its finest quality and abundance. Focusing his attention on Egypt, al-Zarhūnī declares that "it is well known that Egypt is the microcosm that brings together everything that is scattered in the whole entire world." He reports that "there are numerous imams of all the legal schools at all times in Egypt. And they have no other vocation than the determination of that which is permitted and that which is forbidden, and the examination of what happens in religion at all times. They never suspected that sugar manufacturing involves mixing impurities such as blood and the like, despite their preoccupation [*wuqūf*] with inspection of its nature and quality during all stages of production."[93] By emphasizing Egypt as an important supplier of sugar cane and a consumer of imported refined sugar, al-Zarhūnī links Morocco to the Arab East and the wider network of Islamic scholarship.

Drawing on the Egyptian example and some of the previous statements included in his opinion, al-Zarhūnī informs his reader that "Muslim religious scholars throughout the world excelled in investigating the benefit of products that reach us from Christian countries, but they very rarely doubted [their lawfulness]. For the most part, they preferred the opinion that regarded them as legal." Furthermore, al-Zarhūnī asserts, not a single one of them referred to imported sugar as an illegal product, despite its prevalence. He reminds his reader that sugar is indispensable in superb food and that without it a key ingredient in beverages, pastries, and other sweets and desserts is missing.[94] Moreover, those who should be most concerned about the issue are the country's most powerful people (*ahl al-ṣawla*). Indeed, councils of the powerful and influential are markets that attract rumors from remote countries and regions, yet, al-Zarhūnī explains, no one ever mentioned the rumor to them and no one heard them mentioning it. At the present time, al-Zarhūnī advises his reader, there is nothing to do but to forgive the originator of the rumor that provoked doubts in people's hearts based on sheer error.[95]

Al-Zarhūnī concludes this section of his argument by citing a case mentioned in *al-Riḥla al-ʿAyyāshiyya* of al-ʿAyyāshī al-Fāsī that was reported to him by his shaykh, Abū ʿAbdallāh Muḥammad b. Musāhil (d. 1663–64). Sidi ʿAlī al-Khuḍīrī is reported to have held that a musky substance called *zabād*, widely used in perfumes and medicine, is impure because it is the gland secretion of the civet cat, discharged from the musk pouch situated near the urinary tract. Shaykh Muḥammad b. Musāhil reportedly sent for a civet cat and ordered someone to extract the substance in his presence. He witnessed that the spot through which the substance is released was located outside the urinary tract and determined its purity. Al-Zarhūnī concludes by appealing to the reader: "Understand this wisdom and have a good opinion of the religious scholars. Know that they embrace the true religion from God and that they do not speak out of whim." Finally, he repeats the verse of poetry that opens his treatise and serves as a major thread of his argument: "How excellent is he who said: 'Those who passed did not leave with those who remained [distinction in knowledge] // apart from adhering to knowledge obtained through transmission.'"[96]

Conclusion

Al-Zarhūnī's discussion provides unequivocal doctrinal support for his claim that sugar manufactured in Europe is permissible. He signals the end of his treatise with the word *qultu*, "I say":

> [After all that, the best of all people,] people of wealth, culture, knowledge, religion and those who are in government, justice, and education, continue to use different types of sugar, in food and drink, in tea and other beverages. We have personally seen some of them and attained knowledge through trustworthy persons about others, and they continued to use sugar until they passed to the Hereafter. We never heard that anyone of them renounced it or warned anyone else about it. And these are the best of all people, who with their enlightened hearts comprehend things as they are; may God protect them from getting involved in prohibited or even reprehensible occurrences, because, as is well known, they have hearts with which they comprehend things that others fail to understand.
>
> We ask God to inspire us to integrity of conduct, to put us into work for our salvation, to cleanse our hearts and souls, to beautify our outer and inner selves, to protect us with that which He allows against that which He forbids, and not to deny us, on account of our ignorance, His good things, His food and beverage. He is abounding in grace and kindness. Praise be to God who is always worthy of glory. God bless and grant Muḥammad salvation and his noble family and his Companions, the eminent imams. Praise be to God, the lord of the two worlds. This is the end of the material that was available to be assembled. Praise be to God, now and forever.[97]

Subsequent Developments

Upon completing his treatise, al-Zarhūnī was compelled to add the newest developments in the controversy about imported sugar. Sensitive to the gravity of the case and the repercussions of his juridical opinion, he briefly presented new facts that bear a striking resemblance to those of the first affair. "Once more, after a period of time," al-Zarhūnī writes,

> Some merchants received news from merchants [who travel to] countries of the infidels that they saw large ships loaded with the bones of dead animals that are impure and cannot be eaten [*'iẓām al-mayta*] coming from everywhere. It became widely known that [the bones] are brought to be used in refining sugar, [according to the following steps: first,] by burning them until they become ashes, then putting the ashes through fine sieve until they become like flour, and

> finally, dropping them into a cooking pot containing sugar [juice] until they are dissolved in it. At first, when the ashes are dropped into the cooked sugar, they are immersed in it; next they rise and absorb the waste [*khabath*], which is then removed. To purify the sugar, this treatment is repeated. Finally, they pour it into molds until it thickens and dries in them.[98]

Al-Zarhūnī notes that the correct answer to the question of imported sugar was presented above, thereby emphasizing his approval of his first opinion: "These are the facts that were circulated persistently, and the useful material pertaining to its juridical status was mentioned above." He then refers in passing to another rumor that originated with one of the merchants in Marseille, who heard that some of the sugar is purified with human feces [*ʿadhirat al-ādamī*]. The merchant wrote asking for a legal opinion about the issue, stressing that he did not witness the refining process himself but that it was hearsay.

"Consider carefully," al-Zarhūnī continues, "[on the one hand,] these concerns and detailed news from the merchants and [on the other,] the stipulation of the law and the certainty in observing it, and act according to it." In his view, the answer was unequivocal: A rumor may not serve as the basis for any judicial decision. The stipulation of the law is clear and sound and must be applied in the present case. He determines that at present, nothing has been proved that can be used as a basis for a legal decision that would prohibit the consumption of sugar manufactured in Europe. The essence of the issue, he explains, remains the legal presumption regarding the state of affairs, that is, sugar is considered pure and, therefore, permissible. In addition, he comments, according to the preponderant state of affairs, Christians protect their products from impurities that may hurt sales and lead to weak demand or no demand at all. He appeals to his reader as follows: "Choose for yourself what delights and pleases the soul and heart. God takes care of us, and He puts in our hearts the right way to obey Him and the hate to disobey Him. He guides us and protects our religion with His grace and kindness. Peace upon anyone who is bound to Him. May God protect him with His mercy."[99]

FASHIONING A NEW COMPOSITION

Al-Mahdī al-Wazzānī, so I have suggested, was a dynamic and creative compiler of Mālikī wisdom. As the author-editor of a multivolume compilation of fatwās, he treated each text he included in it as an occasion to fashion a new composition. Indeed, I have argued that the creative act of authoring the compilation also involved the study of different works, gathering, assembling, and arranging the selected material in new constructions. In the compilation and arrangement of the material, al-Wazzānī highlights a complex dialogue between the particular historical concerns and practices of his time, on the one hand, and authoritative corpus, long-standing arguments, and methods of disputation pivotal within Mālikī tradition, on the other. It is this feature of the *New Mi'yār* that, in my view, reflects al-Wazzānī's originality and intricate understanding of Mālikī tradition as a dynamic one. In deliberately creating new legal constructions, al-Wazzānī attempted to recover and restore Mālikī thought as essential for the survival of Moroccan society under new, modern conditions. This approach is particularly discernible in the present text.

As al-Wazzānī was copying al-Zarhūnī's treatise into what would become the *New Mi'yār*, he was not satisfied merely with recording his predecessor's manuscript. To the treatise, al-Wazzānī attached four independent texts in a carefully designed arrangement. This intervention included one short poem written by al-Zarhūnī and three separate chapters (*faṣl*, pl. *fuṣūl*) written by al-Wazzānī. The editorial hand of al-Wazzānī that binds the four texts together points to the author's creativity and the innovative nature of his enterprise. The four texts treat the permissibility of three beverages: tea, an intoxicating drink called *mā' al-ḥayāh*, and coffee. The primary object of al-Wazzānī's new composition is to offer a series of legal cases in which the legal presumption regarding the state of affairs, which permits the consumption of these drinks, takes precedence over juridical arguments against consumption.

As I have shown, the growing consumption of tea, alcohol, and coffee in the late nineteenth century did not always meet with the approval of Moroccan authorities and religious scholars. I suggest that, in fashioning a new composition, al-Wazzānī not only rearranged al-Zarhūnī's treatise into a new order by making it a part of mosaic but connected it with other critical issues that were relevant in al-Wazzānī's own time. Thus, the new composition does not simply preserve al-Zarhūnī's sophisticated legal opinion that deems European-manufactured sugar permissible. Rather, it consciously locates al-Zarhūnī's treatise in a new historical context, thereby infusing it with contemporary relevance and, at the same time, offers al-Wazzānī's legal opinions that authorize the consumption of the three beverages the necessary Islamic discursive authority, consequently enabling al-Wazzānī to redefine a Mālikī discourse that accommodates structural and behavioral changes dictated by Moroccan modernity.

A Poem of al-Zarhūnī

First, al-Wazzānī attaches to the treatise a poem written by al-Zarhūnī. In it, he encourages tea drinking and praises it as a virtue that attests to one's adherence to conduct that was passed down through generations. The transition from the end of al-Zarhūnī's treatise to the attached poem is marked briefly. Al-Wazzānī does not identify the source of the material or explain why he included it in this new setting. He simply notes that the poem may clarify the legal opinion discussed previously. Al-Wazzānī quotes the poem as follows:

> Say to anyone who wants to obtain benefits, // gain happiness, and push away distress
> Drink tea and you gain // tall body filled with plenty of happiness
> Especially if you conform to // the good things that were given to us by those who passed away
> Such as Ambergris, fresh butter, clarified butter, // and a trustworthy friend from among the people of praise.[100]

It is worth noting that in his treatise, al-Zarhūnī does not address the link between the spread of sugar and the consumption of tea. However, as I have mentioned, by the time al-Wazzānī was compiling his *New Mi'yār*, tea had established itself as a popular beverage in Morocco and greatly reinforced the demand for sugar. I suggest that by positing a direct connection between the two texts, al-Wazzānī sought to meaningfully link them to the cultural context of his contemporaries and to authorize the tea-and-sugar custom.

First Chapter

Al-Wazzānī mentions that a certain qāḍī, one of his contemporaries, prohibited the drinking of tea and wrote about it. For al-Wazzānī, the reasons offered by the qāḍī for the prohibition of tea, in fact, demonstrate its legality, on the grounds of a legal presumption that considered it permissible (*aṣl al-ibāḥa*). In support of his point, al-Wazzānī quotes the two following verses from the qāḍī's opinion:

> I consider drinking tea today an unethical act that discredits a Muslim's credibility [*jurḥa*] // there is no integrity [*'adāla*] in it
> It was not declared prohibited or reprehensible, but // we considered every foolishness as closely connected to it.[101]

Al-Wazzānī next introduces some useful information about tea. It is, he writes, a plant that grows in China, and its buds and leaves resemble sugar cane.

The tea plant is harvested three times a year. The first harvest, which belongs to the sovereign, is the finest crop. The second harvest goes to the laborers and workers, while the third goes to the rest of the country's population. Merchants bring it to other countries, and this kind of tea, al-Wazzānī comments, is weak with respect to its quality and value, but it has benefits and special attributes. He cites a treatise (*risāla*) on the various advantages of tea drinking:

> Beware of liking wine // and reject the person who serves wine gently,
> Favor drinking tea that gives you pleasure // and is not followed by grief
> In drinking tea there is security and gathering of friendly company // in safety, and there is no safety in drinking wine
> Rather, there are dangers you cannot resist // and pleasures that do not grant benefit and happiness.[102]

Al-Wazzānī continues with another poem in praise of tea drinking, composed by Sulaymān b. Muḥammad al-Shafshāwanī, known as Sulaymān al-Ḥawāt (d. 1816):

> Stop drinking wine, because wine is an intoxicating drink// and according to the law of Islam, all intoxicating drinks are prohibited
> Fall in love with drinking tea because it is // permitted and there is no blame in the permissible
> Become addicted to it because it brings // cure for the soul when illness strikes it
> It provokes vital energy, and extends one's hand in generosity // and therefore all drinkers are honorable
> It lifts the sorrow of the soul privately and publicly // and opens man's eyelid when he sleeps
> It opens the door to the two best desires // which are sexual intercourse and food
> It covers softly the face with redness // as if there are roses watered by clouds in it
> It refines the essence of intellect with sophistication // and uncovers it from the darkness with understanding
> It always removes bad odor from the nose and mouth // and by means of it, one's personality and speech become pleasant
> It slows down ejaculation during sexual intercourse and thus provokes // pleasure, which is the very pinnacle of desire and longing
> It prevents the burning of thirst // and causes the waste in the urine that is toxic for you if held back to flow
> If gas is trapped in the stomach // it dissolves it naturally as well as one could possibly wish

As for its effective influence on digestion, talk about it // and do not be afraid of severe criticism for its usefulness is great
It makes the temperament agreeable in general // by moderating it and by means of it one gets strength
You can have it in the morning or at night // because it has its attributes in both situations
Furthermore, additional benefits [of tea] were experienced // and there are among the imams of the past who spoke about them
Its probity grows and excellence multiplies // if it is refined with drinking companions and a fine cup
It is the greatest pleasure and an elixir to every drinker // not coffee and wine
It is our opinion that nothing else enhances youthfulness // except of Ambergris potion.[103]

Second Chapter

In the second chapter, al-Wazzānī focuses on an intoxicating drink, "*mā' al-ḥayāh* [the water of life], which is produced by distillation [*taqṭīr*]."[104] He begins by explaining that "it is the strongest type of intoxicating beverage [*muskir*], so anyone who drinks wine gives preference to the latter over the former and does not drink it unless wine is not available. The reason for this is that, unlike wine, a small amount of it suffices to induce an intense effect [on body and mind]."[105] Al-Wazzānī now turns to a jurisprudential disagreement within the Mālikī *madhhab* that reveals that despite the obvious impurity of the drink, certain distinguished jurists did not consider it unlawful based on a legal presumption.

The jurisprudential disagreement, as represented by al-Wazzānī, starts with a statement attributed to Shaykh ʿAbdallāh Mayyāra (d. 1662), who claimed that Shaykh Aḥmad Ibn Ghāzī (d. 1513) wrote an excellent and very useful treatise on a beverage named *mā' al-ḥayāh* that is produced by distillation. In his treatise, according to Mayyāra, Ibn Ghāzī did not categorically assert that *mā' al-ḥayāh* is an intoxicating beverage (and therefore forbidden), even though people today generally agree about this. Mayyāra expressed his surprise at the serious violation of a basic religious prohibition, maintaining that "I do not know if it is because of [Ibn Ghāzī's] ignorance about the true nature [*ḥaqīqa*] of intoxication, which is manifested in the loss of reason [*ʿaql*] but not of the senses [*ḥawāss*], as well as exultation and happiness, or for some other reason."[106] Clearly, in the eyes of Mayyāra, Ibn Ghāzī, as a legal expert, had failed.

He should have used his knowledge of the law to forbid the consumption of *mā' al-ḥayāh*. For al-Wazzānī, this jurisprudential disagreement was instructive insofar as it provided an insight into an unambiguous case of impurity in which the legal determination was based upon a legal presumption. After noting that the matter calls for a careful study, he begins his deliberations.

Al-Wazzānī begins by explaining Ibn Ghāzī's opinion. He notes that Ibn Ghāzī held that although *mā' al-ḥayāh* is the most disgraceful (*aqbaḥ*) kind of intoxicating beverage, it is considered forbidden only so long as it contains a drop of intoxicant. If, on the other hand, the intoxicant is removed from it, then, according to Ibn Ghāzī, it should be considered in accordance with the two ways of treating wine as established by Ibn Rushd and Qāḍī 'Iyāḍ. Focusing his attention on the two ways of treating wine, al-Wazzānī cites a second statement attributed to Mayyāra, in which he explains:

> If the intoxicant is removed from the wine, namely, if it is evident that the wine either became thicker in consistency [*taḥajjur*], or if it turns sour and becomes vinegar, then there are two ways to be considered. First, according to Ibn Rushd: if the wine turns sour by itself, then there is no disagreement about its purity. However, if it was turned sour by its owner, then it is associated with efforts [*mu'ānā*] and processing [*mu'ālaja*] [and, therefore, is considered impure]. Second, it was reported by Qāḍī 'Iyāḍ on the authority of Muḥammad Ibn Waḍḍāḥ (d. 899 or 900) that if the wine turns sour either by itself or through processing [it is impure]. Ibn Ghāzī said: As for *mā' al-ḥayāh*, if it is clearly established that the intoxicant has been removed from it, it conforms to the second way in the disagreement about wine turned sour [i.e., the position of Qāḍī 'Iyāḍ], because it is all a matter of processing, and processing is processing.[107]

Put differently, it is clear from Mayyāra's second statement that Ibn Ghāzī considered *mā' al-ḥayāh* an impure drink. In further support of Mayyāra's statement, al-Wazzānī evokes a poem composed by al-Wansharīsī:

> According to Ibn Rushd, that which turns sour by itself should be permitted // in contrast to that which is processed
> Ibn Ghāzī said: *mā' al-ḥayāh* conforms to the second way // if it is clearly established that the intoxicant has been removed.[108]

For al-Wazzānī the case is clear: Ibn Ghāzī viewed *mā' al-ḥayāh* as an impure, intoxicating beverage, as opposed to what was said by Mayyāra. In fact, al-Wazzānī writes, Ibn Ghāzī is frank about considering it an intoxicating beverage; his words suggest that even if it is devoid of intoxicants, it is still considered impure (in agreement with Qāḍī ʿIyāḍ's opinion).[109] Without explicitly saying so, al-Wazzānī implies that Ibn Ghāzī, despite his knowledge of the intoxicating nature of the beverage, did not forbid it based upon a legal presumption. Finally, al-Wazzānī reports that the beverage is still popular in his age. He mentions the distinguished jurist Abū ʿAbdallāh Muḥammad Gannūn, who said that *māʾ al-ḥayāh* is called today *māḥiyā* by the people. Al-Wazzānī concludes the chapter, stating that "no one says that it is not an intoxicating beverage. However, certain religious scholars whose responsibility is to keep the people away from uncertainties [*shubuhāt*] and prohibitions [*muḥarramāt*] are not in agreement about its true nature [*ḥaqīqa*], [and therefore did not forbid it]. Had anyone uncovered its nature, he would not be indecisive about it. God knows best."[110] In other words, even *māʾ al-ḥayāh* that is commonly considered intoxicating is not rejected as prohibited. Since, in the absence of clear evidence that establishes its intoxicating nature, it is safer to assume it to be lawful.

Third Chapter

In the third chapter, al-Wazzānī addresses the question of coffee.[111] He begins his analysis with a revealing discussion attributed to Muḥammad al-Ḥaṭṭāb (d. 1547). In his commentary on Khalīl's *Mukhtaṣar*, al-Ḥaṭṭāb maintains,

> During the present century, i.e., the tenth century of the *hijra*, and slightly before it, a beverage made of the husk of the coffee berry [*qishr al-bunn*], called *qahwa*, appeared, and the people differed in opinion about it. Some, obsessed by it, view drinking it as [a way] to draw closer to God [*qurba*]. Others, destroyed by it, deem it an intoxicating beverage, like wine. The truth is that in its essence, there is no intoxicant. Rather, there is stimulation [*tanshīṭ*] of the soul; it causes, if consumed in large quantities, greed [*ḍarāwa*] that influences the body when it leaves it. It is like getting used to eating meat with saffron and poultry. It affects the body when it leaves it and brings it joy when it is consumed.[112]

Next, al-Ḥaṭṭāb discusses the ways in which coffee drinking interferes with a Muslim's respectability (*ḥurma*). He advances the following five concerns: First, Muslims come together to drink it and pass it around like they do with wine. They clap hands and recite poetry in colloquial language about love and wine. Coffee gives a sensation that reminds us of the effect of wine drinking. Second, some of those who sell it mix it with drugs (*mufsidāt*) such as hashish. Third, coffee is consumed in certain places, which leads to socializing with women who are often engaged in selling it. In addition, it involves listening to slanderous talk, obscene language, and many lies from the despicable people who meet to drink it. Fourth, coffee drinkers are distracted by it and by playing chess and other games found in coffeehouses and miss the Friday prayer. Finally, coffee tends to have harmful bodily effects.[113]

In the last section of his discussion, al-Ḥaṭṭāb asserts that coffee today is increasingly popular and prevalent. Accordingly, the controversy about it had grown. He declares that the fatwās and other writings by religious scholars reveal the disagreement and diverse opinions about it and notes that poems were composed either criticizing it sharply or praising it. In conclusion, al-Ḥaṭṭāb advises his reader to avoid drinking coffee except if it is justified by necessity. However, he establishes that coffee drinking is permitted for anyone who is safe from all the impediments just mentioned that undermine a Muslim's respectability, based upon a legal presumption.[114] The implication of al-Ḥaṭṭāb's account here, in line with al-Zarhūnī's argument, is that the legal determination regarding coffee is based upon a legal presumption that considered it permissible.

Having completed the representation of al-Ḥaṭṭāb's opinion, al-Wazzānī presents his reader with two brief reports about coffee. First, he cites al-Ḥāfiz Ibn Ḥajar (d. 1448), who noted that Shaykh Abū al-Ḥasan 'Alī b. 'Umar al-Shādhilī al-Yamanī (d. 1418) was the first to drink coffee and instructed his followers to drink it to help them stay awake for the nightly devotional ceremonies.[115] Second, al-Wazzānī quotes a report that *bunn* is a tree in paradise planted by seventy thousand angels and named *Silwān*. When God sent Adam down from paradise, where he was leading an enjoyable life, He sent it down with him to the regions of Zeila (*zayla'*) and Ethiopia (*al-ḥabasha*).[116]

Next, al-Wazzānī provides a selection of poems about coffee. He first quotes a poem criticizing coffee:

> I say to my friends, refrain from coffee // and do not sit in a gathering where coffee is served
> It is neither reprehensible [*makrūh*] nor forbidden [*muḥarram*] // however, it became a beverage of every shameless fellow [*safīh*].

He then mentions two poems that praise it:

> You have to drink coffee every hour // in drinking it, my friend, there are five benefits
> Vitality, subsiding, and stopping mucus // illuminating light to comprehend and help mankind.

In addition, others said,

> Coffee is permissible and restores health // God permitted it to the best people.
> If there was any doubt about drinking it// it should not be served at the grave of Muṣṭafā.[117]

At this point, al-Wazzānī's composition ends abruptly. For him, the legal determination regarding the consumption of the three beverages is treated clearly in Mālikī legal theory and must be based upon the legal presumption that permits their consumption.

DISCUSSION

This chapter puts the act of compiling and editing at the center of the writing of the *New Miʿyār*. Al-Mahdī al-Wazzānī did not write all the compositions himself, but he is the author-editor of the *New Miʿyār*. He is the individual singly responsible for the overall composition. And since I am after the work's historical meaning and cultural role, questions pertaining to the work's editorial conception, the selection of its components, and the manner of their treatment are key historical questions. The present composition epitomizes the creative efforts of the author-editor. The acts of selection, juxtaposition, and recombination of discrete texts in new contexts and combinations are powerful instruments for innovation.

I have argued that the prominent characteristic of the *New Miʿyār* is that it engages historical change from within Mālikī legal doctrine and discursive tradition, zealously preserving and reinforcing the Mālikī legal tradition. It carries forward the endeavor to create "new yet old" constructions. In other words, it engages modern needs and pressures that emerged in the context of colonial encroachment through the age-old voices of tradition. Al-Wazzānī's dual loyalty is therein exposed: on the one hand, he wants to address new needs linked to the contemporary context; on the other, he cannot divorce himself from the Mālikī legal tradition.

As the European presence and interference in Moroccan affairs grew, anxieties about economic penetration also increased, especially after the commercial treaty with Britain in 1856. Deep-seated distrust of Europeans and the various detrimental effects of the economic competition bred debates and rumors about new products and tastes that were making their mark in late nineteenth-century Morocco. A case in point is refined sugar imported from

Europe that spread with the popularization of tea drinking in the second half of the nineteenth century. By means of an inventive assemblage of texts, al-Wazzānī fashioned a new composition. His cultural creativity is evident in the freedom with which he borrowed the treatise of al-Zarhūnī, written in the first half of the nineteenth century, and connected it with four other texts that relied on selections from the Mālikī legal tradition. The new narrative expanded upon and deepened the legal argument found in the original treatise and built upon it to authorize the consumption of imported tea and sugar and reinforce the drinking of two other popular stimulant beverages, *mā' al-ḥayāh* and coffee.

Al-Zarhūnī's treatise responded to social discontent that shaped rumors about European-manufactured sugar in the first half of the nineteenth century. The long, detailed, and sophisticated analysis is an unequivocal permission to use imported sugar, based on the authoritative doctrine and legal presumptions of the school. Al-Wazzānī takes the side of al-Zarhūnī and further asserts his opinion in his three original texts, in which he selectively and skillfully authorizes the consumption of tea, *mā' al-ḥayāh*, and coffee. This is not an amorphous collection of texts, with no editorial hand or narrative framework to bind them together. Each text is independent and can stand alone, illustrating and reinforcing the legal issue. Collected together and tied to the other texts in the composition, they create a single textual entity with clear legal intent. Al-Wazzānī's new composition about food, beverage, and patterns of consumption offers us a window into the process of creating a new discursive reality in an open-ended process. Al-Wazzānī was trying to make sense of the new world he inhabited and at the same time to give meaning to moral obligations and legal precedents.

7 ISLAMIC LEGAL TRADITION, CHANGE, AND CONTINUITY

IT MAY BE HELPFUL as a way of closing off this historical investigation to confront the question of the scholarly legacy of al-Mahdī al-Wazzānī and his *New Miʿyār*. To date, al-Wazzānī and his *New Miʿyār* have been hardly recognized by scholars, let alone systematically studied and analyzed. The research process itself—that is, my search for al-Wazzānī in the archives—was potent evidence of this neglect. In archive after archive, librarians typically shrugged me off as I mentioned the subject of my research. Today in Morocco, al-Wazzānī is known as a distinguished Fāsī jurist who skillfully compiled a collection of Mālikī fatwās. His juristic authority is discussed in terms of his affiliation and loyalty to the Mālikī school, and the attributes of the *New Miʿyār* include the gathering together of fatwās from many sources and preserving them in one large compilation.

An explanation for this neglect of al-Wazzānī and his *New Miʿyār* may be attributed to the fact that in 1912, only two years after the publication of the compilation, French and Spanish Protectorates were set up in Morocco. A new era in the history of Morocco was about to begin. Under the Protectorate, the legal system underwent a fundamental transformation. Colonial rule created a dualistic system whereby indigenous courts, including sharīʿa, rabbinical, and tribunals of Berber customary law, functioned in parallel with courts modeled after those in the European legal system. Within this legal pluralism, Islamic law and courts presided mainly over family and inheritance matters, and European bureaucracy oversaw the work of qāḍīs. This meant that the *New Miʿyār* did not assume the cultural meaning and social role that al-Wazzānī intended for it. In my view, this is not an adequate answer. An effective interrogation of precolonial Morocco depends upon the formulation of the questions that seem worth asking and the answers seem worth finding. We need, in other words, to give up constructing an image of Islamic legal tradition as decidedly hostile to change and nonmodern.[1] This has been the theme of my historical investigation here.

The methodology I have used for reading fatwās in this book involves turning the fatwā compilation itself into a subject of systematic exploration and critical discussion. This approach has allowed me to raise fundamental questions about its textual content, literary form and composition, its author and the causes that led him to produce the collection, and its ideological orientation and cultural meaning. Recognizing the significance of the fatwā compilation as a field of research has enabled me to demonstrate its role as a powerful medium for innovation in Islamic tradition.

Subsequently, I have been engaged in a critique of the long-enduring conception that modern Islamic reformist thought in the late nineteenth and early twentieth centuries is characterized by rejection of the practice of adhering to one school of law, opposition to the pervasiveness of the classical teachings, and condemnation of *taqlīd*. I have suggested that the automatic association of modern reformism with reorientation of the sources of law and the practice of *ijtihād* corresponds to the self-portrayal of a few Islamic modernists associated with the network of Muḥammad ʿAbduh and Rashīd Riḍā. As a consequence, for decades, the study of Islamic modernism postulated a distinctive image of Islamic tradition as a fixed set of beliefs and practices that prescribed the recapitulation of the past and understood reform in terms of a rupture with tradition. My general aim has been to sketch out a case that demonstrates that fidelity to a *madhhab* and the authoritative rulings and opinions that had accumulated over centuries of juristic creativity does not exclude the transformation of tradition. In pursuing this concern, my specific aim has been to argue that Islamic ideas of revival and reform were not the privileged intellectual monopoly of thinkers who refuted the authority of the established legal schools and criticized the exclusive adherence to *fiqh* manuals and commentaries. In fact, a jurist who upheld the teachings of his school, practiced *taqlīd* of earlier jurists, and absolutely prohibited *ijtihād* deliberately reshaped the authoritative Mālikī corpus.

My route into the subject has been through al-Mahdī al-Wazzānī's *New Miʿyār* because it is a work of enormous insight into many different concerns simultaneously. As a monument of pre-Protectorate Moroccan cultural patrimony, it illuminates critical elements in the story of Moroccan modernity and historical change. At the same time, it is a work that was actively shaped by the subjective creativity and ideological orientation of its author. Al-Wazzānī was more than a compiler, and his *New Miʿyār* was not simply an act of compilation but one of creativity as well. Finally, the compilation is an exemplary instance of the complex indigenous responses to the new pressures and distinctive changes unleashed by modernity. It has been particularly useful in offering us a way of thinking critically about Islamic tradition and historical change.

Al-Wazzānī's Morocco underwent far-reaching change, including the reorganization of the state apparatus and social structures. Along with these new arrangements, a new rhetoric articulating the change emerged. This new rhetoric insisted on a renewed Islam as an essential condition in addressing the dramatic struggles of the Muslim community created by modernity, on the one hand, and identified Mālikī *fiqh* as deficient, tyrannical, and bearing little relevance to the new historical conditions, on the other. The last quarter of the nineteenth century was marked by fundamental disagreements among Moroccans over the content and meaning of orthodoxy and, by extension, over the norms and practices most effective for the survival of Moroccan society in the context of colonial modernity. Along with and influenced by other scholars, al-Wazzānī engaged this new reformist discourse.

Al-Wazzānī could not have imagined a shift in the legal structures and ideology of the Moroccan state away from the Mālikī legal tradition. Nor did he question the content of Mālikī jurisprudence or its authority to regulate and discipline Moroccan society. A professional Mālikī *faqīh*, al-Wazzānī's powerful response to both discursive and structural changes was to restore and reinforce the authority of Mālikī scholarship by composing a new orthodoxy. He recognized that the key to maintaining the authority of the Mālikī legal tradition in a changing world lies in its regeneration and transformation. For Mālikī knowledge to become more effective, it was necessary for the teachings and opinions to be able to relate to the concerns, dilemmas, and attitudes of the contemporary Moroccan society. His task was the reordering of the age-old voices of Mālikī tradition in light of the modern condition. The *New Miʿyār* served as a medium for inscribing his vision of a reformed Mālikī legal tradition. It was an occasion to deliver his own legal opinions and to set precedents through the knowledge and wisdom he assembled. In it, he addressed questions and concerns arising from the social and economic restructuring of Moroccan society and offered "new yet old" norms that would accommodate the new needs and sensibilities of his contemporaries without violating the boundaries set by the Islamic discursive tradition.

Conceptualizing the *New Miʿyār* as a single textual entity and a comprehensive composition expressing the ideological orientation of its author-editor has been critical to my deliberations in this book. Al-Wazzānī was more than a compiler, and his *New Miʿyār* was not simply an act of compilation. The very act of compiling the collection involved innovation and re-creation as well. Part of what was at stake, clearly, was that the *New Miʿyār* legitimized certain contemporary norms and discourses and delegitimized others. In taking this approach, al-Wazzānī understood the compilation as an act of canonization and authorization of orthodoxy. From this perspective, then, Islamic orthodoxy is constructed through a process of negotiation with a specific historical world. As al-Wazzānī sought to make sense of the new world he inhabited, he shaped new legal interpretations to accommodate changing conditions.

REFERENCE MATTER

NOTES

CHAPTER 1

1. His full name is Abū ʿĪsā Muḥammad al-Mahdī b. Muḥammad b. Muḥammad b. al-Khaḍir b. Qāsim b. Mūsā al-ʿImrānī al-Wazzānī al-Fāsī. All references to the *Miʿyār al-jadīd* in this study are to the Rabat edition.

2. Ḥajjī, *Naẓarāt fī al-nawāzil al-fiqhiyya*, 53.

3. The compilation as a literary genre has a pervasive presence in Islamic literature throughout history. Near the end of the eighth century CE, compilations of classical collections of ḥadīth (legal traditions) and law (juristic opinions and treatises) had already emerged in the Muslim world. See Weiss, *Spirit of Islamic Law*, 15.

4. As a literary form in Mālikī legal scholarship, fatwā collections emerged during the mid-eleventh century. A prominent characteristic of these works is that they bring together the fatwās of a single muftī or of muftīs belonging to one region or city. During the mid-fifteenth century, collections that recorded fatwās issued by various muftīs from different lands formed a new literary trend original to the period. Powers, *Law, Society, and Culture in the Maghrib*, 5. Also see al-Hīlah, "Classification of Andalusian and Maghribī Books of *Nawāzil*," 71–78. ʿUmar al-Jīdī lists the titles of eighty-three Mālikī fatwā collections that represent centuries of Mālikī legal activity. Al-Jīdī, *Muḥāḍarāt fī tārīkh al-madhhab al-mālikī*, 105–10.

5. For the formulation "text-centered society," I am indebted to Moshe Halbertal, *People of the Book*. On the scope and significance of establishing commitment to the past as a way to acquire authority in Islamic thought, see Graham, "Traditionalism in Islam."

6. Al-Wansharīsī, *Al-Miʿyār al-muʿrib wa'l-jāmiʿ al-mughrib ʿan fatāwī ʿulamāʾ Ifrīqiyā wa'l-Andalus wa'l-Maghrib*. There is extensive scholarly literature on the *Miʿyār* of al-Wansharīsī. For the most systematic and influential study, see Powers, *Law, Society, and Culture in the Maghrib*; on the life of al-Wansharīsī and the nature of the work, see ibid., 4–9.

7. *Miʿyār al-jadīd*, 1:6.

8. The *New Miʿyār* is considered by many as the last encyclopedia of Mālikī jurisprudence and its author as the last great compiler of his predecessors' law. See, for example, Berque, "Ville et université," 102.

9. One possible explanation for the delayed interest in the study of the *New Miʿyār* may be that it was available prior to 2000 only in lithograph form. For scholarly works

that have used diverse fatwās from the *New Mi'yār*, see, for example, Ennaji, *Serving the Master*; Laroui, *Les origines sociales*. See also Dialmy, "Femme et discourse au Maroc." For useful studies concerned with the *New Mi'yār*, see, for example, Bourqia, "Droit et pratiques sociales," 131–45; Berque, *Les Nawāzil el muzāra'a du Mi'yār Al Wazzānī*.

10. The *Encyclopedia of Islam* (*EI2*) explicitly highlights these key features of Islamic reformism; see *EI2*, s.v. Iṣlāḥ. For an influential example of this characterization of the modernist project, see Gibb, *Modern Trends in Islam*. For more recent examples, see Nafi, "Rise of Islamic Reformist Thought," 28–60; Kurzman, "The Modernist Islamic Movement," 3–27; D. Brown, *Rethinking Tradition*; Voll, "Renewal and Reform in Islamic History," 32–45.

11. See, for example, Peters, "*Idjtihād* and *Taqlīd* in 18th and 19th century Islam," 131–45.

12. *EI2*, s.v. Iṣlāḥ.

13. This view was reiterated in 2003 by Basheer M. Nafi. See "Rise of Islamic Reformist Thought."

14. For a review of this problem, see Weismann, "Between Ṣūfī Reformism and Modernist Rationalism," 206–37. For example, one of the widely accepted assumptions that has been reiterated in countless works on Islamic modernist reformism is that it originated in Egypt. Weismann argues that in actuality, Damascus played a pivotal role in conceiving and promoting the ideas and principles of Islamic modernism, and "in the first half of the nineteenth century it actually surpassed Cairo as the major locus of learning in the Arab lands." He insists that the Islamic modernist reformism that developed in Ottoman Syria "was not a mere offshoot of the Modernist trend in Cairo, but rather a separate trend that emerged among the reformist-minded *'ulamā'* in the Arab provinces of the late Ottoman Empire" (208). I thank Itzchak Weismann for offering me valuable insights on modern Islamic reformism in Ottoman Syria.

15. Ibid., 206. For example, Weismann argues that contrary to the emphasis of the proponents of Islamic modernism associated with al-Afghānī, 'Abduh, and Riḍā on the Western challenge to Muslim society, the reformists of Damascus were more concerned with the inner degeneration of Islam, associating it with the conduct of the state-patronized 'ulamā' and Ṣūfī shaykhs. Also see Weismann, *Taste of Modernity*.

16. A particularly helpful instance of this conception of Islamic modernist reformism in terms associated with its Egyptian advocates is labeling Abū Shu'aīb al-Dukkālī (d. 1937), an influential Moroccan reformist thinker, "the Muḥammad 'Abduh of Morocco." My worry has been that by subsuming different reformist projects under one label, scholars have often ignored the intellectual differences between thinkers as well as the diverse local contexts in which they lived and operated.

17. Among the many works devoted to this modernist trend are Hourani, *Arabic Thought in the Liberal Age*; Badawi, *Reformers of Egypt*; Keddie, *Sayyid Jamāl ad-Dīn "al-Afghānī"*; Adams, *Islam and Modernism in Egypt*; Kerr, *Islamic Reform*; Kedouri, *Afghani and 'Abduh*.

18. For example, *The Oxford Encyclopedia of the Modern Islamic World* mostly elaborates on 'Abduh's reformism in an article by As'ad AbuKhalil, "Revival and Renewal,"

3:431–34. Dissenting from this approach to Islamic modernism is David Commins, "Modernism," in *Oxford Encyclopedia*, 3:118–23; Kurzman, *Modernist Islam*.

19. See, for example, Haj, *Reconfiguring Islamic Tradition*; Zaman, *The Ulama in Contemporary Islam*; Graham, "Traditionalism in Islam"; Eickelman and Piscatori, *Muslim Politics*, 22–45; Waldman, "Tradition as a Modality of Change," 318–40.

20. Asad, *Idea of an Anthropology of Islam*, 14.

21. Ibid., 14–17.

22. Asad, "Limits of Religious Criticism in the Middle East," 210–11.

23. D. Brown, *Rethinking Tradition*, 3.

24. Ibid., 3–4.

25. The following survey is based on Pennell, *Morocco since 1830*; Burke, *Prelude to Protectorate*.

26. In Morocco, the state, or the Makhzan, usually coincides with the monarchy. The Moroccan monarchy has retained a remarkable longevity over time. Since the ninth century, Morocco has been continuously governed by a sultan. The present dynasty, the ʿAlawī, came to power in the seventeenth century and has monopolized the government ever since. The term "Makhzan" (literally storehouse) refers to the essential task of tax collection, in money or kind, as the foundation of the consolidation of Moroccan royal power. See *EI2*, s.v. Makhzan."

27. On nineteenth-century trade relations between Morocco and Europe, see Miège, *Le Maroc et l'Europe*.

28. For a detailed study on the impact of the protection system, see Kenbib, *Les protégés*.

29. Miller and Rassam, "View from the Court," 25–38.

30. See, for example, the extensive journal of Muḥammad al-Ṣaffār, a member of a Moroccan diplomatic delegation dispatched to France in 1845, in which he gathered detailed and refined information about the mid-nineteenth-century French state and society. S. Miller, *Disorienting Encounters*.

31. On the Makhzan reforms and the opposition to them, see Laroui, *Les origines sociales*, 263–390.

32. Some of these concerns and preoccupations have been the subject of a study by Sahar Bazzaz. Specifically, the 1894 heresy affair of Shaykh Muḥammad al-Kattānī is a compelling example of the contemporary anxieties over religious knowledge and devotional practices. See Bazzaz, *Forgotten Saints*, chap. 2, and "Heresy and Politics in Nineteenth-Century Morocco," 67–86.

33. Bazzaz, *Forgotten Saints*. Although doctrinal and theological debates during this period were informed by the growth of European interference in Moroccan affairs, these conversations were not simply a reaction to the "European challenge." The preoccupation with Islamic revival and reform goes back to the eighteenth and early nineteenth centuries, independent of European influence. I come back to this point in Chapter 3 of the present study, but I find it bearing preliminary consideration here. For a notable example of this pattern of engagement with Islamic tradition, see O'Fahey, *Enigmatic Saint*. I thank Jonathan Katz for this reference.

34. Al-Wazzānī's first fatwā collection is entitled *Al-Nawāzil al-ṣughrā al-musammā bi'l-minaḥ al-sāmiyya fī'l-nawāzil al-fiqhiyya.*

35. On the centrality and effectiveness of the method of juxtaposing different opinions to the same problem as mechanisms of change within Islamic law during the period from the tenth to the nineteenth centuries, see Johansen, "Legal Literature and the Problem of Change," 446–64. Also see Hallaq, "From *Fatwās* to *Furū'*," 29–65; Zomeno, "Stories in the Fatwas and the Fatwas in History," 25–49.

36. There is an extensive scholarly literature on the work of the muftī and the nature of the fatwā, which has provided me with a sophisticated and fruitful source of guidance for my own research and writing. To name but a few studies that informed my work: Tucker, "And God Knows Best," 165–79, and *In the House of the Law*; Powers, *Law, Society, and Culture in the Maghrib*; Hallaq, *Authority, Continuity and Change*, especially 166–235; Masud, Messick, and Powers, *Islamic Legal Interpretation*; Gerber, *State, Society, and Law in Islam*, 79–112; Reinhart, "Transcendence and Social Practice," 5–25.

37. For the formulation "new yet old," I am indebted to Zipora Kagan, "*Homo Anthologicus*, 216 passim.

38. For more on the sources of the *New Mi'yār*, see Berque, *Les Nawāzil el muzāra'a du Mi'yār Al Wazzānī*, 58–65. On the library of the Qarawiyyīn, see Le Tourneau, *Fès avant le Protectorat*, 472–73.

39. For a consideration of some of the conceptual concerns that my study illuminates, see Zomeno, "Stories in the Fatwas and the Fatwas in History." Also see al-Hīlah, "Classification of Andalusian and Maghribī Books of *Nawāzil*."

40. Some of the works that informed my investigation are Rosen, *Law as Culture*, and *The Anthropology of Justice*. Also see Geertz, "Off Echoes," 33–37.

41. Messick, *The Calligraphic State*, 135–52, and "The Mufti, the Text and the World," 102–19. It should be noted that, according to Messick, the muftīship is intimately linked to two other institutions, the school (*madrasa*) and court (*maḥkama*). Together, the three constitute a complex institutional system for the interpretative transmission of Islamic-religious knowledge.

42. Messick, "The Mufti, the Text and the World," 103–4.

43. Messick, *The Calligraphic State*, 151.

44. Messick, "The Mufti, the Text and the World."

CHAPTER 2

1. The literature on the biography and curriculum vitae as sources for historical reconstruction is extensive. For a consideration of varied facets, see *EI2*, s.v.v. Tardjama, Fahrasa; Avila, "Women in Andalusi Biographical Sources," 149–63; Hermansen, "Interdisciplinary Approaches to Islamic Biographical Materials," 163–82; Eickelman, *Knowledge and Power in Morocco*, especially 41–42, and "Traditional Islamic Learning," 35–59; Tucker, "Biography as History," 9–17.

2. For the biographical details, see *Mi'yār al-jadīd*, introduction, 9; al-Fāsī, *Mu'jam al-shuyūkh*, 175. For a more detailed description of the Jbāla region and the social structure of the tribal society in northern Morocco, see *EI2*, s.v.v. Ghumāra, Maṣmūda; Zoug-

gari and Vignette-Zunz, *Jbala*; Temsamani, "The Jebala Region," 14–46. See also Hoffman, *Structure of Traditional Moroccan Rural Society*, 28–30.

3. The 'Imrānī sharīfs of Jabal Ghumāra are the successors and descendants of 'Imrān, a descendant of Mawlāy Idrīs, a descendant of the Prophet's grandson al-Ḥasan. For the biographical details, see al-Fāsī, *Mu'jam al-shuyūkh*, 175; Ḥajjī, *Mawsū'at a'lām al-maghrib*, 8, 2935; al-Ziriklī, *A'lām*, 7, 335. On the 'Imrānī Sharīfs, see Salmon, "Les chorfa Idrisides de Fès," 439–41; al-Bakkārī, *Al-Ashrāf al-'Imrānīyūn bi'l-Maghrib*. See also *EI2*, s.v. Idris I.

4. The *shurafā'* emerged as a privileged social and political group in the Moroccan state and society during the rule of the Marīnid dynasty, toward the end of the thirteenth century. Kably, *Société, pouvoir et religion au Maroc*, 271–91.

5. Burke, "The Moroccan Ulama," 103. Unfortunately, I was unable to consider this information since Burke does not provide a reference to the source he used.

6. The city of Fez is populated with sharīfan families of the Idrīsī line, whose ancestor Mawlāy Idrīs is venerated as the patron saint of Fez.

7. The *ḥurm* of Mawlāy 'Abd al-Salām Ibn Mashīsh extended over a large area that included the saint's shrine and several tribal territories. For an excellent study on the institution of the *ḥurm* in the Moroccan context, see El-Mansour, "The Sanctuary (*Hurm*) in Precolonial Morocco," 49–73.

8. On the city of Wazzān, the *zāwiya*, and the sharīfs, see *EI2*, s.v.v. Wazzān, Wazzāniyya; Keene, *My Life Story*; Aubin, *Morocco of Today*, 361–92; Joffé, "The Zāwiya of Wazzan," 245–89; El-Mansour, "Sharifian Sufism," 69–83.

9. Laghzāwī, "Al-Mumārasa al-thaqāfiyya li'l-zāwiya al-Wazzāniyya," 2:577, 580.

10. *Mi'yār al-jadīd*, 12:25–27.

11. For a discussion of the concept *awliyā' Allāh*, see Cornell, *Realm of the Saint*, xvii–xx.

12. In 1875 the sharīf of Wazzān played a crucial role in the submission of al-Ḥarbī, a rebel in eastern Morocco, and provided him with the customary assurances that allowed him to leave the *ḥurm*. However, Mawlāy Ḥasan chose to disregard the established *ḥurm* customs and imprisoned the rebel. On the al-Ḥarbī incident, see Michaux-Bellaire, "La maison d'Ouezzan," 50–51.

13. Ibid. The implications for the legitimacy of the ruling sultan did not go unnoticed by the French. According to Miège, during the late 1880s some experts among the French diplomatic corps sought to take advantage of the conflict between the sultan and the sharīf of Wazzān and urged the adoption of a policy that would establish the latter as the sultan of Morocco. Miège, *Le Maroc et l'Europe*, 4:233–49.

14. I return in Chapter 4 to the conflict between the Moroccan sultan and the sharīf of Wazzān and consider the role of al-Wazzānī in the affair. Also see Terem, "Al-Mahdī al-Wazzānī."

15. On the Moroccan instructional tradition at the turn of the twentieth century, see, for example, Michaux-Bellaire, "L'enseignement indigène au Maroc," 422–52; Eickelman, *Knowledge and Power in Morocco*, 57–71.

16. *Mi'yār al-jadīd*, introduction, 9; al-Fāsī, *Mu'jam al-shuyūkh*, 176.

17. Al-Wazzānī, *Hādhihī fahrasa*, 10. On the conventional recitational forms in Morocco, see Michaux-Bellaire, "L'enseignement indigène au Maroc," 426.

18. Al-Wazzānī, *Hādhihī fahrasa*, 10. On secondary education, see Michaux-Bellaire, "L'enseignement indigène au Maroc," 434–38.

19. The most widely circulated texts among Moroccan 'ulamā' and students of law were the *Alfiyya* of Ibn Mālik (grammar); *Tuḥfat al-Ḥukkām* of Ibn 'Āsim and *Mukhtaṣar* of Khalīl (Mālikī law). The latter is specifically mentioned by al-Wazzānī in his *Hādhihī fahrasa*.

20. Michaux-Bellaire, "L'enseignement indigène au Maroc," 441; Marty, "L'université de Qaraouiyne," 337.

21. Makhlūf, *Shajarat al-nūr al-zakiyya*, 429–30; al-Ḥajwī, *Al-Fikr al-sāmī*, 633–34; al-'Alawī, *Jāmi' al-qarawiyyīn wa'l-fikr al-salafī*, 82–101.

22. Makhlūf, *Shajarat al-nūr al-zakiyya*, 430–31.

23. Ibid., 431.

24. Ibid., 430; al-Fāsī, *Mu'jam al-shuyūkh*, 80–82.

25. Makhlūf, *Shajarat al-nūr al-zakiyya*, 423; al-Fāsī, *Mu'jam al-shuyūkh*, 131–34.

26. Makhlūf, *Shajarat al-nūr al-zakiyya*, 423; Martin, *Muslim Brotherhoods*, 125–51.

27. Makhlūf, *Shajarat al-nūr al-zakiyya*, 435; al-Fāsī, *Mu'jam al-shuyūkh*, 46–48.

28. Al-Wazzānī specifically recounts these texts in his *fahrasa*, identifying the person-to-person instructional links and establishing the authenticity of the recitational transmission.

29. Al-Wazzānī, *Hādhihī fahrasa*, 9.

30. *Shaykh al-jamā'a* was a jurist recognized for his distinguished level of legal learning as the most qualified member of the community of legal specialists. These jurists were important religious functionaries, involved in appointing judges and prayer leaders. Until the early twentieth century, their activities were outside the sultan's supervision and authority. Under Sultan 'Abd al-'Azīz, the *shaykh al-jamā'a* was appointed by a sultanic decree, reorganizing the office as part of the state bureaucracy. On the office of *shaykh al-jamā'a*, see Laroui, *Les origines sociales*, 101, 195–96.

31. Al-'Alawī, *Jāmi' al-qarawiyyīn wa'l-fikr al-salafī*, 82–101; al-Ḥajwī, *al-Fikr al-sāmī*, 633–34.

32. Laroui, *Les origines sociales*, 101–2.

33. Al-Fāsī, *Mu'jam al-shuyūkh*, 131–34.

34. Ibid., 168–70. Mā al-'Aynayn's works have not been systematically examined, and a large number still remain in manuscript form. For an overview of his writings, see Martin, *Muslim Brotherhoods*, 145–50.

35. As already noted, my conception of Islamic tradition and historical change draws its inspiration from Asad's approach.

36. On the Qarawiyyīn University, see *EI2*, s.v. Ḳarawiyyīn; Porter, "At the Pillar's Base"; al-Tāzī, *Jāmi' al-Qarawiyyīn*; al-'Alawī, *Jāmi' al-qarawiyyīn wa'l-fikr al-salafī*; Delphin, *Fas*; Marty, "L'université de Qaraouiyne"; Péretié, "Les madrasas de Fès," 257–372; Jabre, "Dans le Maroc nouveau," 193–207; Le Tourneau, *Fès avant le Protectorat*, 453–71; Berque, "Ville et université"; Michaux-Bellaire, "L'enseignement indigène au Maroc."

37. Al-ʿAlawī, *Jāmiʿ al-qarawiyyīn wa'l-fikr al-salafī*, 20–56.

38. Eickelman, "The Art of Memory," 487. Also see Eickelman, *Knowledge and Power in Morocco*, 57–71, 91–106.

39. Eickelman, "The Art of Memory," 489–92. Brinkley Messick suggests that this form of instruction through memorization and recitation was established early on in Islam and is emblematic of Islamic textual culture. He identifies the Qur'ān as the paradigmatic recitation-text, which was received orally by the Prophet, who could neither read nor write, and then orally reconveyed to the Companions. See Messick, *The Calligraphic State*, 21–30. For a discussion of the transformation that occurred in content and form of religious learning and authority in contemporary Muslim societies, see, for instance, Eickelman, "Islamic Religious Commentary and Lesson Circles," 121–46.

40. Hallaq, *Authority, Continuity and Change*, chap. 6. Hallaq has observed that the role of qāḍī was not considered to create a reputation of a successful career. In general, judgeship was not seen as a desired position and was associated with a lack of moral standards and deficient integrity. See Hallaq, *Origins and Evolution of Islamic Law*, chap. 8.

41. There is extensive scholarly literature on Maghribi Mālikism. See, among others, Shatzmiller, "Les premiers Mérinides," 109–19; Kably, *Société, pouvoir et religion au Maroc*, and "Legitimacy of State Power," 17–29; Touati, *Entre Dieu et les hommes*; El-Mansour, "Maghribis in the Mashriq," 83–86, and "Moroccan Islam Observed," 208. See also *EI2*, s.v. Mālikiyya.

42. Messick, *The Calligraphic State*, 145.

43. Laghzāwī, "Al-Mumārasa al-thaqāfiyya li'l-zāwiya al-Wazzāniyya," 2:579.

44. Hallaq, *Authority, Continuity and Change*, 168.

45. On the Moroccan ʿ*amal*, see Berque, *Essai sur la méthode juridique*; Toledano, *Judicial Practice and Family Law*; Rosen, *The Justice of Islam*, 24–38.

46. For a consideration of this practice in the Moroccan context, see Powers and Terem, "From the *Miʿyār* of al-Wansharīsī to the *New Miʿyār* of al-Wazzānī," 235–60.

47. Toledano, *Judicial Practice*, introduction; Hallaq, *Authority, Continuity and Change*, 161. Also see Dutton, "Sunna, Ḥadīth, and Madinan ʿAmal," 1–31.

48. Berque, *Essai sur la méthode juridique*, especially 33–42. For a discussion of custom as a legal source in Islamic law, see, for instance, Johansen, "Coutumes locales et coutumes universelles," 29–35; Libson, "Development of Custom as a Source of Law," 131–55. On custom in the Mālikī legal tradition, see al-Jīdī, *Al-ʿUrf wa'l-ʿAmal fī'l-Madhhab al-Mālikī wa-mafhūmuhumā ladā ʿulamāʾ al-Maghrib*.

49. Despite the importance of the ʿ*amal* in Mālikī legal tradition, a systematic investigation of this literature has not yet been attempted in many scholarly works. In light of this lack of studies, further research of the major ʿ*amal* works is required to fully understand its nature and function as a legal source in the Mālikī *madhhab*.

50. *Miʿyār al-jadīd*, introduction, 11.

51. Al-Idrīsī, *Muʿjam al-maṭbūʿāt al-maghribiyya*, 364.

52. Marty, "L'université de Qaraouiyne," 345.

53. Ḥajjī, *Mawsūʿat aʿlām al-maghrib*, 2936.

54. Cornell, *Realm of the Saint*, 3–7, 67.

55. Ibid., 67. See also Cornell, "Faqīh versus Faqīr in Marinid Morocco," 207–24.

56. Some of al-Wazzānī's notable studies include *Bughyat al-ṭālib al-rāghib al-qāṣid fī ibāḥat ṣalāt al-ʿīd fī al-masājid* and *Taqyīd fī jawāz al-dhikr maʿa al-janāza wa-rafʿ al-ṣaut biʾl-haylala*. Also see Bourqia, "Droit et pratiques sociales," 135–38.

57. The text was later published in *Miʿyār al-jadīd*, 12:626–65, under the title *Fī jawāz al-tawaṣṣul ilā Allāh taʿālā bi-awliyāʾhi wa-anbiyāʾhi waʾl-radd ʿalā man ankar dhalika* (On the legality of approaching Allah through his saints and prophets and a refutation of those who deny it). All references to the text are to the published edition.

58. Ibid., 626–27, 638–42.

59. Ibid.

60. Ibid., 628–38.

61. Ibid., 628.

62. *EI2*, s.v.v. ʿUmar b. al-Khaṭṭāb, Al-ʿAbbās b. ʿAbd al-Muṭṭalib.

63. *Miʿyār al-jadīd*, 12:632–33.

64. Masud, Messick, and Powers, "Muftis, Fatwas, and Islamic Legal Interpretation," 17. For a chronological discussion of the juristic discourse of the qualifications of the muftī, see Hallaq, "Iftaʾ and Ijtihad in Sunni Legal Theory," 33–43, and *History of Islamic Legal Theories*, 143–53.

65. *Miʿyār al-jadīd*, 4:286–97. On the issue of *madhhab* boundaries, see Wiederhold, "Legal Doctrines in Conflict," 234–304.

66. *Miʿyār al-jadīd*, 4:292.

67. Jackson, "*Taqlīd*, Legal Scaffolding," 169, 172.

68. Hallaq, *Authority, Continuity and Change*, 85, 88. For another important exploration of the legal practice of *taqlīd*, see Fadel, "Social Logic of *Taqlīd*," 193–233, and "Rules, Judicial Discretion, and the Rule of Law," 49–86.

69. Laghzāwī, "Al-Mumārasa al-thaqāfiyya liʾl-zāwiya al-Wazzāniyya," 2:588.

70. Mujāhid, *Al-Aʿlām al-Sharqiyya*, 405.

71. Michaux-Bellaire, "L'enseignement indigène au Maroc," 446.

72. For the biographical details, see Ḥajjī, *Mawsūʿat aʿlām al-maghrib*, 2936. ʿAbd Allāh Mayyāra was a Mālikī jurist who died in 1662. His most important and well-known work consists of two commentaries on two major *ʿamal* texts. Possibly, one of them is the text mentioned here.

73. Al-Fāsī, *Muʿjam al-shuyūkh*, 176.

74. El-Mansour, "Maghribis in the Mashriq," 98.

75. Al-Manūnī, *Maẓāhir yaqẓat al-maghrib al-ḥadīth*, 2:329.

76. *Al-Manār* 6 (1904): 927–28. See also al-Manūnī, *Maẓāhir yaqẓat al-maghrib*, 2:327–28.

77. On ʿAbduh's fatwā, see Skovgaard-Peterson, *Defining Islam for the Egyptian State*, 123–33; Haj, *Reconfiguring Islamic Tradition*, 146–50.

78. Al-Manūnī, *Maẓāhir yaqẓat al-maghrib*, 2:327.

79. Ibid., 335–38.

80. Ibid., 336–37.

81. Ibid., 361–62.

82. Other religious scholars engaged in the project, according to al-Manūnī, were Muḥammad al-Kattānī, 'Abd al-Ḥayy al-Kattānī, al-'Ābid b. Sūda, and al-'Abbās al-Tāzī.

83. For the Arabic texts, see al-Manūnī, *Maẓāhir yaqẓat al-maghrib*, 2:399–445. For a short discussion of the movement, see Fasi, *Independence Movements*, 87–91. See also Pennell, *Morocco since 1830*, 143–44.

84. Laroui, *Les origines sociales*, 380–82.

85. Because it has a prominent role in the Islamic legal profession and is an agent of legal change, the office of the muftī in Islam has been extensively studied by Western scholars. For a broad orientation, see, for example, Tyan, *Histoire de l'organisation judiciaire*, 219ff.; Masud, Messick, and Powers, *Islamic Legal Interpretation*. Among the many works exploring the office of the muftī in concrete social contexts, see Repp, *The Mufti of Istanbul*; Tucker, *In the House of the Law*; Skovgaard-Peterson, *Defining Islam for the Egyptian State*; Masud, "*Ādāb al-Muftī*," 124–45. In the Islamic West context, see al-Jīdī, *Muḥāḍarāt fī tārīkh al-madhhab al-mālikī*, 91–110; Powers, "Legal Consultation," 85–106.

86. The Moroccan legal system, its structure, institutions, and culture in the pre-Protectorate period, remains a relatively understudied field. For a preliminary study of the Moroccan religious institutions, see Burke, "The Moroccan Ulama." See also Buskens, "Sharia and National Law in Morocco," 92–95.

87. Berque, "Ville et université," 107.

88. For a general discussion of the social origins of the fatwā genre, see, for example, Hallaq, *Authority, Continuity and Change*, 174–80.

89. Al-Fāsī, *Mu'jam al-shuyūkh*, 176.

90. Ḥajjī, *Mawsū'at a'lām al-maghrib*, 2936.

91. S. Miller, *Disorienting Encounters*, 37–38.

92. Mohamed El-Mansour has argued that in the early twentieth century, there were 129 'ulamā' in Fez. Only a few dozen of them occupied positions of power and influence among the sultan and his advisers. "Les oulemas et le makhzen dans le Maroc precolonial," 4.

93. Berque, "Ville et université," 107.

94. Le Tourneau, *Fès avant le Protectorat*, 462; El-Mansour, "Saints and Sultans," 25.

95. For overviews of the Moroccan state and society during the second part of the nineteenth century, see Pennell, *Morocco since 1830*; Burke, *Prelude to Protectorate*.

96. Kenbib, *Les protégés*, 92.

97. Le Tourneau, *Fès avant le Protectorat*, 461–62; El-Mansour, "Les oulemas et le makhzen"; Burke, "The Moroccan Ulama"; K. Brown, "Profile of a Nineteenth-Century Moroccan Scholar," 127–48; Dennerlein, "Legitimate Bounds and Bound Legitimacy," 287–310.

98. Munson, *Religion and Power*, 52–55.

99. On the Abū Ḥimāra rebellion, see al-Khadīmī, "Al-Ḥaraka al-Ḥafīẓiyya," 1:53–57; Gharīṭ, *Fawāṣil al-jumān fī anbā' wuzurā' wa-kuttāb al-zamān*, 110–20; Aubin, *Morocco of Today*, 89–108; Dunn, "The Bu Himara Rebellion," 31–48, and "France, Spain, and the Bu Himara Rebellion," 145–58.

100. Aubin, *Morocco of Today*, 135–39.

101. The fatwā had been composed by Aḥmad b. al-Mawwāz, first secretary of the first minister (*wazīr al-awwal*) Muḥammad al-Mufaḍḍal Gharīṭ. A French translation of the text may be found in "Lettre des oulama," 241–55. For parts of the Arabic text, see al-ʿAlawī, *Jāmiʿ al-qarawiyyīn wa'l-fikr al-salafī*, 127–29.

102. "Lettre des oulama," 247; al-ʿAlawī, *Jāmiʿ al-qarawiyyīn wa'l-fikr al-salafī*, 128.

103. On the circumstances in which ʿAbd al-ʿAzīz established the council of Moroccan notables, and on its discussions and meetings, see al-Khadīmī, "Majlis al-aʿyān," 259–92; Burke, *Prelude to Protectorate*, 68–86; Laroui, *Les origines sociales*, 374–78. For a partial list of the notables who were members of the council, see al-Manūnī, *Maẓahir yaqẓat al-maghrib*, 2:203–4.

104. Burke, *Prelude to Protectorate*, 68–77.

105. Al-Khadīmī, "Majlis al-aʿyān," 266. For the French translation, see "Le fetoua des ʿoulamā de Fès," 141–43.

106. Al-Khadīmī, "Majlis al-aʿyān," 274, 276.

107. Burke, *Prelude to Protectorate*, 86.

108. Ibid., 86–88.

109. On the Mauchamp affair and the events that followed his death, see Katz, *Murder in Marrakesh*, and "The 1907 Mauchamp Affair," 143–66.

110. Laroui, *Les origines sociales*, 386–87.

111. Ibid., 387.

CHAPTER 3

1. Landau-Tasseron, "The 'Cyclical Reform,'" 79–117.

2. Voll, "Renewal and Reform in Islamic History"; Rahman, "Revival and Reform in Islam," 2:632–42.

3. Among the many works devoted to nineteenth-century reformist thought in the Muslim world are Troll, *Sayyid Ahmad Khan*; Metcalf, *Islamic Revival in British India*; Khalid, *Politics of Muslim Cultural Reform*; Commins, *Islamic Reform*; Weismann, *Taste of Modernity*; Nafi, "Abu al-Thana' al-Alusi," 465–94; Zaman, *The Ulama in Contemporary Islam*; Haj, *Reconfiguring Islamic Tradition*, chaps. 3–5.

4. See, for example, al-ʿAlawī, *Jāmiʿ al-qarawiyyīn wa'l-fikr al-salafī*, 66–69, 126–53; Cagne, *Nation et nationalisme au Maroc*, 307–9, 381–82; Zeghal, *Les islamistes marocains*, 40–48.

5. My concern in this book is with al-Ḥajwī's *al-Fikr al-sāmī*. Al-Ḥajwī, it should be noted, presented the principal lines of his argument at a lecture in Fez in 1917. That year, he also wrote the work but continued to make revisions and to add new material until 1939. During this period, he headed the Ministry of Justice, established by the French Protectorate in 1915, and was in charge of all Islamic education, including the primary and secondary schools and the Qarawiyyīn University. It may be argued that due to the later modifications to the work and his ties with the French Protectorate, his perspective should not be considered as evidence of the reformist discourse that al-Wazzānī engaged. To my mind, an investigation of this work as an instance of the discursive changes that marked al-Wazzānī's world is indeed appropriate. In 1889, at the age of

sixteen, al-Ḥajwī started his studies at the Qarawiyyīn and came into contact with al-Wazzānī. In 1904 he was selected, alongside al-Wazzānī, to participate in the council of notables (*majlis al-a'yān*), established by Sultan 'Abd al-'Azīz to discuss the French reform proposal. Later that year, he led a delegation of Moroccan notables, al-Wazzānī included, to Algeria. There can be little doubt that al-Wazzānī was familiar with at least some of al-Ḥajwī's ideas about the cause of Muslim weakness and concerns about the existing Islamic learning institutions and his pedagogical approach. For al-Ḥajwī's biographical details, see *Al-Fikr al-sāmī*, 6–16. On the work itself, see Bin'adāda, *Al-Fikr al-iṣlāḥī fī 'ahd al-ḥimāya*, 102–4.

6. Laghzāwī, "Al-Mumārasa al-thaqāfiyya li'l-zāwiya al-Wazzāniyya," 2:578. For biographical details, see Makhlūf, *Shajarat al-nūr al-zakiyya*, 437.

7. Laghzāwī, "Al-Mumārasa al-thaqāfiyya li'l-zāwiya al-Wazzāniyya," 2:578.

8. Ḥarakāt, *Al-Tayyārāt al-siyāsiyya wa'l-fikriyya bi'l-Maghrib*, 88–90, 117.

9. One striking example of this approach is Abun-Nasr, "The *Salafiyya* Movement in Morocco," 489–502. For important critical engagements with the origins and meaning of salafism and the confusion surrounding it in scholarship, see Haykel, "On the Nature of Salafi Thought and Action," 33–57; Lauzière, "The Construction of *Salafiyya*," 369–89.

10. For a good example of such a thorough investigation of four major eighteenth-century thinkers, see Dallal, "Origins and Objectives of Islamic Revivalist Thought," 341–59.

11. Zeghal, *Les islamistes marocains*, 41.

12. Al-Manūnī, *Maẓāhir yaqẓat al-maghrib al-ḥadīth*, 2:373.

13. On al-Shawkānī, see Haykel, *Revival and Reform in Islam*; on al-Alūsī, see Nafi, "Abu al-Thana' al-Alusi."

14. Chenoufi, "Les deux sejours de Muhammad 'Abduh," 57–96.

15. Cagne, *Nation et nationalisme au Maroc*, 326–31; Munson, *Religion and Power*, 92.

16. Al-Manūnī, *Maẓāhir yaqẓat al-maghrib*, 2:329; Cagne, *Nation et nationalisme au Maroc*, 371.

17. Cagne, *Nation et nationalisme au Maroc*, 372.

18. For studies on Islamic reformist ideas in Morocco in the eighteenth and early nineteenth centuries, see, for instance, Levtzion and Weigert, "Religious Reform in Eighteenth Century Morocco," 173–97; El-Mansour, *Morocco in the Reign of Mawlay Sulayman*, 132–83. Also see Cagne, *Nation et nationalisme au Maroc*, 339–46.

19. This view has been stressed in many works on nineteenth-century Islamic thought. See, for example, Dallal, "Appropriating the Past," 325–58; Haj, *Reconfiguring Islamic Tradition*.

20. For the Arabic text, see al-Manūnī, *Maẓāhir yaqẓat al-maghrib*, 2:376–82. For translation and analysis, see Laroui, *Les origines sociales*, 328–33; Munson, *Religion and Power*, 87–93.

21. See, for example, al-'Alawī, *Jāmi' al-qarawiyyīn wa'l-fikr al-salafī*, 39–56.

22. Al-Ḥajwī, *Al-Fikr al-sāmī*, 704–6.

23. Zeghal, *Les islamistes marocains*, 44.

24. Al-'Alawī, *Jāmi' al-qarawiyyīn wa'l-fikr al-salafī*, 39–56.

25. Ḥarakāt, *Al-Tayyārāt al-siyāsiyya wa'l-fikriyya bi'l-Maghrib*, 12–22.

26. Al-'Alawī, *Jāmi' al-qarawiyyīn wa'l-fikr al-salafī*, 22–25.

27. Ibid., 107.

28. Al-Wazzānī, *Hādhihī fahrasa*, 9.

29. Al-'Alawī, *Jāmi' al-qarawiyyīn wa'l-fikr al-salafī*, 133.

30. Ibid., 29.

31. Ḥarakāt, *Al-Tayyārāt al-siyāsiyya wa'l-fikriyya bi'l-Maghrib*, 16. For a significant scholarly study of the appearance and rapid spread of the genre of *mukhtaṣarāt* in the thirteenth century, see Fadel, "The Social Logic of *Taqlīd*."

32. Al-Nāṣirī, *Kitāb al-istiqsā*, 8:67.

33. Al-Ḥajwī, *Al-Fikr al-sāmī*, 726.

34. Ibid., 705.

35. Ibn Zaydān, *Itḥāf a'lām al-nāss bi-jamāl akhbār ḥādarat miknās*, 3:203.

36. As I have pointed out earlier, in the Mālikī school the authoritative opinions of Mālik b. Anas are assumed to make up the foundations of the court practice.

37. Al-Ḥajwī, *Al-Fikr al-sāmī*, 708–12.

38. Ibid., 706.

39. Al-'Alawī, *Jāmi' al-qarawiyyīn wa'l-fikr al-salafī*, 30–38, 87.

40. Ibid., 157.

41. Ḥarakāt, *Al-Tayyārāt al-siyāsiyya wa'l-fikriyya bi'l-Maghrib*, 34–35.

42. Ibid., 40–42, 87–92; al-Ḥajwī, *Al-Fikr al-sāmī*, 726–28.

43. Al-'Alawī, *Jāmi' al-qarawiyyīn wa'l-fikr al-salafī*, 88.

44. Al-Ḥajwī, *Al-Fikr al-sāmī*, 726.

45. Ibid., 727–28.

46. Al-'Alawī, *Jāmi' al-qarawiyyīn wa'l-fikr al-salafī*, 40.

47. Ibid., 87.

48. Ḥajjī, *Naẓarāt fī al-nawāzil al-fiqhiyya*, 41.

49. Al-Ḥajwī, *Al-Fikr al-sāmī*, 726.

50. 'Alāl al-khadīmī contends that 'Abd al-Ḥafīẓ restricted the number of jurists who were concerned with issuing fatwās to eight. Al-khadīmī, "Al-Ḥaraka al-Ḥafīẓiyya," 355.

51. *Mi'yār al-jadīd*, 12:670–73.

52. Aḥmad bin Khālid al-Nāṣirī was affiliated with the Nāṣiriyya order. See K. Brown, "Profile of a Nineteenth-Century Moroccan Scholar," 128.

53. Abū Shu'aīb al-Dukkālī was a member of the Darqāwi Sufi order and taught in the *zāwiya* of the Nāṣiriyya order. See Munson, *Religion and Power*, 97–98.

54. Mā al-'Aynayn was the leader of the 'Ayaniyya order.

55. Muḥammad b. al-'Arabī al-'Alawī (d. 1964), a leading advocate of Islamic reformist ideas and a teacher of the celebrated nationalist 'Allāl al-Fāsī (d. 1974), was a member of the Tijāniyya order. See Munson, *Religion and Power*, 102–3. On the Tijāniyya, see Jamil Abun-Nasr, *The Tijaniyya*.

56. Ḥarakāt, *Al-Tayyārāt al-siyāsiyya wa'l-fikriyya bi'l-Maghrib*, 56, 62–63, 66, 74–75.

57. On Aḥmad al-Nāṣirī's condemnation of all acts and beliefs containing heresies, see Cagne, *Nation et nationalisme au Maroc*, 346–52.

58. Munson, *Religion and Power*, 98.

59. For example, al-Nāṣirī, *Kitāb al-istiqṣā*, 1:143–44.

60. Al-ʿAlawī, *Jāmiʿ al-qarawiyyīn wa'l-fikr al-salafī*, 109.

61. Ibid., 92.

62. Al-Nāṣirī, *Kitāb al-istiqṣā*, 1:143.

63. For an analysis of al-Kattānī's conflict with the ʿulamāʾ, see Bazzaz, *Forgotten Saints*, 50–81, and "Heresy and Politics in Nineteenth-Century Morocco."

64. Munson, *Religion and Power*, 94, 98.

65. Zeghal, *Les islamistes marocains*, 44.

66. Munson, *Religion and Power*, 86; Cagne, *Nation et nationalisme au Maroc*, 354.

67. Zeghal, *Les islamistes marocains*, 44–47.

68. Al-ʿAlawī, *Jāmiʿ al-qarawiyyīn wa'l-fikr al-salafī*, 151.

69. On the significance of the ḥadīth as the basis of Islamic law, see J. Brown, *Hadith*, 150–66.

70. Touati, *Entre Dieu et les hommes*, 66–70. Touati explicitly acknowledges his debt to Clifford Geertz's conception of *fiqh* as local knowledge (67n101).

71. Both Gannūn and al-Ḥajwī elaborate their insistence on *ijtihād*, especially when they discuss the crisis in *iftāʾ*. For them, the muftī's qualifications and the institution of *iftāʾ* were entirely associated with reason, knowledge of the legal sources, and liberation of thought. The muftī, they argued, had to apply *ijtihād* and had to be a *mujtahid*. See al-ʿAlawī, *Jāmiʿ al-qarawiyyīn wa'l-fikr al-salafī*, 87–88; al-Ḥajwī, *Al-Fikr al-sāmī*, 722–25.

72. Al-Ḥajwī, *Al-Fikr al-sāmī*, 722–23.

73. Ibid., 748.

74. El-Mansour, "Moroccan Islam Observed," 211, and "Maghribis in the Mashriq," 83.

75. Print technology was introduced in Morocco in 1864 by a Moroccan pilgrim who bought a lithographic press in Cairo after completing the ḥajj. During the reign of ʿAbd al-Ḥafīẓ, the government took control of printing. See Abdulrazak, "The Kingdom of the Book," especially 139–47.

76. *Miʿyār al-jadīd*, 1:13–14.

77. Note the Rabat edition's title, *Al-Nawāzil al-jadīda al-kubrā fī-mā li-ahl fās wa-ghayrihim min al-badw wa'l-qurā al-musammā bi'l-miʿyār al-jadīd al-jāmiʿ al-muʿrib ʿan fatāwī al-mutaʾakhkhirīn min ʿulamāʾ al-Maghrib*. The name *al-Maghrib al-Aqṣā* was employed to denote the territory of Morocco as early as the twelfth century. See Kably, "Legitimacy of State Power," 19.

CHAPTER 4

1. The chapter on jihād may be found in *Miʿyār al-jadīd*, 3:3–134. The Islamic legal literature on non-Muslim religious communities is extensive. For a consideration of the legal position of non-Muslims in the Qur'ān, the ḥadīth, and early jurisprudence, see Friedmann, "Classification of Unbelievers in Sunnī Muslim Law and Tradition," 163–95. For a study devoted to the legal stipulations concerning non-Muslims, see Awang, *Status of Dhimī in Islamic Law*.

2. The fatwa may be found in *Miʿyār al-jadīd*, 3:71–76.

3. On the protection system, see *EI2*, s.v. Ḥimāya; Kenbib, *Les protégés*; idem, "European Protections in Morocco," 47–53; idem, "Structures traditionnelles et protections étrangères au Maroc," 79–101. Eric Calderwood has recently called attention to the semantics of the term *ḥimāya*, placing it in the context of late nineteenth-century Morocco. See Calderwood, "Beginning (or End) of Moroccan History," 399–420 passim.

4. Schroeter, *The Sultan's Jew*, 125. On the evolution of the system of consular protection in North Africa, see Pennell, "Treaty Law," 235–56.

5. Al-Manūnī, *Maẓāhir yaqẓat al-maghrib al-ḥadīth*, 1:326–34; Kenbib, *Les protégés*, 215–17.

6. Kenbib, *Les protégés*, 62. By the latter part of the nineteenth century the composition of *ahl al-ḥimāya* included four distinct categories of Moroccans, beneficiaries of consular protection, and extraterritorial rights on Moroccan soil. Miller and Rassam, "View from the Court," 30–31.

7. For a discussion of the various ways by which consular protection undermined the sovereignty of the Makhzan, see, for example, Kenbib, "Protégés et brigands dans le Maroc," 227–48.

8. Schroeter, "Royal Power and the Economy," 92–93.

9. Burke, *Prelude to Protectorate*, 103.

10. On the incident that led the sharīf of Wazzān to request French protection, see Chapter 2 of this study.

11. Kenbib, "Impact of the French Conquest," 56–57.

12. Unfortunately, the fatwā does not contain the specific date on which al-Wazzānī wrote his opinion.

13. Many sultans in precolonial Morocco were trained in Islamic scholarship and Mālikī legal doctrine and possessed the knowledge required to understand the technical language of a legal opinion. For instance, Sultan ʿAbd al-Ḥafīẓ (r. 1908–12) was a student of al-Wazzānī.

14. *Miʿyār al-jadīd*, 3:71.

15. See Makhlūf, *Shajarat al-nūr al-zakiyya*, 386–89. On the office of *shaykh al-jamāʿa*, see Laroui, *Les origines sociales*, 101, 195.

16. It should be noted that the term *amīr* may signify different ranks of authority. Since the present case does not reveal any evidence pertaining to the function of the *amīr*, I choose to identify him with a generic definition as a chief.

17. I have been unable to identify this qāḍī. His *nisba* indicates that he was originally from ʿAnnāba, a town in northern Algeria.

18. Presumably, the qāḍī and his family settled in Tunisia, and as the conflict erupted, the qāḍī sought British protection. On consular protection in precolonial Tunisia, see Clancy-Smith, *Mediterraneans*, chap. 6.

19. *Miʿyār al-jadīd*, 3:72.

20. Ibid. Al-Suhaylī, *Al-Rawḍ al-unuf fī sharḥ al-sīra al-nabawiyya li-ibn Hishām*.

21. *Miʿyār al-jadīd*, 3:72. In all likelihood, al-Riyāḥī refers here to a *ḥadīth*, which may be found in the *Ṣaḥīḥ* of al-Bukhārī. As reported in the *ḥadīth*, Abū Bakr went to Abyssinia at the Prophet's urging to escape persecution by the Quraysh. On his way, however,

he met Ibn al-Daghina, a tribal chief, who was not a Muslim himself but showed good judgment and an admirable impartiality when he willingly offered Abū Bakr protection. The Quraysh recognized al-Daghina's right to grant protection, and Abū Bakr, explicitly protected by a polytheist, returned to Mecca.

22. Ibid.

23. Ibid.

24. Ibid.

25. Ibid.

26. Ibid., 72–73.

27. Ibid., 73.

28. It is possible that al-Wazzānī refers here to al-Ḥajjāj's forceful attack on Mecca; see *EI2*, s.v. al-Ḥadjdjadj b. Yūsuf.

29. *Miʿyār al-jadīd*, 3:73.

30. All references to the Qur'ān in this book are to Ali, trans., *Al-Qur'ān*.

31. *Miʿyār al-jadīd*, 3:73.

32. Ibid.

33. Ibid., 74.

34. Ibid.

35. I have been unable to identify this qāḍī.

36. *Miʿyār al-jadīd*, 3:74.

37. Possibly al-Wazzānī refers here to al-Zayyātī's most popular fatwā collection: *Al-Jawāhir al-mukhtāra fī-mā waqaftu ʿalayhi min al-nawāzil bi-jibāl Ghumāra*. On the author and his work, see Hendrickson, "The Islamic Obligation to Emigrate," 110–20.

38. I have been unable to identify this jurist.

39. *Miʿyār al-jadīd*, 3:74–75.

40. The Sūda family was widely recognized in Fez for generations of learned men who were prominent members of the Fāsī religious elite. A certain Muḥammad al-Tā'udī b. Sūda (d. 1794) was the *shaykh al-jamāʿa*. See Laroui, *Les origines sociales*, 195.

41. Unfortunately, al-Wazzānī does not record here the fatwā of Ibn Manẓūr.

42. *Miʿyār al-jadīd*, 3:75–76.

43. The unquestionable duty of Muslims to obey their rulers and the inherent sinfulness of any rebellion against the established order have been the ruling political positions of Sunnī Islam throughout history. The tacit assumption of these political positions centers around the view that anarchy or challenge of the ruling elite poses a greater danger than does tolerance for coercive powers and violations of Islamic law and morality. On this position in Islamic political thought, see Crone, *God's Rule*, 259–85.

44. *Miʿyār al-jadīd*, 3:76.

45. Ibid.

46. Ibid., 76.

47. Ibid.

48. Ibid.

49. Ibid., 77.

50. Ibid.

51. Ibid.

52. Ibid., 78.
53. Ibid.
54. Ibid., 91–94.
55. Ibid., 91.
56. Ibid., 92.
57. Ibid.
58. Ibid.
59. Ibid., 92–93. It will be recalled that al-Wazzānī himself used both the tradition transmitted by ʿUmar and the reported *ḥadīth* as evidence in his original fatwā.
60. Ibid., 93.
61. Ibid., 93–94.
62. Ibid., 94.
63. Ibid.
64. For a broad examination of the legal discourse, see Khadduri, *War and Peace in the Law of Islam*. Also see March, *Islam and Liberal Citizenship*, 103–33; El Fadl, "Islamic Law and Muslim Minorities," 141–87; idem, "Legal Debates on Muslim Minorities," 127–62; Masud, "The Obligation to Migrate," 29–49. For a study of a recent fatwā that is explicitly concerned with the needs of Muslims living under non-Muslim rule, see Nafi, "Fatwā and War," 78–116.
65. Notably, the historical conditions that emerged during the Christian conquest of Muslim lands in the Iberian Peninsula from the eleventh century until the fall of Granada in 1492 elicited a vital Mālikī discourse. On the slow disintegration of Muslim rule in Iberia, see Miranda, "The Iberian Peninsula and Sicily," 2:406–39; Kassis, "Muslim Revival in Spain," 78–110; Viguera-Molins, "Al-Andalus and the Maghrib," 2:21–47; Harvey, *Islamic Spain*; Meyerson, *Muslims of Valencia*; Mediano, "The Post-Almohad Dynasties," 2:106–43. For works examining the contemporary Mālikī juristic discourse, see Van Koningsveld and Wiegers, "Islamic Statute of the Mudejars," 19–58; K. Miller, "Muslim Minorities and the Obligation to Emigrate," 256–88.
66. Two recent PhD dissertations examine this Mālikī juristic discourse; see Hendrickson, "The Islamic Obligation to Emigrate"; Alan Verskin, "Early Islamic Legal Responses to Living under Christian Rule."
67. The text may be found in *Miʿyār al-jadīd*, 3:28–35.
68. For a survey of the period, see Pennell, *Morocco*, 68–77; Abun-Nasr, *History of the Maghrib in the Islamic Period*, 103–18, 205–27. On the Moroccan legal discourse that emerged in response to the Portuguese occupation, see Hendrickson, "Muslim Legal Responses to Portuguese Occupation," 309–25.
69. El-Mansour, "Maghribis in the Mashriq."
70. Seddon, "Labour Migration and Agricultural Development," 69.
71. Cigar, "Socio-economic Structures," 56, 62.
72. Clancy-Smith, "The Maghrib and the Mediterranean World," 222–49; Kenbib, "Impact of the French Conquest," 48–51.
73. On the legal value of the testimony of witnesses and the assessment of a witness's personal integrity, see Ziadeh, "Integrity (*ʿAdālah*) in Classical Islamic Law," 73–93.

74. The full text of al-Wansharīsī's fatwā is recorded in *al-Jawāhir al-mukhtāra*, a collection of fatwās compiled by 'Abd al-'Azīz al-Zayyātī (d. 1645). On al-Zayyātī and his work, see Hendrickson, "The Islamic Obligation to Emigrate," 110–20. In addition, Hendrickson includes a useful Arabic edition of al-Wansharīsī's fatwā as recorded by al-Zayyātī; see 421–27. Also see idem, "Muslim Legal Responses to Portuguese Occupation."

75. *Mi'yār al-jadīd*, 3:28.

76. Ibid. It should be noted that the term *iṣṭād* that is used to describe the activity pursued with the infidels may signify either fishing or hunting.

77. Ibid.

78. Ibid.

79. Ibid.

80. Ibid., 29.

81. Ibid.

82. Ibid.

83. Ibid.

84. Ibid. The term *ḥurma* (pl. *ḥurumāt*) signifies sanctity or inviolability. The Islamic community who believes in God and upholds the sacred law is among the sacred things of God (*maḥārim*) that must be respected, revered, and honored. As the present fatwā suggests, a Muslim's *ḥurma* is associated with reliability, credibility, and trustworthiness, which played an instrumental role in assessing a witness's testimony. Residing under non-Muslim rule is an offense against the faith and a violation of this sanctity. The notion of respectability seems applicable in this case.

85. During the Reconquista, a period spanning the end of the eleventh century to the fifteenth century, vast Muslim populations in the Iberian Peninsula came under Christian rule. Mudéjars, in Arabic, *mudajjanūn* or *ahl al-dajan*, refer to such Iberian Muslims residing, after the conquest of their territories, in al-Andalus under Christian authorities. Harvey, *Islamic Spain*, 2–5; K. Miller, "Muslim Minorities and the Obligation to Emigrate," 257.

86. *Mi'yār al-jadīd*, 3:29.

87. Ibid.

88. The terms *mukhāṭaba* and *khiṭāb*, which are used interchangeably in the text, refer to a written communication between qāḍīs. One qāḍī may communicate with another by means of a document that corroborates a testimony of a witness or relate evidence pertaining to a claim. Such a document is admissible as evidence in court. Masud, Peters, and Powers, "Qāḍīs and Their Courts," 27–28. For an investigation of the working of this legal instrument in modern Mālikī context, see Layish, "*Shahādat Naql*," 495–516. I thank Aron Zysow for corresponding with me about this issue.

89. *Mi'yār al-jadīd*, 3:29–30.

90. Ibid., 30.

91. Ibid.

92. In this particular context, the term *ṣāḥib* means a jurist who follows the authoritative doctrine of the school, namely, a contemporary of Saḥnūn, a predecessor or even one of Mālik's associates. See Makdisi, *The Rise of Colleges*, 128–29.

93. *Mi'yār al-jadīd*, 3:30.

94. Ibid. I thank Jocelyn Hendrickson for helping me with the translation of this section.

95. Ibid.

96. Ibid., 31.

97. Ibid.

98. Ibid.

99. Ibid.

100. Ibid., 31–32.

101. The fatwā, famously known as *Asnā al-matājir*, was issued in 1491 and recorded in al-Wansharīsī, *Kitāb al-Mi'yār*, 2:119–36. On this fatwā, see Mu'nis, "Asnā al-matājir fi bayān aḥkām man ghalaba 'alā waṭanihi al-Naṣārā wa-lam yuhājir," 1–63; Hendrickson, "The Islamic Obligation to Emigrate."

102. *Mi'yār al-jadīd*, 3:32.

103. Ibid.

104. For a useful biographical sketch of al-Māzarī and a study of his fatwā, see Hendrickson, "The Islamic Obligation to Emigrate," 201–16.

105. *Mi'yār al-jadīd*, 3:32.

106. Ibid., 32–33; Hendrickson, "The Islamic Obligation to Emigrate," 374–75.

107. *Mi'yār al-jadīd*, 3:33.

108. Ibid.

109. Ibid., 34. 'Umar b. Ḥafṣūn (d. 918) led a rebellion that began in 880 against the Umayyad governor of Cordova. Ibn Ḥafṣūn and his supporters, mainly local Christians, challenged the Umayyads almost continuously from the rebellion's inception until 916. *EI2*, s.v. 'Umar b. Ḥafsūn.

110. *Mi'yār al-jadīd*, 3:34.

111. Ibid.

112. On al-Burzulī's collection of *Nawāzil*, see al-Hīlah, "Classification of Andalusian and Maghribī Books of *Nawāzil*," 73–74.

113. *Mi'yār al-jadīd*, 3:34.

114. A translation of this abridged version may be found in Wiegers, *Islamic Literature*, 86–87. For a discussion of the original fatwā, see Hendrickson, "The Islamic Obligation to Emigrate," 219–29.

115. *Mi'yār al-jadīd*, 3:35.

116. Ibid.

117. The original *istiftā'* addressed to al-'Abdūsī includes a specific question about the appointment of Mudéjar judges and the validity of their rulings. Curiously, al-Wazzānī disregarded this issue in the process of editing and abbreviating the *istiftā'*. Hendrickson, "The Islamic Obligation to Emigrate," 220.

118. *Mi'yār al-jadīd*, 3:35.

119. Hendrickson has observed that al-'Abdūsī's fatwā ends with a remark that some jurists in *dār al-Islām* reject the validity of Mudéjar judges appointed by a Christian ruler and their certified documents, arguing that the Muslim community's approval of

these judges cannot be regarded as a voluntary consent. She indicates that by concluding his fatwā with acknowledging instances of disagreement, al-ʿAbdūsī in effect "leaves the matter to the discretion of the receiving judge." Al-Wazzānī's omission of dissenting voices (no matter how brief and unrepresentative) reveals his techniques in connecting earlier texts to the new setting. Hendrickson, "The Islamic Obligation to Emigrate," 221–22. I thank Jocelyn Hendrickson for bringing al-ʿAbdūsī's significant comment to my attention.

120. *Miʿyār al-jadīd*, 3:35.

CHAPTER 5

1. Laroui, *Les origines sociales*, 250–51.
2. Kenbib, *Les protégés*, 14.
3. Between 1871 and 1877 the balance of Moroccan exports over imports was positive, but in 1878 imports increased. From then on, the Moroccan trade deficit widened. In the following decades, although agricultural exports increased briefly during the 1880s, Moroccan exports remained peripheral to European economies. Miège, *Le Maroc et l'Europe*, 3:419; Pennell, *Morocco since 1830*, 88–89; Michel, *Une économie de subsistances*, 1:53–55.
4. K. Brown, *People of Salé*, 124–25.
5. On the Spanish-Moroccan war of 1859–60 and the indemnities imposed on the Moroccan government, see Schroeter, *Merchants of Essaouira*, 132–34.
6. Pennell, *Morocco since 1830*, 72–80.
7. Miège, *Le Maroc et l'Europe*, 2:481, 3:470.
8. Schroeter, *Merchants of Essaouira*, 157–58.
9. Miège, *Le Maroc et l'Europe*, 4:341–42.
10. Kenbib, "Changing Aspects of State and Society," 17–19; Michel, *Une économie de subsistances*, 2:446–48.
11. Schroeter, "Royal Power and the Economy," 90–91. For a detailed discussion of the tanners' rebellion, see Sebti, "Chroniques de la contestation citadine," 283–312.
12. Burke, *Prelude to Protectorate*, 51–53; Michel, *Une économie de subsistances*, 1:85–87.
13. Schroeter, *Merchants of Essaouira*, 197.
14. Brown, *People of Salé*, 123.
15. Holden, *Politics of Food*, 17.
16. Kenbib, "Changing Aspects of State and Society," 17. Also see Ennaji, *Expansion européenne et changement social*, 60–65.
17. In particular, I am thinking of the evidence advanced by Iris Agmon in *Family and Court*, her study on the family in late-Ottoman Jaffa and Haifa.
18. Kenbib, "Changing Aspects of State and Society," 17–19.
19. Ennaji, *Expansion européenne et changement social*, 72–76; Schroeter, *Merchants of Essaouira*, 197–200.
20. Seddon, "Labour Migration and Agricultural Development," 69.
21. Pennell, *Morocco since 1830*, 103.
22. Schroeter, *Merchants of Essaouira*, 198, 214.

23. Brown, *People of Salé*, 120–21. Between 1860 and 1866 imports of cotton cloth made up 30–50 percent of total Moroccan imports. Miège, *Le Maroc et l'Europe*, 2:535.

24. Brown, *People of Salé*, 130–31.

25. Ibid., 121.

26. Ibid., 116.

27. Ibid., 131–32.

28. On the operation of the Islamic law of inheritance, see Coulson, *Succession in the Muslim Family*; Powers, "The Islamic Inheritance System," 11–30.

29. David Powers argues that during the medieval and early modern periods the application of the Islamic law of inheritance was often the last and least important form of property transmission in the family. Powers, "The Islamic Inheritance System," 27–29.

30. The Islamic institution of family endowments has been extensively studied by Western scholars. For a broad overview, see *EI2*, s.v. Waḳf. On Mālikī endowments, see Powers, "The Maliki Family Endowment," 379–406; Layish, "The Mālikī Family *waqf*," 1–32. Some notable studies include Zarinebaf, "Women, Patronage, and Charity in Ottoman Istanbul," 89–101; Deguilhem, "Consciousness of Self," 102–15; Doumani, "Endowing Families," 3–41; Fay, "Women and Waqf," 28–47.

31. Powers and Terem, "From the *Mi'yār* of al-Wansharīsī to the *New Mi'yār* of al-Wazzānī," 239.

32. The fatwā may be found in the *New Mi'yār* in the chapter devoted to *ḥubus*. *Mi'yār al-jadīd*, 8:387–89.

33. Ibid., 387.

34. The cultural logic behind this stipulation is related to the division of labor between men and women in the family. This division assigns the men the role of providing for women, whereas women are not responsible for anyone, not even for themselves. In other words, women are conceived as dependents who are supported by their male relatives or their husbands. On the gendered division of labor, see Tucker, *Women, Family, and Gender in Islamic Law*, 24–25; idem, *In the House of the Law*, 146–47; Agmon, *Family and Court*, 132–33.

35. *Mi'yār al-jadīd*, 8:387.

36. This issue has important consequences for the division of revenues among the beneficiaries. The revenues are not controlled by the members of the oldest generation. A younger generation of descendants may be included in the division of the endowment revenues.

37. *Ḥ'iyāza* is an important legal procedure that regulated a variety of property transactions, as, for example, gifts, bequests, and loans. See *EI2*, s.v. Ḳabḍ.

38. *Mi'yār al-jadīd*, 8:387.

39. Powers, "The Maliki Family Endowment," 399–401. Also see Layish, "The Mālikī Family Waqf," 16–17.

40. *Mi'yār al-jadīd*, 8:387.

41. Ibid.

42. Ibid.

43. Ibid., 387–88. On different hermeneutical strategies employed by jurists in dis-

covering the intent of a founder, see Powers, "The Maliki Family Endowment," 391–94. On the meaning of *lafẓ* in Islamic thought, see Weiss, "Exotericism and Objectivity in Islamic Jurisprudence," 53–71.

44. *Miʿyār al-jadīd*, 8:388.

45. On the linguistic and semantic significance of the term *qarīna* in Islamic legal literature, see Hallaq, "Notes on the Term *qarīna*," 475–80.

46. *Miʿyār al-jadīd*, 8:388.

47. Ibid.

48. Ibid.

49. Ibid. On the legal use and meaning of the particle *wāw*, see Layish, "The Mālikī Family Waqf," 13–14.

50. *Miʿyār al-jadīd*, 8:388.

51. Ibid.

52. Ibid.

53. Ibid., 389.

54. Ibid.

55. On the law of maintenance, see *EI2*, s.v. Nafaḳa; Layish, *Women and Islamic Law*, 91–124; Meron, *L'obligation alimentaire*; Mir-Hosseini, *Marriage on Trial*, 46–49; Tucker, *Women, Family, and Gender in Islamic Law*, 50–52; idem, *In the House of the Law*, 42–44, 58–67.

56. On the absent person, see *EI2*, s.v. Ghāib, Mafḳūd; Tyan, *Histoire de l'organisation judiciaire*, 369; G. Ammar, "De la representation en justice de l'absent," 391–99. Also see Zomeno, "Abandoned Wives," 111–26.

57. The fatwā analyzed here may be found in *Miʿyār al-jadīd*, 4:573–76.

58. Ibid., 573. On legal representation, see *EI2*, s.v. Wakāla; Tyan, "Judicial Organization," 257–59.

59. *Miʿyār al-jadīd*, 4:573.

60. Ibid.

61. On the legal value of a witness's testimony, see Ziadeh, "Integrity (*ʿAdālah*) in Classical Islamic Law."

62. On judicial review, see Powers, "On Judicial Review in Islamic Law," 315–41.

63. *Miʿyār al-jadīd*, 4:573.

64. Ibid.

65. Ibid.

66. Ibid., 573–74.

67. Ibid., 574.

68. Ibid.

69. Ibid., 575.

70. The term *amīn* signifies a guardian or a custodian: a person in a position of trust (*amāna*), charged with power, authority, or control over a thing or a person. Because the husband is entrusted with the responsibility to act for his wife's benefit, his claim of providing maintenance is trustworthy. On *amīn* and the question of liability, see Schacht, *Introduction to Islamic Law*, 147–48.

71. *Mi'yār al-jadīd*, 4:575.
72. Ibid.
73. Ibid.
74. Ibid.
75. Ibid.
76. Ibid., 575–76.
77. Ibid., 576.
78. Ibid.
79. Ibid.
80. Ibid.
81. Ibid., 576–77.

CHAPTER 6

1. Burke, *Prelude to Protectorate*, 23.
2. Miège, *Le Maroc et l'Europe*, 2:535, 3:250; Brown, *People of Salé*, 116–54.
3. Brown, *People of Salé*, 129.
4. Ibid., 130–31.
5. Cigar, "Socio-economic Structures," 63–64.
6. Brown, *People of Salé*, 131–32.
7. Cigar, "Socio-economic Structures," 61, 63–64.
8. Miège, *Le Maroc et l'Europe*, 3:246–51, 398–427; 4:387–96.
9. For example, see Schroeter, "Royal Power and the Economy."
10. Cigar, "Socio-economic Structures," 67.
11. Al-Nāṣirī, *Kitāb al-istiqsā*, 9:221.
12. Ibid., 208.
13. Le Tourneau, *Fès avant le Protectorat*, 554–55.
14. Miège, *Le Maroc et l'Europe*, 4:393.
15. Jouin, "Valeur symbolique des aliments et rites alimentaires," 300; Pennell, *Morocco since 1830*, 76.
16. On the expansion of tea consumption in Morocco and the appeal of tea drinking to Moroccans, see Michel, *Une économie de subsistances*, 2:486–87.
17. The custom of regularly adding sugar to tea probably originated in the Netherlands and England in the late seventeenth century and the early eighteenth century. For a study of the development of the custom and its meaning, see Smith, "Complications of the Commonplace," 259–78.
18. Miège, *Le Maroc et l'Europe*, 3:249, 415; 4:387, 389.
19. Bazzaz, *Forgotten Saints*, 98–99.
20. Cigar, "Socio-economic Structures," 67; Pennell, *Morocco since 1830*, 106.
21. *EI2*, s.v.v. Sukkar, Ḳaṣab al-Sukkar. Also see Mintz, *Sweetness and Power*, 23–24. Mintz's book has been particularly helpful in guiding me through the history of the use of sugar.
22. Galloway, "The Mediterranean Sugar Industry," 180, 188, 193.
23. Geographer J. H. Galloway indicates that the decline of the sugar industry in the

eastern Mediterranean began a century before sugar arrived in Europe from the Atlantic colonies, and sugar production actually flourished in the western Mediterranean during the fifteenth century. He argues that to account for the early decline of the industry in the east and for its increase in the west, "factors other than competition must also be considered; they are warfare, plague, the policies of the Mamluk sultans of Egypt, technological stagnation, and the deterioration of the environment." Ibid., 191. For similar arguments, see Ashtor, "Levantine Sugar Industry," 226–80.

24. Galloway, "The Mediterranean Sugar Industry," 188.

25. Ennaji, *Expansion européenne et changement social*, 85–93.

26. The treatise may be found in *Mi'yār al-jadīd*, 12:520–36.

27. See his biography in al-Ḥajwī, *al-Fikr al-sāmī*, 625.

28. For his biography, see al-Sibtī and Lakhṣāṣī, *Min al-shāy ilā al-atāy*, 165, 187.

29. *Mi'yār al-jadīd*, 12:520.

30. Ibid., 520–21.

31. Sugar is the end product of a complex process of crystallization of the dark juice extracted from sugar cane. The juice is refined by a series of boiling and filtering procedures. Repeated boiling of the juice causes evaporation and sucrose concentration. As the liquid becomes saturated, sugar crystals appear. Mintz, *Sweetness and Power*, 21–22. In Islam, blood is considered a major impurity (*najas*), and its consumption is forbidden. See *EI2*, s.v. Nad̲j̲is.

32. The term *al-aṣl fī al-ashyā'* relates to the issue of determining rules pertaining to objects and acts based upon presumed state of affairs. In the absence of cogent evidence, a legal state of affairs is presumed to continue to be valid. In the present case, sugar is presumed to continue to be permissible so long as there is no proof that changes that presumption. I thank Aron Zysow for corresponding with me about this issue.

33. *Mi'yār al-jadīd*, 12:521.

34. Ibid., 521–22.

35. *Mayta* signifies an animal that has not been ritually slaughtered or that is forbidden for eating as a result of a general prohibition, such as dogs or swine. The flesh and other edible parts of *mayta*, as well as the bones and hair, are considered impure and cannot be eaten. See *EI2*, s.v. Mayta.

36. *Mi'yār al-jadīd*, 12:522.

37. Ibid.

38. Ibid. I thank Aron Zysow for helping me with the translation of this verse.

39. Ibid.

40. Ibid.

41. Ibid., 522–23.

42. Ibid., 523.

43. Under Islamic law, the consumption of lizard is licit and pig is considered impure. Its flesh is thus forbidden, as is the hair. See Waines, *Food Culture and Health*, xxi, xxii; Cook, "Early Islamic Dietary Law," 220–31; *EI2*, s.v. Ḥayawān.

44. *Mi'yār al-jadīd*, 12:523.

45. Ibid. *Khabar* signifies a piece of news, an account, a rumor, or a report that may

be true or false. Given the specific Moroccan context under discussion, I refer to it as a rumor.

46. *Mi'yār al-jadīd*, 12:523.

47. For a consideration of Islamic discourse on the permission to consume food prepared by the People of the Book, see, for instance, Freidenreich, *Foreigners and Their Food*, 131–56.

48. The technical term for this gastric juice is "rennet." Rennet enzymes are produced in the stomach of young animals and play an important role in helping them digest milk. It is also used in cheese making to curdle the milk. The implication here is that cheese curdled with the rennet of a pig should be forbidden. On the legal problem of infidel cheese, see Cook, "Magian Cheese," 449–67.

49. *Mi'yār al-jadīd*, 12:524.

50. Ibid.

51. Al-Zarhūnī's reasoning here presents us with a significant point: Against a preponderant state of affairs that links food manufactured by infidels to impurity, Mālikī jurists, he maintains, did not consider such food as impure. Presumably, the basis for abandoning the preponderant state of affairs was social need and necessity. I thank Aron Zysow for corresponding with me about this issue. Corroboration of this position could be found in Ze'ev Maghen's suggestion that Sunnī jurists did not consider infidels as "intrinsically impure," despite the Qur'ānic verse that links infidels to impurity (9:27). See Maghen, "Close Encounters," 364. In a subsequent discussion, focused on Mālikī juristic discourse in North Africa and al-Andalus in the ninth century, Janina M. Safran argues that Mālikī jurists treated the Christian "as unclean and polluting." See Safran, "Rules of Purity and Confessional Boundaries," 197–212. Drawing on Safran's article, it is possible to explain these two contradictory arguments. According to Safran, the issues, which gave rise to the Mālikī opinions, were serious concerns and anxieties "about the integrity of Islam and the Muslim community in a multiconfessional polity, a concern perhaps accentuated in the ninth century by social flux in al-Andalus. Debates in this period about the impurity and pollution of the Christian in a ritual context may express interest in protecting the community and the faith by emphasizing ritual demarcation" (199).

52. *Mi'yār al-jadīd*, 12:524.

53. The reference to the habit of wetting the yarn by *ahl al-dhimma* alludes to the differences between the Islamic and non-Islamic legal principles and norms governing water law. For the Islamic water law, see *EI2*, s.v. Mā'.

54. Although al-Zarhūnī does not identify the work to which he refers here, it is most likely the *Mukhtaṣar* of Khalīl, which contains the authoritative doctrine of the Mālikī school and became, over the course of centuries, the subject of commentaries and supercommentaries.

55. *Mi'yār al-jadīd*, 12:524.

56. Ibid., 524–25.

57. Ibid., 525.

58. Note that the issue treated here is cleanliness in the ritual sense. Some things may be quite dirty and, from the perspective of Islamic purity rules, be cleansed and,

therefore, ritually valid. On the *ṭahāra* system, see Reinhart, "Impurity/No Danger," 1–24; *EI2*, s.v. Ṭahāra.

59. Waines, *Food Culture and Health*, 183–84. On the origin of an Islamic medico-culinary tradition, see Waines, "Dietetics in Medieval Islamic Culture," 228–40.

60. *Miʿyār al-jadīd*, 12:525.

61. Ibid.

62. Here, al-Zarhūnī refers to *Tadhkirat uli al-albāb waʾl-jāmiʿ liʾl-ʿajab al-ʿujāb*, a medical work that treats diseases and drugs by Dāʾūd al-Anṭākī (d. 1599). See *EI2*, s.v. al-Anṭākī, Dāʾūd b. ʿUmar al-Ḍarīr.

63. *Miʿyār al-jadīd*, 12:525–26.

64. Ibid., 526.

65. Ibid.

66. Ibid.

67. Ibid.

68. The term *waswasa* signifies useless advice or an evil thought prompted by Satan. The implication here is that the Believers need to be concerned with pious thoughts and deeds and avoid dubious and ineffective presumptions. Contemplation of the latter clearly is unlawful.

69. *Miʿyār al-jadīd*, 12:526–27.

70. Islamic law imposes the *ḥadd* punishments for certain crimes specified in the Qurʾān. See *EI2*, s.v. Ḥadd.

71. *Miʿyār al-jadīd*, 12:527.

72. Ibid.

73. *Qadarī* is the name given to a proponent of the human freedom to act in the early period of Islam. See *EI2*, s.v. Ḳadariyya.

74. *Miʿyār al-jadīd*, 12:527.

75. Al-Zarhūnī does not cite God's words as preserved in the Qurʾān. Possibly, he refers to Q. 5:5: "On this day all things that are clean have been made lawful to you; and made lawful for you is the food of the People of the Book, as your food is made lawful for them."

76. *EI2*, s.v. D̲h̲abīḥa.

77. *Miʿyār al-jadīd*, 12:528.

78. Ibid.

79. Ibid.

80. Ibid., 528–29.

81. Note here that al-Wazzānī also wrote a treatise that authorizes the consumption of *ṣāmit*. The text may be found in al-Sibtī and Lakhṣāṣī, M*in al-shāy ilā al-atāy*, 226–28. I was unable to locate the text in the *Miʿyār al-jadīd.*

82. *Miʿyār al-jadīd*, 12:529.

83. Ibid.

84. Ibid.

85. Ibid., 529–30.

86. Powers, *Law, Society, and Culture in the Maghrib*, 29, 62 passim; Fierro, "Idraʾū

l-ḥudūd bi-l-shubuhāt," 209–13 passim; *EI2*, s.v. Shubha; Rabb, "Doubt's Benefit." I thank Aron Zysow for referring me to the last source.

87. *Mi'yār al-jadīd*, 12:530.

88. For Mālikī discussions on the issue of Muslims using the leftover water of Christians, see Safran, "Rules of Purity and Confessional Boundaries;" Halevi, "Christian Impurity versus Economic Necessity," 928–30. I thank David Powers for referring me to the last source.

89. *Mi'yār al-jadīd*, 12:530–31.

90. Ibid., 531–32.

91. Ibid., 532.

92. Ibid., 532–33.

93. Ibid., 533.

94. Ibid.

95. Ibid., 533–34.

96. Ibid., 534.

97. Ibid., 534–35.

98. Ibid., 535.

99. Ibid., 535–36.

100. Ibid., 536.

101. Ibid.

102. Ibid., 537.

103. Ibid., 537–38.

104. *Mā' al-ḥayāh* (in Moroccan dialect, *māḥiyā*; in French, *eau de vie*) is made of figs, dates, grapes, or a mixture of them. Gottreich, *The Mellah of Marrakesh*, 78–79.

105. *Mi'yār al-jadīd*, 12:538. On the prohibition of wine and *sakar*, see *EI2*, s.v. Khamr.

106. *Mi'yār al-jadīd*, 12:538.

107. Ibid.

108. Ibid., 539.

109. Ibid.

110. Ibid.

111. The earliest Arabic reports point to the late fifteenth century as the time when the practice of coffee drinking in coffeehouses established itself in Yemen. Yemenis carried the habit of drinking coffee to other cities of the Middle East. By the first decade of the sixteenth century the widespread adoption of the practice and the presence of coffeehouses throughout the Middle East sparked a serious legal controversy. See Hattox, *Coffee and Coffeehouses*. On the geography of coffee drinking, see Grigg, "The Worlds of Tea and Coffee," 283–94.

112. *Mi'yār al-jadīd*, 12:539.

113. Ibid., 539–40.

114. Ibid., 540.

115. Ibid. See *EI2*, s.v. Ḳahwa.

116. *Mi'yār al-jadīd*, 12:541. Zeila is a port city in Somalia, located on the Gulf of Aden.

117. Ibid. Muṣṭafā is one of the ninety-nine names of the Prophet Muḥammad.

CHAPTER 7

1. Although scholars are well aware of the various critical interventions about the inherent processes of change in Islamic law and the studies that treat attempts to reconcile Islam and modernity, relinquishing the binary traditional/modern construction continues to prove difficult.

BIBLIOGRAPHY

Abdulrazak, Fawzi A. "The Kingdom of the Book: The History of Printing as an Agency of Change in Morocco between 1865–1912." PhD diss., Boston University, 1990.

Abun-Nasr, Jamil. *A History of the Maghrib in the Islamic Period*. Cambridge: Cambridge University Press, 1987.

———. "The Salafiyya Movement in Morocco: The Religious Bases of the Moroccan Nationalist Movement." In *Social Change: The Colonial Situation*, ed. Immanuel Wallerstein, 489–502. New York: John Wiley and Sons, 1966.

———. *The Tijaniyya: A Sufi Order in the Modern World*. London: Oxford University Press, 1965.

Adams, Charles. *Islam and Modernism in Egypt*. New York: Russell and Russell, 1968.

Agmon, Iris. *Family and Court: Legal Culture and Modernity in Late Ottoman Palestine*. Syracuse, NY: Syracuse University Press, 2006.

al-ʿAlawī, Muḥammad al-Fallāḥ. *Jāmiʿ al-qarawiyyīn wa'l-fikr al-salafī, 1873–1914*. Casablanca: Maṭbaʿat al-Najāḥ al-Jadīda, 1994.

Ali, Ahmad, trans. *Al-Qur'ān*. Princeton: Princeton University Press, 2001.

Ammar, G. "De la representation en justice de l'absent. Définition du caractère périodique de l'absence." *Revue Marocaine de Droit* 12 (1960): 391–99.

Asad, Talal. *The Idea of an Anthropology of Islam*. Washington, DC: Center for Contemporary Arab Studies, Georgetown University, 1986.

———. "The Limits of Religious Criticism in the Middle East: Notes on Islamic Public Argument." In *Genealogies of Religion: Discipline and Reasons of Power in Christianity and Islam*, ed. Talal Asad, 200–236. Baltimore: John Hopkins University Press, 1993.

Ashtor, E. "Levantine Sugar Industry in the Later Middle Ages—an Example of Technological Decline." *Israel Oriental Studies* 7 (1977): 226–80.

Aubin, Eugène. *Morocco of Today*. London: J. M. Dent, 1906.

Avila, Maria Luisa. "Women in Andalusi Biographical Sources." In *Writing the Feminine: Women in Arab Sources*, ed. Manuela Marin and Randi Deguilhem, 149–63. London: I. B. Tauris, 2002.

Awang, Abdul Rahman. *The Status of Dhimī in Islamic Law*. Kuala Lumpur: International Law Book Services, 1994.

Badawi, Zaki M. A. *The Reformers of Egypt*. London: Croom Helm, 1978.

al-Bakkārī, ʿAbd al-Salām. *Al-Ashrāf al-ʿImrāniyūn biʾl-Maghrib: Dirāsa Wathāʾiqiyya.* Al-Qunayṭira: Al-Bukīlī li-Ṭibāʿa waʾl-Nashr waʾl-Tawzīʿ, 1996.

Bazzaz, Sahar. *Forgotten Saints: History, Power, and Politics in the Making of Modern Morocco.* Cambridge, MA: Harvard University Press, 2010.

———. "Heresy and Politics in Nineteenth-Century Morocco." *Arab Studies Journal* 10.2–11.1 (Fall 2002–Spring 2003): 67–86.

Berque, Jacques. *Essai sur la méthode juridique maghrébine.* Rabat: Marcel Leforestier, 1944.

———. *Les Nawāzil el muzāraʿa du Miʿyār Al Wazzānī: Étude et traduction.* Rabat: Felix Moncho, 1940.

———. "Ville et université: Aperçu sur l'histoire de l'École de Fès." *Revue Historique de Droit Français et Étranger* 27 (1949): 64–117.

Binʿadāda, Āsya. *Al-Fikr al-iṣlāḥī fī ʿahd al-ḥimāya.* Casablanca: Al-Markaz al-Thaqāfī al-ʿArabī, 2003.

Bourqia, Rahma. "Droit et pratiques sociales: Le cas des nawazil au XIX siècle." *Hespéris-Tamuda* 35 (1997): 131–45.

Brown, Daniel W. *Rethinking Tradition in Modern Islamic Thought.* Cambridge: Cambridge University Press, 1996.

Brown, Jonathan C. *Hadith: Muhammad's Legacy in the Medieval and Modern World.* Oxford: Oneworld Publications, 2009.

Brown, Kenneth. *People of Salé: Tradition and Change in a Moroccan City, 1830–1930.* Cambridge, MA: Harvard University Press, 1976.

———. "Profile of a Nineteenth-Century Moroccan Scholar." In *Scholars, Saints, and Sufis,* ed. Nikki R. Keddie, 127–48. Berkeley: University of California Press, 1972.

Burke, Edmund, III. "The Moroccan Ulama, 1860–1912: An Introduction." In *Scholars, Saints, and Sufis: Muslim Religious Institutions in the Middle East since 1500,* ed. Nikki R. Keddie, 93–125. Berkeley: University of California Press, 1972.

———. *Prelude to Protectorate in Morocco: Precolonial Protest and Resistance, 1860–1912.* Chicago: University of Chicago Press, 1976.

Buskens, Léon. "Sharia and National Law in Morocco." In *Sharia Incorporated: A Comparative Overview of the Legal Systems of Twelve Muslim Countries in Past and Present,* ed. Jan Michiel Otto, 89–138. Leiden, Netherlands: Leiden University Press, 2010.

Cagne, Jacques. *Nation et nationalisme au Maroc.* Rabat: Al-Maʿārif al-Jadīda, 1988.

Calderwood, Eric. "The Beginning (or End) of Moroccan History: Historiography, Translation, and Modernity in Ahmad B. Khalid al-Nasiri and Clemente Cerdeira." *International Journal of Middle East Studies* 44.3 (2012): 399–420.

Chenoufi, Moncef. "Les deux sejours de Muhammad ʿAbduh en Tunisie et leurs incidences sur le réformisme musulman tunisien." *Les Cahiers de Tunisie* 16 (1968): 57–96.

Cigar, Norman. "Socio-economic Structures and the Development of an Urban Bourgeoisie in Pre-colonial Morocco." *Maghreb Review* 6 (1981): 55–76.

Clancy-Smith, Julia A. "The Maghrib and the Mediterranean World in the Nineteenth Century: Illicit Exchanges, Migrants, and Social Marginals." In *The Maghrib in*

Question: Essays in History and Historiography, ed. Michael Le Gall and Kenneth Perkins, 222–49. Austin: University of Texas Press, 1997.

———. *Mediterraneans: North Africa and Europe in an Age of Migration, 1800–1900*. Berkeley: University of California Press, 2011.

Commins, David Dean. *Islamic Reform: Politics and Social Change in Late Ottoman Syria*. Oxford: Oxford University Press, 1990.

Cook, Michael. "Early Islamic Dietary Law." *Jerusalem Studies in Arabic and Islam* 7 (1986): 217–77.

———. "Magian Cheese: An Archaic Problem in Islamic Law." *Bulletin of the School of Oriental and African Studies* 47.3 (1984): 449–67.

Cornell, Vincent J. "Faqīh versus Faqīr in Marinid Morocco: Epistemological Dimensions of a Polemic." In *Islamic Mysticism Contested: Thirteen Centuries of Controversies and Polemics*, ed. Frederick de Jong and Bernd Radtke, 207–24. Leiden, Netherlands: Brill, 1999.

———. *Realm of the Saint: Power and Authority in Moroccan Sufism*. Austin: University of Texas Press, 1998.

Coulson, N. J. *Succession in the Muslim Family*. Cambridge: Cambridge University Press, 1971.

Crone, Patricia. *God's Rule: Government and Islam*. New York: Columbia University Press, 2004.

Dallal, Ahmad. "Appropriating the Past: Twentieth Century Reconstruction of Premodern Islamic Thought." *Islamic Law and Society* 7.1 (2000): 325–58.

———. "The Origins and Objectives of Islamic Revivalist Thought, 1750–1850." *Journal of the American Oriental Society* 113.3 (July–September 1993): 341–59.

Deguilhem, Randi. "Consciousness of Self: The Muslim Woman as Creator and Manager of Waqf Foundations in Late Ottoman Damascus." In *Beyond the Exotic: Women's Histories in Islamic Societies*, ed. Amira El-Azhary Sonbol, 102–15. Syracuse, NY: Syracuse University Press, 2005.

Delphin, Gaetan. *Fas, son université et l'enseignement supérieur musulman*. Paris: Ernest Leroux, 1889.

Dennerlein, Bettina. "Legitimate Bounds and Bound Legitimacy: The Act of Allegiance to the Ruler (*bai'a*) in 19th Century Morocco." *Die Welt des Islam* 41.3 (2001): 287–310.

Dialmy, Abdessamad. "Femme et discourse au Maroc." PhD diss., Université de Picardie, 1987.

Doumani, Beshara. "Endowing Families: Waqf, Property Devolution, and Gender in Greater Syria, 1800–1860." *Comparative Studies in Society and History* 40 (1998): 3–41.

Dunn, Ross E. "The Bu Himara Rebellion in Northeast Morocco: Phase 1." *Middle Eastern Studies* 17 (1981): 31–48.

———. "France, Spain, and the Bu Himara Rebellion." In *Tribe and State*, ed. E. G. H. Joffé and C. R. Pennell, 145–58. Wisbech, UK: Middle East and North African Studies Press, 1991.

Dutton, Yasin. "Sunna, Ḥadīth, and Madinan 'Amal." *Journal of Islamic Studies* 4.1 (1993): 1–31.

EI2 [*Encyclopedia of Islam*]. 2nd ed. Edited by P. J. Bearman, Th. Bianquis, C. E. Bosworth, E. van Donzel, and W. P. Heinrichs. 12 vols. Leiden, Netherlands: Brill, 1960–2005.

Eickelman, Dale F. "The Art of Memory: Islamic Education and Its Social Reproduction." *Comparative Studies in Society and History* 20.4 (1978): 485–516.

———. "Islamic Religious Commentary and Lesson Circles: Is There a Copernican Revolution?" In *Commentaries—Kommentare*, ed. Glenn W. Most, 121–46. Gottingen, Germany: Vandenhoeck and Ruprecht, 1999.

———. *Knowledge and Power in Morocco*. Princeton: Princeton University Press, 1985.

———. "Traditional Islamic Learning and Ideas of the Person in the Twentieth Century." In *Middle Eastern Lives*, ed. Martin Kramer, 35–59. Syracuse, NY: Syracuse University Press, 1991.

Eickelman, Dale F., and James Piscatori. *Muslim Politics*. Princeton: Princeton University Press, 1996.

Ennaji, Mohammed. *Expansion européenne et changement social au Maroc 16–19 siècles*. Casablanca: Edition Eddif, 1996.

———. *Serving the Master: Slavery and Society in Nineteenth Century Morocco*. New York: St. Martin's Press, 1998.

Fadel, Mohammad. "Rules, Judicial Discretion, and the Rule of Law in Naṣrid Granada: An Analysis of *al-Ḥadīqa al-mustaqilla al-naḍra fī al-fatāwā al-ṣādira 'an 'ulamā' al-ḥaḍra*." In *Islamic Law: Theory and Practice*, ed. Robert Gleave and Eugenia Kermeli, 49–86. New York: I. B. Tauris, 1997.

———. "The Social Logic of Taqlīd and the Rise of the Mukhtaṣar." *Islamic Law and Society* 3.2 (1996): 193–233.

El Fadl, Khaled Abou. "Islamic Law and Muslim Minorities: The Juristic Discourse on Muslim Minorities from the Second/Eighth to the Eleventh/Seventeenth Centuries." *Islamic Law and Society* 1.2 (1994): 141–87.

———. "Legal Debates on Muslim Minorities: Between Rejection and Accommodation." *Journal of Religious Ethics* 22.1 (1994): 127–62.

al-Fāsī, 'Abd al-Ḥafīẓ. *Mu'jam al-shuyūkh al-musammā riyāḍ al-jannah*. Beirut: Dār al-Kutub al-'Ilmiyya, 2003.

Fasi, Allal. *The Independence Movements in Arab North Africa*. Translated by Hazem Zaki Nuseibeh. New York: Octagon Books, 1970.

Fay, Mary Ann. "Women and Waqf: Property, Power, and the Domain of Gender in Eighteenth Century Egypt." In *Women in the Ottoman Empire*, ed. Madeline C. Zilfi, 28–47. Leiden, Netherlands: Brill, 1997.

"Le Fetoua des 'oulamā de Fès." *Archives Marocaines* 3 (1905): 141–43.

Fierro, Maribel. "Idra'ū l-ḥudūd bi-l-shubuhāt: When Lawful Violence Meets Doubt." *Hawwa* 5.2–3 (2007): 208–38.

Freidenreich, David M. *Foreigners and Their Food: Constructing Otherness in Jewish, Christian, and Islamic Law*. Berkeley: University of California Press, 2011.

Friedmann, Yohanan. "Classification of Unbelievers in Sunnī Muslim Law and Tradition." *Jerusalem Studies in Arabic and Islam* 22 (1998): 163–95.

Galloway, J. H. "The Mediterranean Sugar Industry." *Geographical Review* 67.2 (1977): 177–94.

Geertz, Clifford. "Off Echoes: Some Comments on Anthropology and Law." *Political and Legal Anthropology Review* 19.2 (1996): 33–37.

Gerber, Haim. *State, Society, and Law in Islam: Ottoman Law in Comparative Perspective*. Albany: State University of New York Press, 1994.

Gharīṭ, Muḥammad al-Mufaḍḍal. *Fawāṣil al-jumān fī anbā' wuzurā' wa-kuttāb al-zamān*. Fez: Al-Maṭba'a al-Jadīda, 1927.

Gibb, H. A. R. *Modern Trends in Islam*. Chicago: University of Chicago Press, 1947.

Gottreich, Emily. *The Mellah of Marrakesh: Jewish and Muslim Space in Morocco's Red City*. Bloomington: Indiana University Press, 2007.

Graham, William A. "Traditionalism in Islam: An Essay in Interpretation." *Journal of Interdisciplinary History* 23.3 (1993): 495–522.

Grigg, David. "The Worlds of Tea and Coffee: Patterns of Consumption." *GeoJournal* 57.4 (2002): 283–94.

Haj, Samira. *Reconfiguring Islamic Tradition: Reform, Rationality, and Modernity*. Stanford, CA: Stanford University Press, 2009.

Ḥajjī, Muḥammad. *Mawsū'at a'lām al-maghrib*. Beirut: Dār al-Gharb al-Islami, 1996.

———. *Naẓarāt fī al-nawāzil al-fiqhiyya*. Rabat: Al-Jam'īya al-Maghribiyya li-Ta'līf wa'l Tarjama wa'l-Nashr, 1999.

al-Ḥajwī, Muḥammad b. al-Ḥasan. *Al-Fikr al-sāmī fī tārīkh al-fiqh al-islāmī*. Beirut: Al-Maktaba al-'Aṣriyya, 2006.

Halbertal, Moshe. *People of the Book: Canon, Meaning, and Authority*. Cambridge, MA: Harvard University Press, 1997.

Halevi, Leor. "Christian Impurity versus Economic Necessity: A Fifteenth-Century Fatwa on European Paper." *Speculum* 83 (2008): 917–45.

Hallaq, Wael B. *Authority, Continuity and Change in Islamic Law*. Cambridge: Cambridge University Press, 2001.

———. "From *Fatwās* to *Furū'*: Growth and Change in Islamic Substantive Law." *Islamic Law and Society* 1 (1994): 17–56.

———. *A History of Islamic Legal Theories: An Introduction to Sunnī uṣūl al-fiqh*. Cambridge: Cambridge University Press, 1997.

———. "Ifta' and Ijtihad in Sunni Legal Theory: A Developmental Account." In *Islamic Legal Interpretation*, ed. Muhammad Khalid Masud, Brinkley Messick, and David S. Powers, 33–43. Cambridge, MA: Harvard University Press, 1996.

———. "Notes on the Term *qarīna* in Islamic Legal Discourse." *Journal of the American Oriental Society* 108.3 (1988): 475–80.

———. *The Origins and Evolution of Islamic Law*. Cambridge: Cambridge University Press, 2005.

Ḥarakāt, Ibrāhīm. *Al-Tayyārāt al-siyāsiyya wa'l-fikriyya bi'l-Maghrib khilāla qarnayn wa-nisf qabla al-ḥimāya*. [Morocco?]: s.n., 1985.

Harvey, L. P. *Islamic Spain, 1250 to 1500*. Chicago: University of Chicago Press, 1990.

Hattox, Ralph S. *Coffee and Coffeehouses: The Origins of a Social Beverage in the Medieval Near East*. Seattle: University of Washington Press, 1988.

Haykel, Bernard. "On the Nature of Salafi Thought and Action." In *Global Salafism: Islam's New Religious Movement*, ed. Roel Meijer, 33–57. London: Hurst, 2009.

———. *Revival and Reform in Islam: The Legacy of Muhammad al-Shawkānī*. Cambridge: Cambridge University Press, 2003.

Hendrickson, Jocelyn N. "The Islamic Obligation to Emigrate: Al-Wansharīsī's *Asnā al-matājir* Reconsidered." PhD diss., Emory University, 2009.

———. "Muslim Legal Responses to Portuguese Occupation in Late Fifteenth-Century North Africa." *Journal of Spanish Cultural Studies* 12.3 (September 2011): 309–25.

Hermansen, Marcia K. "Interdisciplinary Approaches to Islamic Biographical Materials." *Religion* 18 (1988): 163–82.

al-Hīlah, Muḥammad al-Ḥabīb. "Classification of Andalusian and Maghribī Books of Nawāzil from the Middle of the Fifth to the End of the Ninth Century A. H." In *The Significance of Islamic Manuscripts*, ed. John Cooper, 71–78. London: Al-Furqān Islamic Heritage Foundation, 1992.

Hoffman, Bernard G. *The Structure of Traditional Moroccan Rural Society*. The Hague: Mouton, 1967.

Holden, Stacy E. *The Politics of Food in Modern Morocco*. Gainesville: University Press of Florida, 2009.

Hourani, Albert. *Arabic Thought in the Liberal Age, 1798–1939*. Oxford: Oxford University Press, 1983.

Ibn Zaydān, ʿAbd al-Raḥmān. *Itḥāf aʿlām al-nāss bi-jamāl akhbār ḥādarat miknās*. 5 vols. Rabat: Al-Maṭbaʿa al-Waṭaniyya, 1929–33.

al-Idrīsī, Idrīs al-Qayṭūnī. *Muʿjam al-maṭbūʿāt al-maghribiyya*. Salé: s.n., 1988.

Jabre, F. "Dans le Maroc nouveau: Le role d'une université islamique." *Annales d'Histoire Économique et Sociale* 51 (1938): 193–207.

Jackson, Sherman. "Taqlīd, Legal Scaffolding and the Scope of Legal Injunctions in Post-formative Theory." *Islamic Law and Society* 3.2 (1996): 165–92.

al-Jīdī, ʿUmar b. ʿAbd al-Karīm. *Muḥāḍarāt fī tārīkh al-madhhab al-mālikī fī al-gharb al-islāmī*. Rabat: Manshūrāt ʿUkāẓ, 1987.

———. *Al-ʿUrf wa'l-ʿAmal fī'l-Madhhab al-Mālikī wa-mafhūmuhumā ladā ʿulamāʾ al-Maghrib*. Rabat: Ṣundūq Īḥyāʾ al-Turāth al-Islāmī al-Mushtarak, 1984.

Joffé, E. G. H. "The Zāwiya of Wazzan: Relations between Shurafāʾ and Tribe at the Advent of Colonial Occupation." In *Jbala: Histoire et société*, ed. Ahmed Zouggari and Jawhar Vignette-Zunz, 245–89. Casablanca: Wallada, 1991.

Johansen, Baber. "Coutumes locales et coutumes universelles aux sources de juridiques en droit Musulman Hanafite." *Annales Islamologiques* 27 (1993): 29–35.

———. "Legal Literature and the Problem of Change: The Case of the Land Rent." In *Contingency in a Sacred Law: Legal and Ethical Norms in the Muslim Fiqh*, ed. Baber Johansen, 446–64. Leiden, Netherlands: Brill, 1999.

Jouin, J. "Valeur symbolique des aliments et rites alimentaires à Rabat." *Hésperis* 44 (1957): 299–327.

Kably, Mohamed. "Legitimacy of State Power and Socioreligious Variations in Medieval Morocco." In *In the Shadow of the Sultan*, ed. Rahma Bourqia and Susan G. Miller, 17–29. Cambridge, MA: Harvard University Press, 1999.

———. *Société, pouvoir et religion au Maroc à la fin du Moyen-Age*. Paris: Maisonneuve et Larose, 1986.

Kagan, Zipora. "*Homo Anthologicus*: Micha Joseph Berdyczewski and the Anthological Genre." In *The Anthology in Jewish Literature*, ed. David Stern, 211–25. Oxford: Oxford University Press, 2004.

Kassis, Hanna E. "Muslim Revival in Spain in the Fifth/Eleventh Century: Causes and Ramifications." *Der Islam* 67.1 (1990): 78–110.

Katz, Jonathan. *Murder in Marrakesh: Émile Mauchamp and the French Colonial Adventure*. Bloomington: Indiana University Press, 2006.

———. "The 1907 Mauchamp Affair and the French Civilizing Mission in Morocco." *Journal of North African Studies* 6 (2001): 143–66.

Keddie, Nikkie. *Sayyid Jamāl ad-Dīn "al-Afghānī": A Political Biography*. Berkeley: University of California Press, 1972.

Kedouri, Elie. *Afghani and ʿAbduh: An Essay on Religious Unbelief and Political Activism in Modern Islam*. New York: Humanities Press, 1966.

Keene, Emily. *My Life Story*. London: Edward Arnold, 1911.

Kenbib, Mohammed. "Changing Aspects of State and Society in 19th Century Morocco." In *The Moroccan State in Historical Perspective, 1850–1985*, ed. Abdelali Doumou, 11–27. Dakar: Codesria, 1990.

———. "European Protections in Morocco, 1904–1939." In *Morocco and Europe*, ed. George Joffé, 47–53. London: University of London Press, 1989.

———. "The Impact of the French Conquest of Algeria on Morocco (1830–1912)." *Hespéris-Tamuda* 29 (1991): 47–60.

———. *Les protégés: Contribution à l'histoire contemporaine du Maroc*. Casablanca: Najah El Jadida, 1996.

———. "Protégés et brigands dans le Maroc du XIXe siècle et début du XXe." *Hespéris-Tamuda* 29.2 (1991): 227–48.

———. "Structures traditionnelles et protections étrangères au Maroc au XIXe siècle." *Hespéris-Tamuda* 22 (1984): 79–101.

Kerr, Malcolm H. *Islamic Reform: The Political and Legal Theories of Muḥammad ʿAbduh and Rashīd Riḍā*. Berkeley: University of California Press, 1966.

Khadduri, Majid. *War and Peace in the Law of Islam*. Baltimore: Johns Hopkins University Press, 1955.

al-Khadīmī, ʿAlāl. "Al-Ḥaraka al-Ḥafīẓiyya, 1894–1912." PhD diss., 2 vols., Muḥammad V University, 2001–2.

———. "Majlis al-aʿyān wa-mshrūʿ al-islāhāt al-faransiyya bi'l-maghrib sana 1905." In *Al-Islāḥ wa'l-mujtmʿ al-maghribī fī al-qarn al-tāsiʿ ʿashr*, 259–92. Rabat: Kullīyat al-Adāb, 1983.

Khalid, Adeeb. *The Politics of Muslim Cultural Reform: Jadidism in Central Asia*. Berkeley: University of California Press, 1998.

Kurzman, Charles. "Introduction: The Modernist Islamic Movement." In *Modernist Islam, 1840–1940*, ed. Charles Kurzman, 3–27. New York: Oxford University Press, 2002.

———, ed. *Modernist Islam, 1840–1940*. New York: Oxford University Press, 2002.

Laghzāwī, 'Abd al-Ilah. "Al-Mumārasa al-thaqāfiyya li'l-zāwiya al-Wazzāniyya: Mu'ālaja fī al-tafkīk wa'l-tarkīb." PhD diss., 3 vols., Muḥammad V University, 1996.

Landau-Tasseron, Ella. "The 'Cyclical Reform': A Study of the *Mujaddid* Tradition." *Studia Islamica* 70 (1989): 79–117.

Laroui, Abdallah. *Les origines sociales et culturelles du nationalisme marocain (1830–1912)*. Casablanca: Centre Culturel Arabe, 1993.

Lauzière, Henri. "The Construction of *Salafiyya*: Reconsidering Salafism from the Perspective of Conceptual History." *International Journal of Middle East Studies* 42 (2010): 369–89.

Layish, Aharon. "The Mālikī Family *waqf* according to Wills and Waqfiyyāt." *Bulletin of the School of Oriental and African Studies* 46.1 (1983): 1–32.

———. "*Shahādat Naql* in the Judicial Practice in Modern Libya." In *Dispensing Justice in Islam: Qadis and Their Judgments*, ed. Muhammad Khalid Masud, Rudolph Peters, and David S. Powers, 495–516. Leiden, Netherlands: Brill, 2006.

———. *Women and Islamic Law in a Non-Muslim State: A Study Based on Decisions of the Sharī'a Courts in Israel*. New York: John Wiley, 1975.

Le Tourneau, Roger. *Fès avant le Protectorat*. Rabat: Éditions la Porte, 1987.

"Lettre des oulama de Fez." *Bulletin de la Société de Géographie d'Oran* 23 (1903): 241–55.

Levtzion, Nehemia, and Gideon Weigert. "Religious Reform in Eighteenth Century Morocco." *Jerusalem Studies in Arabic and Islam* 19 (1995): 173–97.

Libson, Gideon. "On the Development of Custom as a Source of Law in Islamic Law." *Islamic Law and Society* 4.2 (1997): 131–55.

Maghen, Ze'ev. "Close Encounters: Some Preliminary Observations on the Transmission of Impurity in Early Sunnī Jurisprudence." *Islamic Law and Society* 6.3 (1999): 348–92.

Makdisi, George. *The Rise of Colleges: Institutions of Learning in Islam and the West*. Edinburgh: Edinburgh University Press, 1981.

Makhlūf, Muḥammad b. Muḥammad. *Shajarat al-nūr al-zakiyya fī ṭabaqāt al-mālikiyya*. Beirut: Dār al-Kitāb al-'Arabī, 1975.

El-Mansour, Mohamed. "Maghribis in the Mashriq during the Modern Period: Representations of the Other within the World of Islam." *Journal of North African Studies* 6.1 (2001): 81–104.

———. "Moroccan Islam Observed." *Maghreb Review* 29 (2004): 208–18.

———. *Morocco in the Reign of Mawlay Sulayman*. Wisbech, UK: Middle East and North African Studies Press, 1990.

———. "Les oulemas et le makhzen dans le Maroc precolonial." In *Le Maroc actuel: Une modernisation au miroir de la tradition?*, ed. Jean-Claude Santucci, 3–15. Paris: Éditions du Centre National de la Recherche Scientifique, 1992.

———. "Saints and Sultans: Religious Authority and Temporal Power in Precolonial Morocco." In *Popular Movements and Democratization in the Islamic World*, ed. Masatoshi Kisaichi, 1–32. London: Routledge, 2006.

———. "The Sanctuary (*Hurm*) in Precolonial Morocco." In *In the Shadow of the Sultan: Culture, Power, and Politics in Morocco*, ed. Rahma Bourqia and Susan Gilson Miller, 49–73. Cambridge, MA: Harvard University Press, 1999.

———. "Sharifian Sufism: The Religious and Social Practice of the Wazzani Zawiya." In *Tribe and State*, ed. E. G. H. Joffé and C. R. Pennell, 69–83. Wisbech, UK: Middle East and North African Studies Press, 1991.

al-Manūnī, Muḥammad. *Maẓāhir yaqẓat al-maghrib al-ḥadīth*. 2 vols. Beirut: Dār al-Gharb al-Islāmī, 1985.

March, Andrew F. *Islam and Liberal Citizenship: The Search for an Overlapping Consensus*. Oxford: Oxford University Press, 2009.

Martin, B. G. *Muslim Brotherhoods in Nineteenth-Century Africa*. Cambridge: Cambridge University Press, 1976.

Marty, Paul. "L'université de Qaraouiyne." *Bulletin du Comité de L'Afrique Française* 34 (1924): 329–53.

Masud, Muhammad Khalid. "*Ādāb al-Muftī*: The Muslim Understanding of Values, Characteristics, and Role of a *Muftī*." In *Moral Conduct and Authority: The Place of Adab in South Asian Islam*, ed. Barbara Daly Metcalf, 124–45. Berkeley: University of California Press, 1984.

———. "The Obligation to Migrate: The Doctrine of *Hijra* in Islamic Law." In *Muslim Travellers: Pilgrimage, Migration, and the Religious Imagination*, ed. Dale Eickelman and James Piscatori, 29–49. Berkeley: University of California Press, 1990.

Masud, Muhammad Khalid, Brinkley Messick, and David S. Powers, eds. *Islamic Legal Interpretation: Muftis and Their Fatwas*. Cambridge, MA: Harvard University Press, 1996.

———. "Muftis, Fatwas, and Islamic Legal Interpretation." In Masud, Messick, and Powers, *Islamic Legal Interpretation*, 3–32.

Masud, Muhammad Khalid, Rudolph Peters, and David S. Powers. "Qāḍīs and Their Courts: An Historical Survey." In *Dispensing Justice in Islam: Qadis and Their Judgments*, ed. Muhammad Khalid Masud, Rudolph Peters, and David S. Powers, 1–44. Leiden, Netherlands: Brill, 2006.

Mediano, Fernando Rodriguez. "The Post-Almohad Dynasties in al-Andalus and the Maghrib (Seventh–Ninth/Thirteenth–Fifteenth Centuries)." In *The New Cambridge History of Islam*, ed. Maribel Fierro, 2:106–43. Cambridge: Cambridge University Press, 2010.

Meron, Ya'akov. *L'obligation alimentaire entre époux en droit Musulman Hanéfite*. Paris: Librairie Générale de Droit et de Jurisprudence, 1971.

Messick, Brinkley. *The Calligraphic State: Textual Domination and History in a Muslim Society*. Berkeley: University of California Press, 1993.

———. "The Mufti, the Text and the World: Legal Interpretation in Yemen." *Man* 21 (1986): 102–19.

Metcalf, Barbara Daly. *Islamic Revival in British India: Deoband, 1860–1900*. Princeton: Princeton University Press, 1982.

Meyerson, Mark D. *The Muslims of Valencia in the Age of Fernando and Isabel: Between Coexistence and Crusade*. Berkeley: University of California Press, 1991.

Michaux-Bellaire, E. "L'enseignement indigène au Maroc." *Revue du Monde Musulman* 15 (1911): 422–52.

———. "La maison d'Ouezzan." *Revue du Monde Musulman* 5 (1908): 23–89.

Michel, Nicolas. *Une économie de subsistances le Maroc précolonial*. 2 vols. Cairo: Institut Français D'Archéologie Orientale, 1997.

Miège, Jean-Louis. *Le Maroc et l'Europe (1822–1906)*. 4 vols. Paris: Presses Universitaires de France, 1961–64.

Miller, Kathryn A. "Muslim Minorities and the Obligation to Emigrate to Islamic Territory: Two Fatwās from Fifteenth-Century Granada." *Islamic Law and Society* 7.2 (2000): 256–88.

Miller, Susan G. *Disorienting Encounters: Travels of a Moroccan Scholar in France in 1845–1846—the Voyage of Muḥammad aṣ-Ṣaffār*. Berkeley: University of California Press, 1992.

Miller, Susan G., and Amal Rassam. "The View from the Court: Moroccan Reactions to European Penetration during the Late Nineteenth Century." *International Journal of African Historical Studies* 16.1 (1983): 25–38.

Mintz, Sidney W. *Sweetness and Power: The Place of Sugar in Modern History*. New York: Penguin Books, 1985.

Miranda, Ambroxio Huici. "The Iberian Peninsula and Sicily." In *The Cambridge History of Islam*, ed. P. M. Holt, Ann K. S. Lambton, and Bernard Lewis, 2:406–39. Cambridge: Cambridge University Press, 1970.

Mir-Hosseini, Ziba. *Marriage on Trial: A Study of Islamic Family Law*. New York: I. B. Tauris, 2000.

Mujāhid, Zakī Muḥammad. *Al-A'lām al-Sharqiyya*. Beirut: Dār al-Gharb al-Islāmī, 1994.

Mu'nis, Ḥusayn, ed. and trans. "Asnā al-matājir fi bayān aḥkām man ghalaba 'alā waṭanihi al-Naṣārā wa-lam yuhājir." *Revista del Instituto Egipcio de Estudios Islámicos en Madrid* 5 (1957): 1–63.

Munson, Henry. *Religion and Power in Morocco*. New Haven, CT: Yale University Press, 1993.

Nafi, Basheer M. "Abu al-Thana' al-Alusi: An Alim, Ottoman Mufti, and Exegete of the Qur'an." *International Journal of Middle East Studies* 34 (2002): 465–94.

———. "Fatwā and War: On the Allegiance of the American Muslim Soldiers in the Aftermath of September 11." *Islamic Law and Society* 11.1 (2004): 78–116.

———. "The Rise of Islamic Reformist Thought and Its Challenge to Traditional Islam." In *Islamic Thought in the Twentieth Century*, ed. Suha Taji-Farouki and Nafi M. Basheer, 28–60. New York: I. B. Tauris, 2004.

al-Nāṣirī, Aḥmad b. Khālid. *Kitāb al-istiqsā li-akhbār duwal al-maghrib al-Aqṣā'*. 9 vols. Casablanca: Dār al-Kitāb, 1956.

O'Fahey, R. S. *Enigmatic Saint: Ahmad Ibn Idris and the Idrisi Tradition*. Evanston, IL: Northwestern University Press, 1990.

The Oxford Encyclopedia of the Modern Islamic World. Vol. 3. Edited by John L. Esposito. New York: Oxford University Press, 2001.

Pennell, C. R. *Morocco: From Empire to Independence*. Oxford: Oneworld Publications, 2003.

———. *Morocco since 1830: A History*. New York: New York University Press, 2000.

———. "Treaty Law: The Extent of Consular Jurisdiction in North Africa from the Middle of the Seventeenth to the Middle of the Nineteenth Century." *Journal of North African Studies* 14.2 (2009): 235–56.

Péretié, M. A. "Les madrasas de Fès." *Archives Marocaines* 18 (1912): 257–372.

Peters, Rudolph. "*Idjtihād* and *Taqlīd* in 18th and 19th Century Islam." *Die Welt des Islams* 20.3–4 (1980): 131–45.

Porter, Geoffrey David. "At the Pillar's Base: Islam, Morocco, and Education in the Qarawiyin Mosque, 1912–2000." PhD diss., New York University, 2002.

Powers, David S. "The Islamic Inheritance System: A Sociohistorical Approach." In *Islamic Family Law and the State*, ed. Chibli Mallet and Jane Connors, 11–30. London: Graham and Trotman, 1993.

———. *Law, Society, and Culture in the Maghrib, 1300–1500*. Cambridge: Cambridge University Press, 2002.

———. "Legal Consultation (Futyā) in Medieval Spain and North Africa." In *Islam and Public Law*, ed. Chibli Mallat, 85–106. London: Graham and Trotman, 1993.

———. "The Maliki Family Endowment: Legal Norms and Social Practices." *International Journal of Middle East Studies* 25.3 (1993): 379–406.

———. "On Judicial Review in Islamic Law." *Law and Society Review* 26.2 (1992): 315–41.

Powers, David S., and Etty Terem. "From the *Mi'yār* of al-Wansharīsī to the *New Mi'yār* of al-Wazzānī: Continuity and Change." *Jerusalem Studies in Arabic and Islam* 33 (2007): 235–60.

Rabb, Intisar A. "Doubt's Benefit: Legal Maxims in Islamic Law, 7th–16th Centuries." PhD diss., Princeton University, 2009.

Rahman, Fazlur. "Revival and Reform in Islam." In *Cambridge History of Islam*, ed. P. M. Holt, K. S. Lambton, and B. Lewis, 2:632–42. Cambridge: Cambridge University Press, 1970.

Reinhart, Kevin. "Impurity/No Danger." *History of Religions* 30.1 (1990): 1–24.

———. "Transcendence and Social Practice: Muftis and Qadis as Religious Interpreters." *Annals Islamologiques* 27 (1993): 5–25.

Repp, R. C. *The Mufti of Istanbul: A Study in the Development of the Ottoman Learned Hierarchy*. Oxford: Ithaca Press, 1986.

Rosen, Lawrence. *The Anthropology of Justice: Law as Culture in Islamic Society*. Cambridge: Cambridge University Press, 1989.

———. *The Justice of Islam*. Oxford: Oxford University Press, 2000.

———. *Law as Culture: An Invitation*. Princeton: Princeton University Press, 2006.

Safran, Janina M. "Rules of Purity and Confessional Boundaries: Maliki Debates about the Pollution of the Christian." *History of Religions* 42.3 (2003): 197–212.

Salmon, M. G. "Les chorfa idrisides de Fès." *Archives Marocaines* 1 (1904): 425–53.

Schacht, Joseph. *An Introduction to Islamic Law*. Oxford: Oxford University Press, 1982.

Schroeter, Daniel J. *Merchants of Essaouira: Urban Society and Imperialism in Southwestern Morocco, 1844–1886*. Cambridge: Cambridge University Press, 1988.

———. "Royal Power and the Economy in Precolonial Morocco: Jews and the Legitimation of Foreign Trade." In *In the Shadow of the Sultan: Culture, Power, and Politics in Morocco*, ed. Rahma Bourqia and Susan Gilson Miller, 74–102. Cambridge, MA: Harvard University Press, 1999.

———. *The Sultan's Jew: Morocco and the Sephardi World*. Stanford, CA: Stanford University Press, 2002.

Sebti, Abdelahad. "Chroniques de la contestation citadine: Fès et la revolte des tanneurs (1873–1874)." *Hespéris-Tamuda* 29.2 (1991): 283–312.

Seddon, David. "Labour Migration and Agricultural Development in Northeast Morocco: 1870– 1970." *Maghreb Review* 4.3 (1979): 69–77.

Shatzmiller, Maya. "Les premiers mérinides et le milieu religieuse de Fès: L'introduction des médrasas." *Studia Islamica* 43 (1976): 109–19.

al-Sibtī, ʿAbd al-Aḥad, and ʿAbd al-Raḥmān Lakhṣāṣī. *Min al-shāy ilā al-atāy: Al-ʿādah wa'l-tārīkh*. Casablanca: Maṭbaʿat al-Najāḥ al-Jadīda, 1999.

Skovgaard-Peterson, Jakob. *Defining Islam for the Egyptian State: Muftis and Fatwas of Dār al-iftā*. Leiden, Netherlands: Brill, 1997.

Smith, Woodruff D. "Complications of the Commonplace: Tea, Sugar, and Imperialism." *Journal of Interdisciplinary History* 23.2 (1992): 259–78.

al-Suhaylī, ʿAbd al-Raḥmān b. ʿAbd Allāh. *Al-Rawḍ al-unuf fī sharḥ al-sīra al-nabawiyya li-ibn Hishām*. Mutlan, Pakistan: Al-Maktaba al-Fārūqīyya, 1977.

al-Tāzī, ʿAbd al-Hādī. *Jāmiʿ al-Qarawiyyīn: Al-masjid wa'l-jāmiʿa bi madīnat fās*. 3 vols. Beirut: Dār al-Kitāb al-Lubnānī, 1972.

Temsamani, Abdelaziz Khalouk. "The Jebala Region: Makhzan, Bandits and Saints." In *Tribe and State*, ed. E. G. H. Joffé and C. R. Pennell, 14–46. Wisbech, UK: Middle East and North African Studies Press, 1991.

Terem, Etty. "Al-Mahdī al-Wazzānī." In *Islamic Legal Thought: A Compendium of Muslim Jurists*, ed. Oussama Arabi, David S. Powers, and Susan Spectorsky, 435–55. Leiden, Netherlands: Brill, 2013.

Toledano, Henry. *Judicial Practice and Family Law in Morocco*. Boulder, CO: Social Science Monographs, 1981.

Touati, Houari. *Entre Dieu et les hommes: Lettrés, saints et sorciers au Maghreb (17e siècle)*. Paris: Recherches d'Histoire et de Sciences Sociales, 1994.

Troll, Christian W. *Sayyid Ahmad Khan: A Reinterpretation of Muslim Theology*. New Delhi: Vikas, 1978.

Tucker, Judith E. "And God Knows Best: The Fatwa as a Source for the History of Gender in the Arab World." In *Beyond the Exotic: Women's Histories in Islamic Societies*, ed. Amira Sonbol, 165–79. Syracuse, NY: Syracuse University Press, 2005.

———. "Biography as History: The Exemplary Life of Khayr al-Din al-Ramli." In *Auto/Biography and the Construction of Identity and Community in the Middle East*, ed. Mary Ann Fay, 9–17. New York: Palgrave, 2001.

———. *In the House of the Law: Gender and Islamic Law in Ottoman Syria and Palestine*. Berkeley: University of California Press, 1998.

———. *Women, Family, and Gender in Islamic Law*. Cambridge: Cambridge University Press, 2008.

Tyan, Emile. *Histoire de l'organisation judiciaire en pays d'Islam*. 2nd ed. Leiden, Netherlands: Brill, 1960.

———. "Judicial Organization." In *Law in the Middle East: Origin and Development of Islamic Law*, ed. M. Khadduri and H. J. Liebesny, 236–78. Washington, DC: The Middle East Institute, 1955.

Van Koningsveld, P. S., and G. A. Wiegers. "The Islamic Statute of the Mudejars in the Light of a New Source." *Al-Qantara* 17.1 (1996): 19–58.

Verskin, Alan. "Early Islamic Legal Responses to Living under Christian Rule: Reconquista-Era Development and 19th-Century Impact in the Maghrib." PhD diss., Princeton University, 2010.

Viguera-Molins, Maria Jesus. "Al-Andalus and the Maghrib (from the Fifth/Eleventh Century to the Fall of the Almoravids)." In *The New Cambridge History of Islam*, ed. Maribel Fierro, 2:21–47. Cambridge: Cambridge University Press, 2010.

Voll, John O. "Renewal and Reform in Islamic History: *Tajdid* and *Islah*." In *Voices of Resurgent Islam*, ed. John L. Esposito, 32–47. Oxford: Oxford University Press, 1983.

Waines, David. "Dietetics in Medieval Islamic Culture." *Medical History* 43.2 (April 1999): 228–40.

———. *Food Culture and Health in Pre-modern Islamic Societies*. Leiden, Netherlands: Brill, 2011.

Waldman, Marilyn Robinson. "Tradition as a Modality of Change: Islamic Examples." *History of Religions* 25 (1986): 318–40.

al-Wansharīsī, Aḥmad. *Al-Miʿyār al-Muʿrib wa'l-jāmiʿ al-mughrib ʿan fatāwī ʿulamā' Ifrīqiyā wa'l-Andalus wa'l-Maghrib*. Printed ed. 13 vols. Rabat: Ministry of Culture and Religious Affairs, 1981–83.

al-Wazzānī, al-Mahdī. *Bughyat al-ṭālib al-rāghib al-qāṣid fī ibāḥat ṣalāt al-ʿīd fī al-masājid*. Lithograph. Fez: Lithographic Press, n.d.

———. *Hādhihī fahrasa*. Lithograph. Fez: Al-Maṭbaʿa al-Ḥajariyya, 1896.

———. *Al-Nawāzil al-jadīda al-kubrā fī-mā li-ahl fās wa-ghayrihim min al-badw wa'l-qurā al-musammā bi'l-miʿyār al-jadīd al-jāmiʿ al-muʿrib ʿan fatāwī al-muta'akhkhirīn min ʿulamā' al-Maghrib*. Lithograph. 11 vols. Fez, 1910. Printed ed., 12 vols. Rabat: Ministry of Culture and Religious Affairs, 1996–2000.

———. *Al-Nawāzil al-ṣughrā al-musammā bi'l-minaḥ al-sāmiyya fī'l-nawāzil al-fiqhiyya*. Lithograph. 4 vols. Fez, 1900–1901. Printed ed., 4 vols. Rabat: Ministry of Culture and Religious Affairs, 1992–93.

———. *Al-Nuṣḥ al-khāliṣ li-kāffat al-muslimīn bi'l-tawaṣṣul ilayhi ta'ālā bi-aṣfiyā'ihi al-muqarrabīn*. Lithograph. Fez: Lithographic Press, n.d.

———. *Taqyīd fī jawāz al-dhikr ma'a al-janāza wa-raf' al-ṣaut bi'l-haylala*. Lithograph. Fez: Lithographic Press, n.d.

Weismann, Itzchak. "Between Ṣūfī Reformism and Modernist Rationalism—a Reappraisal of the Origins of the Salafiyya from the Damascene Angle." *Die Welt des Islams* 41 (2001): 206–37.

———. *Taste of Modernity: Sufism, Salafiyya, and Arabism in Late Ottoman Damascus*. Leiden, Netherlands: Brill, 2001.

Weiss, Bernard G. "Exotericism and Objectivity in Islamic Jurisprudence." In *Islamic Law and Jurisprudence*, ed. Nicholas Heer, 53–71. Seattle: University of Washington Press, 1990.

———. *The Spirit of Islamic Law*. Athens: University of Georgia Press, 1998.

White, James Boyd. *Justice as Translation: An Essay in Cultural and Legal Criticism*. Chicago: University of Chicago Press, 1990.

Wiederhold, Lutz. "Legal Doctrines in Conflict: The Relevance of Madhhab Boundaries to Legal Reasoning in the Light of an Unpublished Treatise on *Taqlīd* and *Ijtihād*." *Islamic Law and Society* 3.2 (1996): 234–304.

Wiegers, Gerard Albert. *Islamic Literature in Spanish and Aljamiado*. Leiden, Netherlands: Brill, 1994.

Zaman, Muhammad Qasim. *The Ulama in Contemporary Islam: Custodians of Change*. Princeton: Princeton University Press, 2002.

Zarinebaf, Fariba. "Women, Patronage, and Charity in Ottoman Istanbul." In *Beyond the Exotic: Women's Histories in Islamic Societies*, ed. Amira El-Azhary Sonbol, 89–101. Syracuse, NY: Syracuse University Press, 2005.

Zeghal, Malika. *Les Islamistes marocains: Le défi à la monarchie*. Paris: Éditions La Découverte, 2005.

Ziadeh, Farhat J. "Integrity (*'Adālah*) in Classical Islamic Law." In *Islamic Law and Jurisprudence*, ed. Nicholas Heer, 73–93. Seattle: University of Washington Press, 1990.

al-Ziriklī, Khayr al-Dīn. *A'lām*. Beirut: Dār al-'Ilm li'l-Malāyin, 1979.

Zomeno, Amalia. "Abandoned Wives and Their Possibilities for Divorce in Al-Andalus: The Evidence of the *Wathā'iq* Works." In *Writing the Feminine: Women in Arab Sources*, ed. Manuela Marin and Randi Deguilhem, 111–26. London: I. B. Tauris, 2002.

———. "The Stories in the Fatwas and the Fatwas in History." In *Narratives of Truth in Islamic Law*, ed. Baudouin Dupret, Annelies Moors, and Barbara Drieskens, 25–49. New York: I. B. Tauris, 2008.

Zouggari, Ahmed, and Jawhar Vignette-Zunz, eds. *Jbala: Histoire et société*. Casablanca: Wallada, 1991.

INDEX

Mālikism: and custom, 32; as idiom of identity, 68, 189; and Sufism, 33
Al-Manār, 39–40, 54
El-Mansour, Mohamed, 68, 187, 191
Al-Manūnī, Muḥammad, 41, 191
Marrakesh, 29, 45, 49, 83, 145
Marseille, 166
Mashriq/Arab East, 39–41, 53–54, 68, 164
Maṣmūda, 21–22. *See also* Berbers; Ghumāra
Mauchamp, Émile, 49, 192
Mayta (an animal that is forbidden for eating), 148, 159, 165, 205. *See also* Bones; Sugar
Mayyāra, Abdallāh, 39, 170–171, 190
Al-Māzarī, Abū 'Abdallāh, 102–104, 110, 155, 200
Mecca, 40, 53–54, 197. *See also Ḥājj*; Ḥijāz
Meat, 40, 157, 172
Medina, 54, 152
Mediterranean, 51, 94, 100, 142, 145, 205
Merad, Ali, 3
Merchants: Christian and European, in Morocco, 77, 113, 114, 144; Muslim, 2, 44, 77, 93–94, 113, 115, 137, 142–144, 147, 162–163, 165–166
Messick, Brinkley, 13, 30, 76, 186, 189. *See also* Muftīship
Miège, Jean-Louis, 113, 142, 144, 187
Migration and migrants: from Rif, 115; rural-urban, 114–115, 137
Millaf (wool blanket), 154
Miller, Susan, 44
Al-Mi'yār, Kitāb, 2, 11, 73, 105, 107, 122, 183. *See also* Al-Wansharīsī
Monopolies, 112–113
Mudawwana, of Saḥnūn. *See* Saḥnūn
Mudéjars, 96–97, 102, 199, 200. *See also* Documents; Judgment; *Khiṭāb*; Qāḍī
Muftī, 1, 9–10, 13, 24, 27, 29–30, 34–35, 37, 41–44, 57, 61–63, 67–69, 71–72, 76, 79–80, 89, 91, 93–94, 102, 106, 109, 119–124, 127–139, 146, 183, 186, 190–191, 195. *See also* Fatwā; *Istiftā'*; Messick; Muftīship; *Mustaftī*; Qāḍī
Muftīship, 13, 27, 76, 186. *See also* Messick
Muḥammad the Prophet, 3, 8, 21, 26, 29, 31, 35, 47, 52, 68, 80, 82–85, 90, 96, 106, 146–147, 152, 154–156, 160–161, 165, 189, 196, 208; descendants of, 8, 21, 187. *See also Ḥadīth*; *Sunna*
Mujaddid (renewer), 52. *See also* Renewal
Mujtahid (jurist who exercises independent reasoning), 31, 35, 68, 195. *See also Ijtihād*; *Taqlīd*
Mukhtaṣar, of Khalīl. *See* Abridgment; Khalīl b. Isḥāq
Munson, Henry, 45
Muqallid (jurist who practices "blind imitation"), 37, 162. *See also Ijtihād*; *Mujtahid*; *Taqlīd*
Mushrik (polytheist), 41, 80–81, 83, 89, 96, 106, 197. *See also Shirk*
Musk, 153, 159, 164
Mustaftī (questioner), 42, 86, 93–95, 133. *See also* Fatwā; *Istiftā'*; Muftī
Muwaṭṭā', of Mālik, 11, 25, 58, 60–61, 68. *See also* Mālik b. Anas

Nafaqa (maintenance), 16, 125–134, 138–139, 203. *See also* Abandoned wife; Absent husband; *Amīn*; Brother-in-law; *Wakīl*
Naṣīḥa, 62, 80, 83; *Naṣīḥat ahl al-Islām*, 55, 65. *See also* Al-Kattānī, Muḥammad bin Ja'far
Al-Nāṣirī, Aḥmad b. Khālid, 52, 56–58, 63–65, 67, 143
New Mi'yār (al-Mi'yār al-jadid), 1–2, 7–17, 32, 44, 53, 55–56, 63, 70–76, 78, 86, 93–94, 105–106, 108–109, 111, 117, 124, 127, 129, 134, 141, 145–146, 167–168, 174, 177–180, 183–184, 186; as a compilation, 1, 10–12, 16, 44, 71–72, 180; as a New Mālikī orthodoxy, 7, 14–15, 56, 73, 75–76, 179–180; preface, 70–71, 109; sources of, 11, 32; structure of, 10; title of, 2, 72–73. *See also* Al-Wazzānī, Al-Mahdī

Olive oil, 112, 155, 159
Oran, 115
Orthodoxy, 5–6, 69, 73, 75, 179; *New Mi'yār* as, 7, 14–15, 56, 73, 75–76, 179–180. *See also* Asad
Oujda, 46, 49